Testimonials for *My First Last Year*

The gift you will receive from My First Last Year is not only the inspiring example of Roger Leslie's courageous vulnerability as a spiritual warrior, but also its potent reminder that we have every reason to trust in each step of our inner and outer journey by realizing that we are inwardly equipped with all that we need to fulfill it.
—**Dr. Michael Bernard Beckwith,**
author of *Life Visioning*

My First Last Year *is written with such utter authenticity of heart that I couldn't stop reading! How precious a gift it will be to Roger Leslie's readers.* —**Anita Rehker** (Agape Intl. Spiritual Ctr.)

With My First Last Year, Roger Leslie is an offspring of the marriage between Henry David Thoreau and Benjamin Franklin.
—**Dr. Wade Dorman**

Concealed behind that brilliant smile and congenial demeanor lie the intelligently woven stories of a man who has gone through much more than one might readily assume. Roger Leslie is a relevant voice of our times. —**Francis Roberson**

Thanks for everything you taught us. We will never be the same!
—**Dyla Gutierrez**

I owe a great deal to this man. He truly inspired me, and taught me that you can do anything that you put your mind to.
—**Codey Church**

Dr. Roger Leslie is the most inspiring and loving teacher I ever had. He helped us all become more confident and kind. It is no surprise that he is doing so many amazing things.
—**Anna Anguiano Smith**

Books Published by Roger Leslie

Spiritual inspiration *My First Last Year,* Paradise, 2015

Character education resource *Teach Me SUCCESS*, Bayou, 2015

Performing arts reference book *Film Stars and Their Awards: Who Won What for Movies, Theater, and Television*, McFarland, 2008

YA biography *Eagle on Ice: The Antarctic Adventure of Teenager Paul Siple*, Vantage Press, 2008 (co-authored with Patricia Potter Wilson)

Novel study guide and test book *Saurcana* Teachers' Sourcebook, Seaworm, 2005

Biography *Isak Dinesen: Gothic Storyteller,* Morgan Reynolds, 2004

Motivational book *Success Express for Teens,* Bayou, 2004

Novel *Drowning in Secret,* Absey & Company, 2002

Library text *Center Stage: Library Programs that Inspire Middle School Patrons,* Libraries Unlimited, 2002 (co-authored with Patricia Potter Wilson)

Library text *Igniting the Spark: Library Programs that Inspire High School Patrons,* Libraries Unlimited, 2002 (co-authored with Patricia Potter Wilson)

Library text *Premiere Events: Library Programs that Inspire Elementary Patrons,* Libraries Unlimited, 2001 (co-authored with Patricia Potter Wilson)

History book *Galena Park: The Community that Shaped its own History,* published by Galena Park archivist Sue Elkins Edwards, 1993 (co-authored with Sue Elkins Edwards)

Order any book through my website, rogerleslie.com or the publishers' sites:

Absey & Company:	absey.biz
Bayou Publishing:	bayoupublishing.com
Libraries Unlimited:	abc-clio.com
McFarland:	mcfarlandbooks.com
Morgan Reynolds:	morganreynolds.com
Paradise Publishing:	paradisepublishinghouse.com

My First Last Year

Roger Leslie, PhD

Paradise Publishing
Spring, Texas
2015

Copyright © 2015 by Roger Leslie

All Rights Reserved

All rights reserved. No part of this book may be reproduced or transmitted in any form or by any means, electronic or mechanical. This includes photocopying or recording by any information storage or retrieval system, without written permission from the publisher.

Paradise Publishing, LLC
P.O. Box 132542
Spring, TX 77393

www.ParadisePublishingHouse.com
www.RogerLeslie.com

Hard Cover / Jacket — 978-1-941680-00-1
Perfect Binding — 978-1-941680-01-8
eBook MOBI — 978-1-941680-02-5
eBook ePub — 978-1-941680-03-2

Roger Leslie, 1961 -
    1. Conduct of Life. 2. Spirituality -- United States -- Biography. 3. Life and Death. 4. God -- Metaphysical Understanding. 5. Dreams and Dream Interpretations.
        p. 272 cm.
            ISBN 978-1-941680-00-1 (hard cover / jacket)
            ISBN 978-1-941680-01-8 (perfect)
            ISBN 978-1-941680-02-5 (ebook MOBI)
            ISBN978-1-941680-03-2 (ebook ePub)

SUMMARY: In response to a spiritual dream, an author and librarian lives a year as if it were his last, setting goals, recording insights, and sharing lessons about savoring each day and fulfilling one's destiny.
LOC: BL 72. Dewey: 210 or 920.

NOTE: All events described in this autobiographical work were shared through the perceptions of the author. Some people depicted are not identified by their real name.

Book Packager and Project Coordinator — Rita Mills
www.BookConnectionOnline.com
Editors — Susann and Wade Dorman
Cover Photo — Shasta Rose
Cover Concept — Rita Mills & Martin Vives

The paper used in this publication meets the requirements of the American National Standard for Permanence of Paper for Printed Library Materials Z39.48-1984.
Printed in the United States of America

Dedication

*To you, my readers, and the Allsoul
connection that makes us one.*

Table of Contents

PROLOGUE
The Shadow of Who I Was ix

CHAPTERS
1. Renaissance 1
2. Slowing Down to Focus 11
3. Making Connections 17
4. Connecting to Others on the Physical and Spiritual Planes 29
5. Spiritual Awakenings 39
6. In the Midst of Spiritual Magic 55
7. Flying, Growing, and Seeing Signs along the Journey . . 69
8. Creating Beauty 83
9. A Gift Fit for Angels 97
10. The Truth is Below the Surface 107
11. Say "Yes" to Every Inspiration 111
12. Narrowing My Focus 121
13. Rewiring Thoughts 123
14. Spiritual Millionaires 131
15. Awakening to Enlightenment 137
16. True Prosperity 145
17. Live from Your Soul 147
18. Two Whacks on the Side of the Head 153

19.	In Heartbreak, Soul's Beauty	159
20.	Legacies and Signs	169
21.	The Presence of the Past	183
22.	The Bigger Picture	195
23.	We are to Live Our Mission	197
24.	My Faith is Tested	201
25.	The Courage to Love	211
26.	SUCCESS	219
27.	The Entire Picture	233

EPILOGUE
Up Next 241

APPENDICES
People Connected to Roger Leslie 245
General Index 248
Dream Chronicle 252

PROLOGUE

The Shadow of Who I Was

What would you do if you only had one year left to live? That challenge came to me in a dream last night, followed by these instructions: *Live the next year as if it were your last. Strive to be present every moment. Savor each day of the next year as if that calendar date were the last time you'd experience it.*

But the dream was not self-serving. It requested further action. *As you live from this focused perspective, notice what you learn, and record your experiences, insights, and philosophies. Write them to empower readers on their own journey. Make your life an example for others to relish their own.*

I woke this morning knowing that if I accepted the challenge, my life would never be the same.

My inspiration was partly schooled by Randy Pausch's *The Last Lecture*, a powerful, life-enhancing testimonial to the eternal strength of spirit that he offered as a message to his children and his college students just before he succumbed to pancreatic cancer. After viewing the lecture and reading his book, I thought, why wait for such a prognosis? Live the life you dream now.

This inspiring dream instructed me how. It concluded with these empowering directives: *Be bold. Set priorities. Do only what really matters and let the rest go.*

Knowing that Pausch had shared his life lessons while dying helped me realize what a generous gift my dream was providing. If I accepted the challenge I could do what the dying must—review their life, determine what matters, and pare it down to only the essentials. But as a healthy man, I could sustain the benefits of living fully each day without the physical trauma and emotional upheaval that often comes with catastrophic illness. To live this year as if it were my last demanded I surrender everything that isn't paramount. Now.

To fulfill the instructions of helping others confirmed that the challenge wasn't encouraging me to become recklessly self-absorbed. While maintaining the context of my life, I could transform myself from the *inside*. Just imagining the challenge made my life seem more precious and valuable. I suspected I would learn to appreciate *everything* more. I would be called to abandon all pettiness. I would know what matters because I'd have no time to waste on what doesn't.

My inspiration made clear my mission: *Don't wait until you're about to die to really live. Live now and pass it on.*

That day I accepted the challenge. Because I understood my instructions to mean I was to live, not die, for 365 days, I didn't want to think of this as my last year. But if I learned what I thought life was teaching me through this experiment, then this year could serve as a template for how to live the rest of my life, no matter how long that was. This could be, instead, my first last year.

This new spiritual journey began within four days of the 25th anniversary of another rebirth that gave Jerry and me a new lease on life after our first real brush with mortality. Jerry and I met in an education class at the University of Houston in August of 1983. I was single; Jerry had a partner named Patrick. Throughout the following year, Jerry and I grew closer, but we remained only friends as his relationship with Patrick dissolved. In August of 1984 Jerry and I became a couple. A few months later, Patrick called Jerry to say he was very sick. This was the era when a frightening immune disease that was killing throngs of gay men had recently been identified as acquired immune deficiency syndrome—AIDS.

Many of Patrick's friends were already dead or dying, and the healthy ones didn't seem willing to help, so Jerry and I took Patrick to the hospital. We didn't know what was wrong with him, and although we were too afraid to say it aloud, we all feared the worst. While Patrick had tests run, Jerry and I sat silently in the waiting room, terrified that Patrick's prognosis was fateful news for all of us. If he did have AIDS, then he was going to die. That result was inevitable in the mid-1980s. More personally, chances were almost certain that he had given it to Jerry, and Jerry had passed it on to me.

We spent agonizing hours waiting for the prognosis. I don't know where Jerry was the entire time—maybe pacing in a different area of the hospital. But I recall lying on a gray vinyl sectional in the empty waiting room in the middle of the night. The television mounted on the wall overhead blared, but those sounds were drowned out by the fearful prayers in my head. I was 23, terrified and still on the graveled beginnings of a spiritual path that I began traveling when I was 16.

Back then I struggled with the philosophies of a religion that had me reaffirm, at church of all places, where I came to be spiritually fed, that I was unworthy of God, and that being gay, a mere construct of my physiological composition, separated me from the spiritual sustenance for which I hungered. During those teen years I sunk into a depression so dark it was shadowless. In time I rose to the surface and learned, if not to sail, at least to stay afloat. Now all the old fears and doubts about who I was as a spiritual being reemerged, as I wondered if the consequence of falling in love with a beautiful soul like Jerry was punishable by death.

When the doctor finally returned, he said Patrick was a very, very sick man, but he did not have AIDS. He had Bell's palsy, a dysfunction of the cranial nerve that destroys a patient's ability to control facial muscles. Jerry and I exhaled in relief. We weren't exposed to the AIDS virus, and Patrick's condition was treatable.

After Patrick's release, Jerry and I took him to his apartment. He eventually started recovering with the help of other friends, and Jerry and I moved on with our own life.

In 1985, Jerry and I both completed our certification work to be educators and secured teaching positions in adjacent school districts. Jerry had been married previously and had two children, Cory and Rebecca. The kids stayed with us that summer, as they would every summer, and we all shopped for "furchiler" (as Rebecca called it) to fill our first apartment.

In late August, I came home from my first day as a teacher excited about my new profession. I found Jerry seated on one of the beds upstairs crying. The heaviness of his countenance felt thick and frightening.

He didn't even look at me when he spoke. "Patrick called me a few minutes ago. He has AIDS."

Nothing was the same after that moment. Our death knell had rung. We went from being young men embarking on new careers with a lifetime ahead of us to waiting and watching for signs of illness that spelled certain death. That perspective pervaded everything. From that moment on, although we functioned and made it through our days with students, with colleagues, with family, and with our kids, we were already scarred by our belief that we were diseased and dying.

While hiding the news from everyone, Jerry and I relied entirely on each other to see us through this black, traumatic period. At this time, people weren't sure how AIDS was spread, and it was still generally accepted that close contact with someone might infect them, too. As a result, we withdrew even further into a life of just the two of us, even avoiding holding the kids very much. If we hugged anyone, we did it briefly, afraid that extended contact might infect them. We no longer kissed the kids, or if we did it was a light evasive brush against their cheek so we wouldn't transmit death to them.

In our fear, we mistakenly believed that avoiding getting tested perpetuated hope. Often depressed and frightened, we kept watching for a skin lesion to burst that delusion. Looking back, our decision made no sense, because happiness requires courage. Happiness cannot surface from a pool of fear.

More than a full year after Patrick's fateful phone call to Jerry we decided the life we had created by avoiding the truth was not worth living. For even the potentially brief remainder of our life to have any quality, we had to muster the courage to get tested. By fall of 1986, there were clinics that did AIDS tests anonymously so that patients weren't immediately in danger of losing their jobs if they tested positive. Jerry found one of those clinics in Montrose. After 16 months of dying spiritually and emotionally, we finally acted from bravery and went to a clinic to get tested.

It took a full week to receive our results. When we returned to the clinic, the counselor called us in together. Was that a good sign because we didn't need the confidentiality required of a negative prognosis? Or was is a bad sign because these counselors knew that sharing fatal news with a couple together gave them a chance to console one another?

The counselor seemed to stare at our test results forever before he finally lifted his eyes and told us, "You both tested negative."

We sat dumbstruck, not quite grasping his message: was it negative, as in the news was bad, or "negative" in that we weren't dying? "Does that mean we don't have AIDS?" we asked.

"It means that this test reveals no exposure to the virus. If either of you has had sexual contact with another partner in the past few weeks, you might want to come back and get tested again."

We hadn't. We wouldn't.

"But according to these results, you're both well." Finally he smiled. "Now go and live your lives." I wondered how he knew we hadn't in so long.

Outside the clinic, shuddering with tears, we embraced. "Thank You, God! Thank You, God," we whispered through our first clear breath in over a year.

In that moment I felt transformed. I was born again. God gave me a new lease on life. I determined to savor it graciously and gratefully forever.

That decision brought an instant transformation that challenged many old ways of thinking. I still had much to learn about relishing life and being continuously gracious and grateful. But I was so committed to it that it became the foundation of my life.

The first last year inspiration that came last night has invited me to leap from another life-changing threshold. I say "Yes!" I believe living this year as if it were my last will add the penthouse floors of that earlier spiritual construct. Over the next 365 days I want to live as a soul even better than I do now. By savoring the present and doing only what feels meaningful, I hope to intensify the spiritual light my soul adds to what I call the Allsoul, which is comprised of everything living—every pulse, spark, and energy—what collectively I understand to be God. Half of my lifetime ago, I had a year of dying; now I am committed to a year where I really live.

My First Last Year

Renaissance

Day 1: November 12

There is no greater spiritual gift than explicit instructions for living a rich and meaningful life. In my dream last night, I was told: *Live the next year as if it were your last. Strive to be present every moment. Savor each day of the next year as if that calendar date were the last time you'd experience it.*

This gift, Spirit assured, was not just for me.

As you live from this focused perspective, notice what you learn, and record your experiences, insights, and philosophies. Write them to empower readers on their own journey. Make your life an example to help others.

Any great inspiration demands immediate action, so as soon as I awoke I began writing. In the quiet of the morning, I recorded the instructions spelled out in the dream, feeling already as though I had begun a new life.

How appropriate that my first activity was a Renaissance wedding. My husband Jerry, minister of Unity Circle of Light in The Woodlands, Texas was officiating, and I was a groomsman. Every detail of the wedding fit a Renaissance theme, including all participants' wardrobe. The bride sewed Jerry a tan friar's robe with a thick rope belt. For the groomsmen she made shirts with billowing sleeves, a

that closed with crisscrossing strings, and boot covers I loved
because they looked Shakespearean. A wedding guest later observed
that if I were holding a quill I could be Shakespeare for the day. As a
soul who dreams of leaving my legacy through my writing, I couldn't
have been more excited.

The two hour drive to the festival offered plenty of time for me to tell Jerry about my first last year inspirations. One of Jerry's many endearing qualities is his willingness to feel deep emotion and allow tears to flow. His eyes welled as I shared the message Spirit sent me: this is it. I have one year to get everything in that matters most—to live fully, to shine my light for anyone who needs it, and to express my affection to everyone who has given me the most meaningful and life-sustaining gift of all—their love.

During the ride Jerry and I brainstormed new goals that we could achieve together. Immeasurably grateful to still have our parents, and all in relatively good health for being in or near their 80s, we imagined plans with them.

Travel with MawMaw and PawPaw.

Jerry's mother, whom I call MawMaw as her grandchildren do, had mentioned last summer that she and PawPaw had never been to Savannah and would really like to go. Jerry and I love to help other people make their dreams come true. We decided back then that during our next spring break, we could take them to Georgia. That plan just got cemented.

Plan a surprise visit for Mom with her friend, Barbara.

Jerry and I take my mom with us to Michigan every summer to spend several days with Mom's aunts, Ciocia Honey {Ciocia (*chuh-chuh*) is the Polish term for aunt} and Ciocia Stas (*stosh*), and her cousins, Debbie, Nancy, and Arlene in our favorite little town in Michigan. Because Mom won't fly any more, we've been driving. For the trip this year, we already planned to increase our travel time for a more leisurely road trip. It's been nearly 20 years since Mom has seen her friend Barbara in Ohio. We could stop there for a surprise reunion.

Take our dream Mediterranean cruise.

Jerry and I had a glorious wedding at Emerald Lake Lodge in British Columbia 23 years into being a couple. We had hoped to take a honeymoon cruise through the Mediterranean. Because it took us a few years to pay for the wedding, we postponed the trip until we paid the wedding bills and saved for the honeymoon. This goal changed that priority. Lack of money can no longer be a reason for postponing something. I have a year to really live. In my lifetime, I want to take that Mediterranean cruise with Jerry. I will contact our travel agent, Rita, to initiate a plan soon.

Send gifts or loving notes to extended family.

As I work on prosperity, I get creative ideas to keep from spending money that needs to be going toward current bills. While calculating the cost of several Thanksgiving cards, I realized I could save money buying one packet of autumn stationery and sending letters instead of cards. If I find something attractive, I'll do that. If not, the important part is the message, not the paper. I don't want a card with somebody else's message. I am a writer, for God's sake (and I mean that literally, not as an idiom). Even if it's on plain white typing paper, it could be perfect. What matters is to express my gratitude for them and make sure they get the message.

Start giving away personal belongings to those I love.

My sister Judy loves penguins. I've had some penguin Christmas decorations that she's admired for years. I'm giving them to her this Christmas. My 8-year-old niece Maycee loves books as much as I do. I have a collection of books I treasure. I want her to have a piece of that treasury. I'm going to give her one of my favorite books with the others I've already bought her for Christmas.

The list continued:

> *For Christmas, give a small, meaningful gift to everybody in our immediate families.*
> *Regularly get together with friends for dinner.*
> *Buy my sweet cousin Debbie the Curious George Christmas ornament I saw at the Hallmark Shop last week.*

In her mid-50s, Deb loves Curious George. I imagine that ornament bringing her joy for years to come whenever she decorates her house for the holidays.

> *Contact Gene Hackman and ask him to write the Foreword to my latest movie reference book, Actors and the Academy Awards.*
> *Send Aunt Lenore the turn-of-the-century photos of her in-laws that I acquired last summer.*
> *Take Mom Christmas shopping as we used to.*

That was the start of the list.

Arriving at our destination, I burst from Jerry's copper colored Dodge Caliber. "This is Day 1," I told Jerry. "Let's make it unforgettable."

As we walked the festival grounds toward the open-air wedding chapel, I had a magical experience that occurs whenever I feel spiritually open. Everybody I saw looked familiar. Gazing at hundreds of faces, I felt sure I'd seen each one before. When I first experienced this phenomenon, years ago, I tried to recall where I'd seen the people before, or wondered who else that person resembled. But I learned through my spiritual journey that, as a soul, I already know everybody because I am part of them and they're part of me. Today, as before, I was seeing a reflection of my own soul in everybody I passed.

While Jerry choreographed the event with the wedding coordinator, I felt physically depleted. I had a colonoscopy the previous day and suffered from an upset stomach this morning. Also, my blood sugar level drops sometimes. When I feel suddenly depleted, eating revives me. We'd passed pretzel vendors dressed as squires, so I went in search of a soft pretzel.

I had to go several directions before catching up with one of the vendors. I bought a pretzel, sat on an empty bench around a broad-trunked oak, and felt better as soon as I began eating. After I took only a few bites, a teenage boy approached. "Were you ever a teacher?"

"I was."

"In Galena Park?"

"At the high school."

That's when, a few paces behind the boy, I saw one of my former students. I ran up to her and hugged her. "Yes, I recognize you. Remind me of your name."

"Gloria," she said.

"Gloria, I do remember you," and I was glad I had a specific story from our past to ensure her that I did indeed remember her after twenty years.

Because Jerry and I are very sociable, and because we both have multiple careers that keep us in front of the public, we run into somebody we know nearly everywhere we go. Reconnecting with former students revives one of my favorite periods in life. As a teacher I opened my heart to students as expansively as I could. Whenever I imagine myself at my very best, I think of me in those days when I woke up every morning excited to hurry back to school and see what I could do next for my kids.

That feeling bubbled anew when I saw Gloria, reinforcing that I'm on the right track with this year's journey. It will place me in the spiritual epicenter of loving energy and teach me how to love with greater strength and abandon than I've known before.

After visiting with Gloria and finishing my pretzel I felt revived and ready to take the next step in this new process by creating some magic. Turns out I didn't have to do anything to materialize that thought except stay in the mindset of being present and grateful. The bride and groom, Kate and Darryl, had planned such an elaborate wedding that it felt mystical from beginning to end. It started with a procession from the Renaissance entrance gate to the chapel at the back of the festival grounds. I'm a happy guy, and I know my energy can overwhelm, so I usually temper it around others. During the procession, however, I let my light shine.

Way in front, flanked by festival guides in Renaissance regalia, Jerry led the wedding party toward our destination. Behind Jerry a white, floral laced horse-drawn carriage transported the bride and groom. I processed in the middle of the lines of wedding attendants behind the carriage, which included three groomsman (I was number three), bridesmaids, a maiden of the woods brandishing a rustic staff, the bride and grooms' granddaughters dressed as magical fairies, and right in front of me, their grandsons who would present the coat of arms of each ancestral line depicted on felt banners suspended from poles.

I don't know where my bridesmaid partner went, but I ended up walking alone among the paired attendants. Along the route, the herald announced our party. "Make way for the bride and groom," he bellowed. People stopped and watched, smiling and snapping photographs and holding little children in their arms and pointing in our direction until their eyes caught sight of us and their expressions bloomed. With my smile beaming, my heart flooded with light and lightness.

The grandsons in front of me started waving back to the spectators who waved to them. Then I saw the maiden of the woods, a woman about my age, wave to the crowds, too. Initially I felt self-conscious about waving, so I didn't.

Instead I walked, beaming till my cheeks nearly blocked my view, and thought, How blessed is this! The first day of the best year of my life starts with a parade, and I'm in it. I'm dressed for a Renaissance, my renaissance, in a brand new costume that someone made for me. The weather is gloriously bright but comfortably cool as Houston autumns at their best can be. As far as I can see, people are lined up along the processional path. I'm overflowing with joy, they're filled with a mirrored exhilaration, and I'm floating in this energy of love and excitement.

I let go of that last shred of inhibition and started waving, too. I waved to toddlers with their faces painted, I waved to an elderly man in a wheelchair whose eyes couldn't look straight ahead. I waved to a group of special needs children chaperoned by camp counselors in matching t-shirts. And I waved to everybody whose camera pointed in my direction.

The wedding went beautifully. As Jerry officiated the ceremony, I sent my love to him and to Kate and Darryl. It occurred to me what a miracle life is, and I thought about the fact that the first miracle Jesus performed was at a wedding. How appropriate it was that the first day of my miraculous new year of life should begin with a rite centered around love.

The reception followed in a vine-draped enclosure where caterers served turkey legs, a variety of meats, roasted corn on the cob, baked potato chips, and fruit cocktail. Usually when I eat out, even at a wedding, I choose what seems healthiest. With my new goal in mind as a guide for decision-making, I wanted to fully experience this event, including what fits the occasion. I couldn't let the opportunity pass without choosing a turkey leg. Further down the buffet line, I saw the roasted corn on the cob, which I love. But my digestion had been so unsettled since the colonoscopy that I even took an Immodium before we left the house that morning. I know corn is tough to digest and, momentarily, considered skipping it. Then I realized, what if this is the last wedding I ever attend? Am I going to avoid eating what I love because it might not sit well with my stomach later?

That insight reminded me of a story I had read in my favorite class, sophomore English. In the story a sickly old man feels pretty good one day and so has an adventure with his grandson. At the end of the day, he becomes very ill because of their excursion.

The grandson feels guilty for not stopping his grandfather from venturing out in his frail condition, but the old man assured him, "I would not have traded this experience for anything. A life lived too safely is a life not lived." The grandfather dies sooner because he had the adventure. Though I appreciated the story at the time, I couldn't embrace it because I was too afraid to live any way but safely.

So many years later I sensed remnants of that old fear still lingering inside me, and I wanted to set myself free of it. As a small step toward embracing that grandfather's philosophy, I ate what I wanted.

I tore into the turkey leg with the gusto (but a little less barbarism) of Henry VIII. I ate the corn on the cob. Usually I'm disciplined and avoid desserts. After the bride and groom cut the cake I took the piece of chocolate cake with the most icing. Instead of rebelling, my stomach actually rejoiced in my choices. This was going to be a good year.

On the way home, I reminded Jerry that we needed to stop at the grocery store to pick up some dog food.

"Dressed like this?" he asked.

"Sure, it'll be an adventure. Besides, it's the season of the Renaissance Festival. I think people will figure out why we're in costume."

It was actually fun to go through the grocery store dressed as we were. An older woman stared at us with persistent curiosity, and it made it easy to look right at her, smile, and greet her warmly. Living from this new perspective was already giving us an excuse to live a little more freely.

We arrived home to find one of our dachshunds, Joey, in severe pain. We'd been nursing him back to health since he herniated a disk over Labor Day weekend. We thought our prayers, attention, and the last round of medicines he's finished three days ago finally brought recovery. Now a new setback.

Despite my long day in the sun, I felt energized and motivated to get Joey immediate help. Our vet's pharmacy isn't open on Saturday evenings, but I called the office determined to get Joey a refill on his pain medication and his anti-inflammatory. By no accident, my faith confirms, the receptionist said that Joey's vet was the one on call, and he just happened to be there performing an emergency surgery.

"Could I please get the refills now? Our dog is really hurting."

"If I can catch Dr. Coogan, I'll ask if he would renew the prescription, but it usually takes 24 to 48 hours for the renewals to go through."

"If it would help I'll come to the clinic and wait. When he passes, I could talk to him."

She chuckled and assured me that wasn't necessary. But I think she noted my clarity. I believe it helped motivate her to be more proactive about finding Dr. Coogan.

Twenty minutes later she called back. Joey's prescriptions were ready.

On the way to pick them up I wondered how I'd pay for them. We still had a $200.00 balance from the oral surgery Joey and his brother, our red dachshund, Rex had in August. I had negotiated to pay our bill in full by Thanksgiving. These refills would cost $65.00, which I didn't have in my checking account. Charging the combined balance would only transfer the debt to a creditor that charged interest. So I prayed for a better solution. My $100 emergency stash came to mind.

I bought the prescriptions with the $100.00 and had the receptionist apply the change to our outstanding bill. From an apparent setback came little miracles. l left the clinic with Joey's prescriptions from a closed pharmacy on a Saturday night and had even chipped away at a debt I was determined to clear in less than two weeks.

At home I coaxed Joey to take the pills without his usual resistance. In 45 minutes the pills took effect. He started moving his head and contentedly licking Rex's leg.

Jerry, like his family, hails from Arkansas, and is an intense Razorback fan. Usually Jerry watches games in one room while I write, pursue personal goals, or work to maintain of our life in another. Open to a new mindset, I sat on the couch and petted Joey and Rex and watched the game with Jerry. Throughout, I stayed focused on the present. Frequently I looked over at Jerry and enjoyed him enjoying the game. I liked the feel of each dog's coat against my palm—slender Joey's black hair is smooth and sleek, while portly Rex's has a coarse blend of brown, red, and gray covering occasional waves of fat that have increased since the dogs turned 11. This was me actually sitting still and not feeling anxious to *do* something. In this attitude, I discovered that I had chosen what was most important—be with those I love. On this initial night of my first last year, it struck me that the clock was ticking away my time in this world. That realization coursed through my mind, heart, and body with an overwhelming hunger to relish the human experience of being alive now.

At bedtime, one of us didn't sleep on the couch with Joey, as we often took turns doing when he wasn't well. The previous night Joey had gotten sick on our king sized bed, and those linens were in the washer and dryer. The four of us on a queen sized guest bed is not an ideal sleeping arrangement, but Jerry and I wanted us all together. I drifted off that night with my hand on Jerry's shoulder, Rex against my leg, and Joey, as always, in the crook of my arm.

Day 1: on the physical plane, it seemed a day of ups and downs, with the wedding and then Joey's illness and pain. Spiritually, there was no up, no down, just growth, expansion. Faith is a warm, well-lit sanctuary. Anywhere you go in that space provides the ideal place to nestle.

2

Slowing Down to Focus

Day 2: November 13

On Sundays Jerry and I usually go to church together, but today I stayed home in case our ailing Joey needed me. I spent the entire morning and part of the afternoon writing the first day's entries with Joey curled against my leg and Rex on the other end of the couch burrowed under a throw.

After I finished writing, I called my mother to begin taking action on the goals I recorded in the car yesterday. For many years my mom and I spent one day in mid-December Christmas shopping. By then we had all our gifts bought so we could leisurely wander the mall taking in the music, observing the bustle of last-minute shoppers, and then sharing a meal at a favorite, quiet restaurant.

Discouraged by health setbacks, she has been declining my invitations in recent years. This time, rather than ask, I told her how much I would enjoy reviving our tradition. She can't walk far anymore without getting out of breath, so before she could elaborate on that first argument for not going, I told her we could go anywhere, even to quaint Old Town Spring where we could sit and people watch, or to a single antique warehouse that we've enjoyed browsing through before. The warm, positive approach worked: she accepted the invitation. I had already begun making progress on the first goals I'd set for my first last year.

After dinner that evening I wrote my first Thanksgiving letter. I have a gracious aunt I look up to as a spiritual role model because she is joyfully devout. So I wrote a letter with no news, just reminiscences of times we'd shared and affirming descriptions of how much her faith has inspired me. My loving gesture felt positive, but not new. I frequently write heartfelt notes to people I love or people who have made an impact on my life.

On one hand, I knew my letter would be well-received, as I'd expressed such sentiments to her in the past. On the other, this loving gesture didn't require the boldness my inspiration recommended. To give this year an extraordinary pulse, I needed to take more chances and regularly stretch and risk teetering to the most precarious tips of the limbs of life. To remain vibrant this year and learn new lessons of the soul required actions I never before had the courage to take.

Day 3: November 14

I left for work at my usual time but wanted to mail my aunt's letter, a detour that added about six minutes to my long commute to the school where I am librarian. I raced out the door, glad I remembered to bring my week's worth of lunches, the satchel I take most everywhere, and the box of children's novels I'm analyzing as part of the research for another book I'm writing called *Teach Me SUCCESS*.

Only after I'd swung by the post office and reached the first freeway four miles from home did I remember leaving on the counter a newly bound copy of my dissertation I had told my dad I'd give him at our monthly dinner that night. Running about ten minutes late already, I couldn't go back for the dissertation without being late for work. I am a stickler for punctuality, so knowingly making myself late was not an option. As I drove to school, my mind spewed a ticker tape of different solutions. I could rush home after work, grab the dissertation, and then get to the restaurant to meet Dad. That idea was impractical, as going home would add at least 40 minutes to my trek from school to the restaurant.

The school where Jerry works as a counselor is much closer to the restaurant than is our house. Maybe I could arrange for him to take the dissertation to work, and I could race to his school and get the dissertation from him, then hurry to the restaurant. In this problem-solving mode, my mind reeled so that I was not at all present with my ride to work. A sliver of insight opened new awareness. It didn't matter that I had intended to bring Dad the dissertation. I didn't have it. I would see him the following week when the family gathered on Thanksgiving. So I had forgotten the dissertation the last time we met, which itself is unusual for me. Forgetting something, especially after having placed it right next to everything else I remembered to take this morning, left me disappointed in myself.

Through my limiting thoughts, I saw an invitation for growth. By being more flexible, I wouldn't create unnecessary dilemmas. I accepted that I didn't have the dissertation, and I would not give it to Dad tonight. Although I always want to be impeccable with my word, I can also demonstrate better discernment. The point of our dinners is to enrich our father/son bond. Alternative solutions shot through my brain. When the most obvious resounded—apologize and tell my dad I'd bring it next time we met—I realized that focusing on solutions to what really wasn't a problem had only distracted my attention for the ride to work.

On the horizon stretched a long pink ribbon of sky. I took some relaxing breaths. Despite still running 10 minutes late, I coasted to the speed limit and watched the sky dissolve to white as I neared my campus. No longer in hyperspeed, I savored the journey, and signed in at work on time.

In my office I still had baby shower gifts for a colleague named Jacob. Several weeks ago, the social studies department planned a shower for Jacob and his expectant wife. Men seldom attend faculty showers, and I'm the librarian, not a social studies teacher, but I wanted to contribute. The day of the shower, Jacob's wife went into labor, so the social studies teachers decided to forego the shower in lieu of one large gift from them.

With the shower canceled, I didn't give Jacob the gift. Any time I felt inspired to take it to him anyway, I decided I'd waited too late. My new quest to pack full-out living in this one year meant completing unfinished acts of kindness. I saw an opportunity to be generous and brave. Giving a gift is obviously generous, but in this case it was brave, too. I felt embarrassed to bring Jacob a gift so long after his baby arrived and the rest of our colleagues acknowledged the birth. On the way to Jacob's classroom, I knew I needed to start surrendering limited thoughts and emotions that no longer served me. With so little time left to live and to bless others, I had a new rule: don't let feeling self-conscious or embarrassed keep me from taking action. If I'm inspired to do something, or even if I just feel like it, I must do it full-out without worrying if someone else is judging me, or, more importantly, without judging myself.

Just knocking on Jacob's classroom door cleared every emotion except the joy of giving. I handed him the gift with an apology for being so late. His grateful expression told me there is no wrong time to be generous.

Twice that morning I had misjudged time. Despite running late to work, I slowed to enjoy my commute and arrived on time anyway. I had been holding a gift I thought was too late to give Jacob, only to discover that kindness is always welcome. Another lesson bubbled to the surface and popped in my awareness: quit designing my life around deadlines. There's only one, and I'm 362 days from it.

That evening my dad chose Logan's Road House for our monthly father/son dinner. He likes Logan's because they serve buckets of peanuts, and patrons are free to toss the shells on the floor. When I entered, Tim McGraw's "Live Like You Were Dying" was playing. I had thought of the song when I started my first last year the other day. It seemed a fitting theme song then; it felt like an appropriate confirmation now.

During our dinner conversation, I really watched Dad sitting across from me. I made a conscious effort to maintain extended eye contact, and I focused on listening to everything he said instead of anticipating how I would respond, or letting an activity around us distract me. While being more attentive, I discovered that my eyes tend to laser onto people's mouths when they talk, rather than their eyes. But I looked into my dad's eyes and relished feeling connected to him. My dad and I are very similar in personality, in looks, and demeanor. I often tell people I am my dad—30 years later. As I studied his eyes in the shadow of the overhead light, they looked black.

"Dad, what color are your eyes?"

"They used to be blue."

"But they're darker now, aren't they?"

He confirmed that they were.

Even during past one-on-one dinners where we shared very personal opinions and insights, I had been only half present. I was listening and learning, but not seeing. Given the new awareness, I felt called to do both, with him and with everyone I encounter.

On the way home, I didn't listen to a motivational program or Oprah radio as I often do, but rode in silence, another practice that helps me stay centered and present. Traffic around the 610 loop was so backed up past The Galleria shopping center that I came to a complete stand-still on the freeway. I opened my windows to experience the breeze. It was 77 degrees out. A cool November wind was stirring through town. Exhilaration shot through me. Normally on beautiful days, I leave my windows open as I drive down residential streets, but then close the windows when I reach freeway speeds.

Even as I accelerated to 60 M.P.H. past the traffic congestion, I left my windows open. The wind hit my ears so hard that I would normally have closed the windows. But I wanted the sensory experience even with the slight discomfort. It helped me feel present. So I left the windows open all the way home and marveled how the earliest stages of this year's spiritual journey expanded my appreciation for the physical. Sensory experiences reminded me how vibrant life is, and how grateful I am to be aware that I'm living it.

3

Making Connections

Day 4: November 15

In a profound dream last night I searched to discover, "What is the core of the universe?" My answer came through a song. Immediately upon posing the question I heard "Oh, Holy Night" from Jerry's pristine tenor voice. Jerry, a professional singer, melts hearts with his ballads. In a single song, his intonations can dissolve everything but pure beauty. Among all the numbers in his repertoire I love, his rendition of "O, Holy Night" always touches me to the core. There was my answer: the core of the universe is the soul. I access it through beauty. Because the song's context focuses on serenity at the birth of Jesus, who symbolizes for me the manifestation of Spirit in physical form, I knew my yearlong journey would bring monumental spiritual leaps. I felt more excited about this process, and more spiritually alive than ever before.

Long ago, Jerry recorded a Christmas CD with a quartet called The Yuletiders. He sang lead on "Oh, Holy Night." I put the CD in my car and played the song continually throughout the long commute to my campus.

Work as a writer and high school librarian has been exceptionally busy this year. Usually juggling even fewer responsibilities would overwhelm me. Although inspirations from dreams and meditations keep adding more goals than I've ever pursued simultaneously, I feel empowered rather than fragmented or drained.

In this process I've been more in tune with my surroundings and my body, and I have been open to doing things differently to savor more experiences. For all the years I've worked at my school, I have eaten fruit, yogurt, and a granola bar for lunch because it's healthy and I can keep working at my desk while eating. Today the administration treated the staff to a free Thanksgiving lunch from the school cafeteria. Normally I wouldn't use time I could be working to go all the way to the cafeteria to get it. Even more importantly, I wouldn't want to ingest all those extra calories and carbs. But this time when I received the generous offer of a free lunch, I embraced the opportunity. At noon, I went directly to the cafeteria and accepted the whole meal without asking for smaller portions of the dressing, requesting that they leave off the gravy, or refusing the roll as I usually would. I accepted it all and felt grateful for the opportunity to experience some of the flavors of the upcoming holiday more than a week early.

I thought I might join some other faculty members in the cafeteria, but none were there, so I returned to my office, closed the door as I always do, and then did something new. I ate without working. I wanted to experience the meal—to note the textures of the food, inhale the aroma of the dressing and milky brown gravy, and taste what I was eating rather than focusing on some project until I looked down and discovered my plate was empty without giving my conscious mind a clue that my body had just consumed a delectable meal that would sustain it for hours.

Even with the break in momentum of my work, I achieved all my daily goals. Most exciting was learning how to secure charitable contributions from local businesses. I'll be hosting a reception for 50 teachers currently analyzing children's award-winning chapter books with me for my upcoming book, *Teach Me SUCCESS* (www.BayouPublishing.com). I felt propelled by the joy I imagined them feeling when I surprised them with gift cards from local restaurants and stores.

On the way home I listened to the entire Yuletides CD. It buoyed my spirit to be touched by Christmas joy more than a week before Thanksgiving. When I was growing up, Christmas season officially began when my dad played his Philadelphia Philharmonic album that starts with a rousing rendition of "O, Come, All Ye Faithful." Every year when we go to my sister's house for Thanksgiving dinner, she has the song cued to start as we walk in her front door.

Listening to Christmas songs in mid-November started the blessed season early for me. I shared the experience with Jerry that evening, and we laughed about his rule that he doesn't like anything about Christmas to happen until after Thanksgiving. I'm glad that's his rule, and not mine.

Because I got paid today, I stopped by the animal clinic and fulfilled my promise to pay our outstanding bill by Thanksgiving. Our dogs' vet was standing alone at the front desk, a first among all our visits. We discussed Joey's current health regimen for treating the slipped disk in his back, and then I asked him about his plans for Thanksgiving with his daughter, Hannah. I felt a sudden shift as he opened up to me and shared a struggle he was currently having with his ex-wife wanting to move with Hannah to another city. Between confessional statements he would stammer and say, "I don't know why I'm telling you this." But in the same beat, he'd continue.

Jerry and I had spent Cory and Rebecca's childhood creating ways to maintain a close relationship with them even though they lived hours away, so my responses came fluidly and naturally. I could sense that what I shared was lifting the heaviness in his heart, and I clipped an extended bit of advice with the simple affirmation, "You'll do whatever's best for Hannah."

"Yes!" he beamed, "Of course. Whatever's best for Hannah." He shook my hand. "Thank you. Talking to you really helped."

For the past few weeks I'd been discouraged that I didn't have the money to pay our vet bill when he treated the dogs. I spent too much time wondering if I'd have enough money left on payday to cover the bill in full. Now I knew I was meant to show up on this particular day.

Day 5: November 16

I woke early today to exercise using my home weight bench as has been my routine lately. For months Jerry has considered getting back into an exercise regimen and even working out with me. This morning, he was awake as I headed to the weight room.

"I think I'll join you," he offered, and we worked out together. Even better, he joined me in my next routine of meditating. I sat in my usual prayer chair and Jerry sat in the matching wingback beside it. Joey rested against my legs the entire meditation, and Rex sat in Jerry's lap.

My days are always extraordinarily busy at work as I am at different stages of writing five books in addition to running a high school library. My favorite activity is the writing. I start each session by meditating in order to slow down my mind and refocus my attention from the external world to the internal universe inhabited by my characters. To pave the way for writing *One Sister Left the Gun*, a novel I'm dedicating to Baka and her sisters, I begin my meditation by inviting them into my soul and listening for their guidance. On those rare days I feel tired or uninspired, my grandmother reminds me, "All you ever have to do is show up. The characters will do the rest." And the ideas flow again.

With so much going on at work today, I only had the energy to show up. I sat at my writing desk, went into a brief meditation, and began revising. My excitement peaked instantly. Today I had reached the disquieting scene that introduces the character with the gun. The story pulled me effortlessly into the session and revived creativity.

When I finished writing, I paused to appreciate how the universe was guiding me. I didn't have the resources to pay our vet until the day he needed my counsel. I reached a revitalizing scene in my manuscript the day I thought I would be too tired to be productive. My efforts to be alert every moment of this year already helped me recognize that needs are met in perfect time.

For the rest of the day I helped students research. Since beginning my first last year, I've concentrated on looking students in the eye and affirming them in my heart. To every class, I sent out little blessings. My goal is always to be positive and encouraging with students, but I feel that this new journey has helped me amplify the spiritual energy—without embarrassment, as my new rule dictates.

Today I pursued another goal I set on the way to the Renaissance wedding. Last summer I inherited several antique family photographs, including shots of ancestors I barely knew. Among them was a late cousin of my grandmother closely related to my Aunt Lenore. Months ago I wondered if she would like to have those photographs, but I never took action. Today I sent a letter offering them to her.

I stayed so late at school leading a literary analysis group for *Teach Me SUCCESS* that I arrived home too tired to journal about the day. I didn't judge. Instead I reaffirmed to Jerry how much I valued his support in making this the best and most memorable of years. I went to sleep committed to processing the journey by writing about it in the morning.

Day 6: November 17

I know this quest has now seeped into my subconscious. Last night I dreamed that I went into a store holding Joey. Vendors were selling Christmas decorations, so I searched for a memento to help make this holiday exceptional. One glass-encased display included a metal lunch box with Peanuts characters playing in a village. Most prominent was Linus, a character with whom I have always identified. Like him, I aspire to be kind to the underdog (in *A Charlie Brown Christmas*, only he is consistently kind to Charlie Brown) and to always have the wisdom to know what really matters (Linus articulated the true meaning of Christmas).

In the dream, I wanted to add this lunchbox to my vintage metal lunchbox collection. Even though it cost $30.00 I didn't have, I was determined to buy it as a memento of my first last Christmas.

Clearly my mind has built barriers against prosperity. But my determination in the dream convinces me my subconscious is working its way through them.

A disquieting emergency faculty meeting prompted me to send a loving message to a colleague. This year our school acquired a new administrator. Today he was absent, and in his place the former principal gathered the staff into the auditorium before school and cryptically explained that the new administrator had neither been arrested nor formally accused of anything, but was removed from campus and was on leave pending an investigation. We received no other details but were instructed to say nothing to the local media waiting hungrily across the street.

I barely know the new administrator. Last year colleagues at my school who had worked with him at another campus were thrilled he transferred to our high school. I greeted him last spring on his first campus visit, and I have spoken briefly to him on a few other occasions. Although I had no details about what happened, I felt inspired to email him. My act of bravery today would be to write a loving message to that administrator.

Subject: A Note of Encouragement.

Dear Mr. _____,

I'm sending you a note of encouragement to help you through your current challenge. I haven't heard any details about what is happening, so I cannot address any issue that you might be facing on the physical plane.

But always more important is what is happening on the spiritual plane. From there I can assure you that you will come through this temporary experience a stronger, wiser, and more enlightened man no matter what life brings.

Know that I am praying for you right now and I am visualizing with bright, positive expectation the very best results that can happen for you.

We are all one in spirit, and any energy you need to support and guide you is coming forward this very second with dazzling, powerful force. Let it lift you, and let it show you the way to make whatever decisions that you know spiritually are right. Rest assured that the only result that can happen is whatever is best for you and all concerned.

All is well. All is well. All is well.

For me, sending this email required bravery because I do not know the man, so I had no idea how he would receive it. At work I moderate expressing my spiritual philosophies so as not to overwhelm or repel anyone. But writing the email felt so spiritually empowering that I released all doubts or judgments and shared what I believe about spiritual versus physical reality. Composing this email, I sensed how I have been holding back, tempering my actions and energy so that I don't offend. But by not wanting to stand out, I was also not standing up—for who I am, for what I believe, and for what I have to share with the world.

I know that whoever is ready to hear a message will receive it in the spirit in which it is shared. I also know that I create the energy field that surrounds me, drawing into that field those who match it so that it strengthens and expands. Anyone not in that field is seldom even aware that I'm around because they're occupying their own energy field.

So I sent the email with the commitment to hereafter let my light shine. While remaining diligent and sensitive to the people around me, I will be more fearless about sharing my message that we are all spiritual beings in the perfect place and time no matter what is happening on the physical plane.

Recently I was listening to Oprah interview an author on the radio. She asked him if he thought the world was becoming a better, more spiritually enlightened place.

I would answer that question, "There is nothing but spiritual enlightenment. We are all already in paradise. We're each awakening to that awareness in our own time, through unique lessons, and in different ways. There is nothing to make better in the world because everything is already perfect. It always has been; it always will be. That's how it was created. Only our perceptions of that spiritual reality are susceptible to the illusion that anything is less than perfect. Any suffering that occurs in this world is from our erroneous thinking, and of our limited perception of not taking in the big picture of all that is.

"Even the biblical story of Jesus' crucifixion is not tragic when seen in the context of the whole Easter story. Two days after the crucifixion came resurrection, which symbolizes enlightenment of everything that pulsates with the energy of life. As I live and learn and expand in spiritual understanding, I feel ever clearer that everything is in divine order. Always."

So I am willing to risk people thinking I am strange or too happy or too anything. I am now, more than ever before, committed to sharing good news and letting any eager or willing heart ready to join my circle of influence add to that energy and help more people wake up to realize they're in paradise.

Between classes in the morning, one of the teachers who had been bringing her seniors to the library approached me. "I need to be rescued."

I hugged her.

She confessed her frustration with unruly students, most of whom were distracted and chatting up rumors about the administrator who was removed from campus. I asked her if she was open to praying with me. She was.

We walked to the research area her classes had been using. We held hands and I led us in a prayer for the students to feel affirmed and loved by us and to feel secure with the adults who *were* on campus taking care of them. Then we blessed the space in the library to be a sanctuary of peace and focus for students to work. For the first time that day, the library was empty. Not one patron milled about and no one entered until the bell rang for the next class to begin.

When the first two young men from her class arrived, the teacher turned to me and smiled. "I already know the prayers worked. These are my two best students." For the rest of the day, students were great.

An inspiration that I previously dismissed was to send a thank-you note to the doctor who performed my colonoscopy last Friday. I judged it as over-the-top to send a formal thank-you note to the doctor, but I never did see him after he performed the screening. He gave Jerry my positive results and then, when I came out of the anesthetic, a nurse wheeled me out front and Jerry drove me home. Deciding it was a loving thing to do, I let go of the judgment I had about the gesture being too much and sent a small thank-you card. As it was on its way, I imagined the pleasant surprise the doctor would experience and felt joyful for ultimately not letting the opportunity pass.

Day 7: November 18

I started my workday by meditating and then revising another chapter of *One Sister Left the Gun* (forthcoming... www.ParadisePublishingHouse.com). Occasionally my mind frets about not making swifter progress on the manuscript, but I have learned this lesson. I must trust that everything unfolds in perfect time.

Jerry and I each left work early to head to his parents' house in East Texas for a special weekend. Although the Roberts family has an annual reunion every December, Jerry and I seldom see his mother's side of the family. A few weeks ago, Jerry suggested to his mom a reunion with her relatives. Now we were traveling to East Texas to spend the night with Jerry's folks before heading further north the next morning for the reunion.

This trip began a week's vacation from school for me. I am on such a roll with my writing that I intend to continue working throughout the week, a shift from my usual routine of relinquishing all work during vacation times. On part of the northbound trip, I read to Jerry from the book I've been reading each morning at breakfast, Napoleon Hill's *Think and Grow Rich*.

I used to avoid writing spiritual books because I didn't believe my ideas added new insights to the body of knowledge already published. But noting the philosophical similarities between Hill's book from 1937 and many current publications, I appreciated the value of continual exposure to ideas. A familiar concept expressed in a fresh voice can give it new meaning for me, and reignite my passion for spiritual exploration. Even re-reading books I know well can spark fresh insights related to my current life experiences.

Constant exposure to spiritual ideas allows them to seep into our subconscious, reach our superconscious, and allow our soul to reflect them on the physical plane. One literary theory suggests that there are only seven stories retold in different ways in each original work. Similarly, there are basic Truths that we are all learning, and learning, and learning, and eventually absorbing until they are authentically ours.

When I wrote *Success Express for Teens* (www.RogerLeslie.com), I knew I had something original to say to teen readers because I was drawing from 30 years of personal growth. Writing for adults proved a dilemma. On one hand, when I would lock into a new insight that transformed me to a higher spiritual plane, I wanted to share it with people who had not yet learned it. On the other hand, once I took in the spiritual insight, the wisdom no longer seemed new. Instead it felt so natural that my mind accepted it as a universal and obvious truth. By sharing revelations from my unique experiences, I offer an original perspective on universal ideas. The truth may be obvious, but my context might give it the dimension to help readers grasp it.

As powerful spiritual forces, we can create self-fulfilling prophecies in the physical realm. Consequently, throughout this past week, I have worried about what message I'm sending the universe by holding the vision that this is my last year. However, I'm not living this experience to die well. I am living as if this is my first last year to live well, and to place in my conscious mind the demand to never be lackadaisical about any new day. So I am reframing this experience to focus less on its being the *last* time I experience each day, but living each 24-hour period as if it's the *only* time I am experiencing it. So this is not my last November 18, but I am living it as though I have never had a November 18 before. If I don't ever have one again, I will have made one November 18 a day I truly lived.

This desire is not new, although this expression of it is. Back in 1985 my lifelong friend Jeanette gave me a book of days, an empty calendar book with adjacent pages of famous works of art. After first receiving it, I set a goal to fill that book so that, by the time I died, I would have done something extraordinarily memorable every day of the calendar year. I still have the book, but I haven't added a landmark memory in years. Some pivotal events I commemorated include the day I acquired my first dog, Max, who is with me in spirit always. He remains the most steadfast and grounding force of love to see me through the volatile years when I was first discovering myself spiritually. At the time I suffered much from my own limited belief that I was a mere physical being with little control over challenges, joys, and disappointments from a world moved by unpredictable forces. Through his beautiful example, he showed me that nothing is stronger or simpler than love and loyalty. In my book of days, I also recorded my grandmothers' deaths, publication of my early books, and unique family celebrations.

I need to pull out the book and update it with events from the recent past. During the cycle of this experiment, I want to fill my days with experiences that warrant inclusion in my book of days. A blessed life is proactively driven. Through initiative come opportunities to touch lives and remind people what they have always known as spiritual beings—we fuel the fire of our own passion for life through others' encouragement and example.

The quest seems altogether natural. When we are our true selves, life is easy. All drama on the physical plane is merely children fussing in front of a looking glass, not seeing themselves as they arrived here in this life as spiritual energy, but as helpless, or spoiled, or self-centered entities wondering where their mother is, and worrying that their own needs are not being met. I hope sharing my spiritual insights awakens a revolution in the numbed, fearful hearts of those still focusing on chaos.

I envision a quantum shift to help the world of form reflect more accurately the bliss of the eternal, spiritual plane. Beyond the borders of our own geography, we are all beloved members of a universal citizenship. I trust that tracing my year-long journey will shine light throughout the physical plane wherever it is needed most.

4

Connecting to Others on the Physical and Spiritual Planes

Day 8: November 19

The Vestal reunion was as soul-nourishing an experience as I've ever had with Jerry's extended family, mostly because I showed up differently. Though it may seem odd to anyone not in my situation, I have held back being myself around Jerry's family to honor his gradual self-acceptance as a gay man.

Until his thirties, Jerry fought his natural inclinations. He presented himself as a straight man, got married, had children, and became minister of a mainline Christian denomination that condemned homosexuals. What courage it ultimately took to leave a ministry where he was so admired to restart a life true to himself.

Jerry waited nearly 10 years after we became a couple to come out to his immediate family, and he has still never spoken about himself or us to some relatives. Until he told them himself, I honored Jerry's coming out process by acting merely as his friend. Many of Jerry's relatives, especially on his dad's side, are charismatic, fundamentalist Christians who live in small towns. Though I've attended every Roberts reunion since 1985, I still taper my energy and, as a colleague once noted about me, selectively "hide my light under a bushel."

The Vestals are laid-back and approachable. I had only seen most of them a few times before at family gatherings or hospital visits. I attended the funeral of Jerry's Aunt Lorette, held graveside on a chilly Christmas Eve ten years ago. Interestingly, Lorette's daughters had selected as the music for her funeral the version of "Silent Night" that Jerry recorded with The Yuletiders.

Intent on making the Vestal reunion a first last year experience, I lifted that bushel and let my light shine. Despite not knowing most of the attendees and rarely spending time with them, I interacted with everyone without fear of recrimination or suspicion or judgment for being Jerry's husband rather than just a friend. In conversation, I referred to Rebecca as "our daughter" and Cory as "our son." In that freer emotional space, ideas to affirm people came as naturally as they usually do. The feedback I received felt astounding. It was as though Spirit kept speaking through the voices of Jerry's relatives, grinning widely and saying, "Yes, Roger. This is the man I made you to be. You are serving others by being yourself, finding the best about them, and telling them what you see."

And I did. If I thought a cousin looked beautiful, I told her. If I felt positive energy from a relative, I complimented him or her, not with spiritual terminology, but with phrases such as, "Wow, you seem so happy you just glow," or even as simple as "I like the way you look at things. That inspires me."

I felt real connections with several of Jerry's cousins, a few of whom told me they wanted to take me home with them so I could keep building up their self-esteem. My passion is to inspire others. The desire circulates naturally through me because it's what I came to this life to do. How deep-breath, face-to-the-sun, eyelids gently closed blissful it felt to be myself among people I know Jerry loves so dearly. It occurs to me now that I probably could have been myself much longer ago, and doing so might have helped Jerry build confidence in himself more quickly, too.

I know better now, so I'm acting on that wisdom. It's making all the difference.

Day 9: November 20

On our weekends in East Texas, Jerry and his parents often take a side trip to the Shreveport, Louisiana casinos. I'm not much for gambling, so I usually stay at his parent's house to watch television, assemble a jigsaw puzzle, and eat whatever I want. Those rare times I do go, they head to the slot machines while I find an unobtrusive corner to write or read. Knowing they would go this morning, I wondered, as a day I wanted to make memorable, whether I should go with them.

I know I'm working on prosperity, but I'll admit here that I literally did not have a single dollar in my wallet. I gave the last one away to the young man who cleaned my windshield at the carwash on Thursday. So I decided to stay home and realized I wouldn't be alone if I wrote to you. Yes you, the reader. From my spiritual perspective, I've already formed a bond with you. Just as I spend time in meditation with my grandmother and her sisters before writing my novel, I sense you with me as I journal. Neither of us is alone.

This perspective fits my spiritual belief. For a flash, my spark of divinity leaps from Spirit's sun and shines. For a flash, your spark of divinity catches it. In physical time, my flash will take the year to experience and record what I learn. Your spark will flash after you are drawn to this work, acquire a copy, read it, and are touched by it. In spiritual time, which is spatial, not linear, we're already in relationship. What you were seeking during my first last year, I am being called to write. Your needs are resonating with me now, even though in the physical realm you may awaken to them years from now. An unenlightened person might think I am alone sitting on a plush green area rug typing on my laptop on a cool Sunday morning in Texas. You and I know better.

So thanks for spending this time with me and for inspiring me. It's quiet here right now. Joey and Rex are sprawled on the couch. Joey's lying on his back, a rarity for a dog usually too timid to let himself be that vulnerable, and portly Rex rests on his left side, his sweet little face brushed against the sofa cushion. They're both partly covered by a Christmas throw Jerry's mom pulled out early. They're so fast asleep neither stirs or even snores.

Feeling such peace right now, sensing my connection to you, my reader, overcomes me with emotion. Often in the past I ruined the quiet solitude meant to blanket me in bliss by thinking I was alone. I know better now. I'm warmed by the belief that you are present, and I am now visualizing many experiences on book tours when you approach me, refer precisely to this section of the book and share your version of what happened spiritually from your piece of the Allsoul. Let your spark shine, dear friend. Someone out there right now is catching a glimpse of it and feeling inspired because you had the courage to be you.

Day 10: November 21

This was a great football weekend for Jerry and his family. Not only did the Razorbacks win, but other teams ahead of them in the ranking also lost, likely moving the Hogs up to fifth in the nation. When we visit Jerry's folks, they have sports on television nonstop. His parents will watch whatever sport comes on. If there were a little league Lithuanian lacrosse tournament, they'd watch for a few seconds, discuss what's going on, determine which team they admire more and which players are worth rooting for, then get so involved in the game that they'd make watching it a few hours of high-energy entertainment.

I rarely enjoy competitive sports. As a swimmer in high school, I learned that competition can be an effective motivator for self-improvement. But scenarios where one group of people feels victorious at the expense of another's disappointment run counter to what I want to create in my life.

I know Jerry once dreamed of having a spouse share his love of sports, but I never developed the passion. I tried. During our first year together I memorized the rules from a book about football fundamentals and could demonstrate the referees' gestures. When I watch games with Jerry and his family, I can get swept into the excitement of a game, but my heart is not in it like theirs. I appreciate what a bonding experience watching and discussing football is for them. Unfortunately for Jerry, neither knowledge nor exposure spiked my interest.

I mention this now because today I decorated the house for Christmas. Just as Jerry wanted a spouse to share his enthusiasm for sports, I held romantic ideas of sharing the experience of decorating for the holidays. Early on, Jerry did try to indulge me. We used to select a live tree together. He would even put the hooks on the ornaments and lay them on the coffee table so I could hang them on the tree. But I could tell from the earliest years that Jerry didn't share my spark for it. I would be decorating the tree, turn around, and Jerry would have disappeared into the bedroom upstairs. I'd find him watching TV or sleeping. In time, I realized it was easier to decorate for Christmas alone.

Our jobs eventually created a perfect opportunity for that to work. For several years Jerry has been scheduled to work the Monday and Tuesday of Thanksgiving week, while my district gives us the entire week off. The first time that happened, I surprised Jerry that Monday and decorated the entire house before he came home from work. As he entered, I had the tree fully adorned with lights set on random twinkle; stockings for Jerry, the kids, the dogs, and me hanging from the mantle; and various displays around the living areas, from my Christmas book arrangement on the hearth, our Disney and Muppet characters on the kitchen ledge, our dog-themed tabletop tree in the living room, and even the bathroom festooned with a Christmas shower curtain and Night Before Christmas hand towels. Jerry is always great about acknowledging what I do, and I know he appreciates my efforts to create a joyful holiday atmosphere.

Jerry revels in favorite childhood memories that took place at football stadiums and has perpetuated his love of sports with our children, Cory and Rebecca. Similarly I reignite my boyhood excitement for the holidays by reviving my own traditions. While decorating, I re-watch favorite movies and Christmas episodes from sitcoms I first loved as a child. Even in the warmth of Texas in November, those shows revive memories of chilly Michigan winds and snow crunching underfoot.

It was once exciting for Jerry and for me to imagine sharing with one special someone a boyhood experience that meant so much. It's been empowering to surrender that dream and sustain our lifelong love of something with others or alone. Making this observation today reinforces what matters most. I can create my own joy, made easier because I have such a loving spouse.

But in my first last year, re-watching the shows I've always loved stirred a disquieting realization. For worldly pleasures, "always" has an expiration date. I can bring past joys into the present, but I am not guaranteed an indefinite future to relive them. With only now, I have to appreciate more fully what I have this time, and experience it as if I would never see it again. This insight shifted my tradition. I still played the old shows as I decorated, but the tasks lasted longer because I frequently stopped working during my favorite movie scenes to fully engage in the action, or to laugh at sitcom jokes that have long delighted me.

Like many people in our culture, I am a skilled multitasker. I can work on many projects simultaneously and complete them all quickly with excellent results. But the number of tasks we juggle is directly proportionate to the amount of focus our mind can give each. We can do various jobs well, but we can be wholly present with only one at a time. Multitasking may not jeopardize the quality of results, but it always fragments the quality of our experience completing them. I don't want to simply finish this last year well; I want to savor it as it transpires. That requires attending fully to each moment and making it new. I learned today that such focus can make any experience fresh, even reviving joys I've known a lifetime.

Day 11: November 22

At Panera Bread this morning, I met with my publicist. Each interaction with Doris grows more insightful and spiritual. This time, I suggested we start with prayer. We took each other's hands and I prayed for us to be instruments of enlightenment as our collaboration manifested all our professional dreams.

"I think my next mission involves palliative care," she shared later in the meeting. She came to that conclusion after multiple experiences of attending to loved ones as they died.

In one case, she was the only relative in the room. Soon after family members left, her ailing aunt started taking intermittent gasps. Doris called in the nurse, who told her that this was the beginning of the end. The nurse pointed out the patient's blue fingertips, an indication that the body's systems were shutting down. After her aunt died when Doris was alone with her, the nurse told her, "Do you realize what a gift you've been given? Patients choose when they will ultimately go. The fact that she waited until everybody else left means that she chose you to see her out of this life."

Doris shared with me that, since we last saw each other a year ago, she had been the sole person present for three family members' deaths, and her brother was about to make his transition after a long bout with brain cancer. She didn't know how this new experience would manifest, but she felt a spiritual tug telling her that she had a gift for being a loving presence when people died.

I told her that it was no mistake that we should get on this topic. "My grandmother and her four sisters visit regularly in my meditations. Some of them died long ago; two are still living. But they all show up equally alive in my spiritual sanctuary. I'm fascinated. The border between the physical and spiritual worlds has become beautifully blurred for me."

Then I recapped what I journaled to you earlier about the big picture and Easter weekend: Death in the moment only seems sad, and circumstances tragic, until we take in the spiritual view and realize that everything, even the individual seconds of loss that feel so sad and empty, is aligning for ultimate good. What is not important—usually our expectation about how things should be—evaporates. What matters gets stronger and more meaningful as we awaken spiritually and become more wholly aware. By meeting's end, we both shone a little brighter.

After our meeting, I swam at the gym. This year I set a 3-part fitness goal. I completed the cardio dimension in October and the weight training facet early this month. Today's 2500 meter swim puts me less than 10,000 meters from success. Without the goal, I could easily have foregone working out to concentrate exclusively on my writing. But goal setting commits us to act on inspirations. Further, goals hone our creativity by demanding that we find original approaches when life, as it often does, brings other opportunities our way.

As always, after working out I feel invigorated, leaner, happier and more alert. The positive effects of the workout usually linger throughout the next day. What a worthwhile tradeoff to spend an hour or two productively and enjoy results for about 48. My first last year quest is also a goal of sorts. I imagined the residual blessings looming longer and more broadly than I'd first imagined.

After my swim I met Jerry and two assistant principals from his school at Guadalajara's Mexican restaurant. This entire year Jerry and both of these colleagues have been disheartened by the toxic atmosphere at their school. I spent most of my evening encouraging them and sharing insights that could help them recreate their situation.

"You ought to be a motivational speaker," one AP said.

I wondered why so many people are still not aware of my writing and speaking history. My disappointment convinced me to do more public speaking and market my career better.

I live to encourage people. It's so easy to forget how powerful and empowering we are. Everything we want is waiting for us if we have the wisdom to accept it and the courage to claim it. While sharing this perspective with Jerry's colleagues, I knew I could be more dynamic in acknowledging and accepting the prosperity that I seek. It is here for me to claim right now. I know I am proactively taking steps, and sometimes leaps, toward fulfilling my destiny by writing and speaking to help others make their dreams come true. I feel that it has already come to pass on the spiritual plane for me. I will watch for a reflection of that truth in the physical world.

5

Spiritual Awakenings

Day 12: November 23

Most Friday nights, Jerry and I get together with friends at our favorite restaurant. Tonight we made plans with longtime pals Dennis, Ann Marie, and their son John. Eager to do something generous, I wanted to treat dinner. Without cash on hand to pay for it, I decided to charge the meal and figure out how to pay for it later. Warning bells blared in my head. To create prosperity, I shouldn't incur a debt without a plan to pay it off. I got creative and sought another way to be generous. I searched through my Christmas gift drawer and found multiple copies of a Jim Brickman CD I bought for stocking stuffers. From a prosperity perspective, it was exciting to realize that even before I decided what to do for someone else, I had gifts available. This act of generosity required only that I wrap the gift and give it to them at dinner.

We've all dined at this restaurant so long we know the wait staff, and their personal histories. Two of our favorites are Alfonso, who only rarely gets to go home to Mexico over the holidays to be with his family, and Marita, who is facing health challenges but continues to work two jobs to put her niece through college.

At dinner Jerry and I had the same inspiration: give Alfonso and Marita each $100 as a thoughtful holiday gesture. Although I don't yet know where we'll get the extra cash to give our favorite servers, the discovery of a gift for Dennis, Ann Marie, and John tells me I already have the resource. By thinking a little deeper I'll discover that God has already provided for me.

Whenever I want to do something and don't know how, I picture the core of my faith, sometimes tiny as a mustard seed, deep in my soul. There I know that God already has provided the answer. God never gives me the wisdom to ask a question before I have access to the answer in a way I can grasp right now. Life never presents a challenge until the path to reach the next level of enlightenment is already clearly lighted.

Day 13: November 24

To start the holiday season with generosity, I have gathered small gifts for the family members who'll attend the Thanksgiving dinner hosted by my sister, Judy and her spouse, Phil. It seemed natural and appropriate to fill this day with gratitude, so I lived from that spiritual perspective all day.

I felt blessed to be with Jerry and my family. Mom has been in rare high spirits lately, Dad said he's feeling well, and Judy and Phil prepared a beautiful meal we all relished.

Everyone enjoyed the presents. I gave Mom a Barry White CD. Back in the seventies she had a Barry White album, but had to sneak down to the basement and listen to it after we went to bed because the lyrics were too provocative for us kids to hear. Judy collects penguins and keeps fun books of wisdom in her guest bathroom, so I was delighted to give her a penguin book of wisdom. I bought Phil an insulated cup so he could drink coffee on the way to work on cold mornings. Dad, always proud of his heritage, loved his Christmas ornament with a Polish eagle on the front, and the story of its history on the back.

Jerry and I left the Thanksgiving gathering after 9:00 p.m. Driving away, I regretted not calling both of my brothers, as it would have been loving to connect with them on this holiday of gratitude. Once we arrived home, it would be too late to call my brother Randy, who lives in a later time zone. Then it occurred to me that Jerry could text him as I drove so he would at least receive a communication from us while it was still Thanksgiving Day. When Jerry finished, he then texted my brother Ray, too, who lives near Houston but spent the holiday with his wife's family.

Lesson learned: With very little creative energy, we can always find a way to achieve a loving act.

Day 14: November 25

I've been thinking about Elizabeth Gilbert's travels in her book, *Eat, Pray, Love* and sensing that my own experiences need to grow bigger than they have been. I like what I'm doing, and I like the spiritual perspective from which I am living. Still I sense that I'm on the threshold of something much grander than what I've done so far.

Tonight Jerry and I watched a pre-recorded episode of *Oprah's Soul Series Sunday*. Interestingly, one segment was dedicated to *The Oprah Winfrey Show* episode with Elizabeth Gilbert. While watching I felt a message reassure me. When I compared my spiritual quest with Elizabeth's, I thought mine should be more global. Then I realized that most people do not have the money, drive, inclination, or time to drop their lives and travel the world for a year discovering themselves. Most need and want to do it right where they are and begin now. So I felt reassured that I don't need to do anything massive to touch the souls of millions who are seeking guidance, inspiration, or even a whispered acknowledgment of their soul. What a great service I would provide by living my spiritual journey as it shows up for me, and then writing about it.

Watching the interview brought another inspiration. If we don't act on inspirations, the spark dies. As a friend succinctly affirmed, "Miracles have expiration dates." If you let enough sparks of inspiration fade without taking action and owning them, the opportunities move on and become someone else's miracle.

I will do an extraordinarily loving and generous act this holiday. After I decorated my house with the mementoes I value most, I went through what's left in the bins to give most of it away. Initially I thought of donating items to a needy family we adopt through my school. But as the pile of decorations grew to include games and toys and clothes and household items, I became excited about touching many lives.

Why not take everything to my library and let students get them as they wish? I could designate a section of the library as a Christmas store where students shop for free! I even have time to invite other teachers to donate items, too.

I learned something interesting in the process of imagining what this dream could become. My mind wanted to thwart the inspiration. It brought up doubts. Who would want a game that's already been opened? What if students who don't need items come and take them just because they can, and they don't go to people in need? Immediately I saw my idea shift from *Thy Will Be Done* to *My Will Be Done*. As a man of faith, I want to put ideas into action and trust that the spiritual energy of God will move the love where it's needed most. I must learn to trust that when I act on inspiration, I may be a vessel for fulfilling someone's dream. Despite what my ego would like to believe, I didn't start this loving action. The energy of it began with someone else's prayer. By responding to the call, I'm agreeing to participate in something bigger than me.

Looking at the boxes full of gifts that could bring many families joy helped me appreciate a form of my prosperity I'd overlooked. My abundance is not restricted to a number in a checkbook ledger or the thickness of my wallet. In one day I collected piles of items from my home that can indelibly touch the hearts of others. I feel empowered by even the anticipation of sharing generously, and I feel freer having more room in my closets.

Day 15: November 26

Last night Jerry and I decided it'd be fun to go to Starbucks this morning and use a gift card from one of his students. I woke first and, without thinking, punched on our coffee pot. When Jerry awoke I remembered our Starbucks plan. With Mr. Coffee brewing, we almost lulled ourselves into staying home. Then I remembered my first last year and felt determined to follow through on our original plan. I punched off the coffee, we threw on some clothes, and enjoyed two mocha lattes, and a slice of ginger bread and lemon pound cake. Being among people filled me with joyful energy. When I went to the counter to pick up our drinks, I kidded with a female customer waiting there and could feel the energy between us intensify.

Three men sat at a small round table beside us. I didn't recognize the language they spoke, but having them nearby added a cosmopolitan diversity that expanded the breadth of our experience.

Thanks to an early payday, I could complete another goal I set as I began my first last year. Jerry and I bought Christmas gifts for the Michigan relatives we vacation with every July. Besides presents for the great aunts and cousins we see annually, we shopped for their spouses and children so everyone would receive something. We found presents for almost everyone, but had more shopping to do.

That afternoon I wrapped what we bought and stacked them in the den. Without all the presents for any one household, I packaged what I could and formed a new pile for mailing. Meantime, I gathered more Christmas puzzles and decorations to donate at my library. In the corner, a stack of antique pictures waited for me to sift through to find photos to send Aunt Lenore.

Previously such a mountain range of incomplete activities would have left me anxious. This time, instead of seeing the piles as clutter I needed to clear, I recognized them as ideas brimming to life. I enjoyed the emotional freedom of letting each project evolve in its own natural time.

I used this insight as a personal metaphor. There are areas of my life that I would like to see reach fruition. For example, I would already like to have the financial abundance to do even more for us and for others. But I'm not there yet. I am exactly where I am, taking this new journey with you, readers, living for this year, growing each day, and processing new insights through this book. What an emancipating adventure! That's how I used to envision wanting my life to become, an enriching, soul-satisfying adventure. For some periods in my past, life temporarily became exactly that. Now, while focusing on being fully present, it feels that way every moment.

Note to self: don't look at now and think it represents my future. Be in the moment and live life as it evolves. What I have today may last a lifetime or only five minutes. But when I live each moment, I don't need to fear losing what I have now. Tomorrow will evolve just as I will, so it won't look as it looks now. It will be no better or worse, for the essence of perfection is not comparative. It just is.

Today, I have an obstacle course of boxes and donations and photographs towering with the promise of bringing others joy. This is the Christmas season. How lucky I am to have been inspired. How wise that I took action. How blessed to live for a few days with a tangible sign of love in progress.

The key to all happiness and success is to access our inspirations and then act on them. It'll shake things up. In order to enjoy acting on multiple inspirations simultaneously, I had to change how I perceived my present moment. One man's clutter is another's joy. I can see my growth by contrasting those two men. They were both me.

Day 16: November 27

In his church message Jerry shared my plans to donate personal items for students at my school. After the service, two congregates asked if they could donate, too. Already, my single inspiration was growing. Who knows what the library Christmas store will ultimately offer students? As the momentum built, so did the excitement of those who would contribute.

We return to work tomorrow after our Thanksgiving break. Jerry is still debating a career change, as he knows his current job no longer requires the spiritual gifts he wants to share daily. I usually give myself more down time than I took this Thanksgiving break, but I'm not concerned. My idea of living is being active, doing and enjoying and relishing and experiencing and being present. Sometimes that means being as busy as that last string of verbs implies. Other times it means becoming still and attuning to my soul. Either way—busy or relaxed, vibrant or peaceful—it is about awareness and presence and gratitude.

It's 5:30, so I have a few more hours to enjoy the last evening of this break. I'll start by going through one more Christmas bin to find treasures to pass on. What a lesson! While seeking a more abundant life, I find a lifetime of prosperity to give away. Recognizing that I'm in the cycle of abundance makes me a very rich man, indeed.

Day 17: November 28

I returned to work with an avalanche of new challenges threatening to bury me. For this afternoon's meeting with one literary analysis group for *Teach Me SUCCESS*, I emailed a reminder to the members. I haven't heard back from anyone, but I'm hoping they show. Further, I've received inaccurately formatted analysis results from other groups. That required more emails and troubleshooting.

But the biggest boulder fell when one group leader called to say that she was dropping out and that her group had accomplished none of their objectives. Such a bombshell would normally have overwhelmed me. I would have been congenial to the bailing group leader, but it would have taken effort to sound sincere while my mind fretted about how to wring from my schedule another new obligation.

Committed to loving every minute of this year, I took a breath and refused to let worry overtake me. Instead of making a snap decision, I asked the teacher to give me time to consider my next steps. During our conversation she shared feeling unappreciated by the group she was leading.

"Would you consider filling in as a reader in a group led by someone else?" I asked. She readily agreed.

When I hung up the phone, I bellowed, "Arrgh! Now what do I do?" Strangely, the knee-jerk reaction felt disingenuous. Spiritual strides from my first last year quest kept me feeling grounded. The plates underfoot had shifted and locked my foundation more sturdily into place, but without an earthquake, only a mere tremor.

My mind still swum from the overwhelming prospect of leading a sixth group, having to read and analyze seven more books, and—the most challenging part of the entire process—coordinating schedules with other educators to meet and reach consensus on our findings.

But naturally throughout the day, good news dripped into the project like an intravenous lifeline. Another reader emailed me that she analyzed all the books for her group and would help another if needed. I received the literary analysis from another group that got the process right the first time.

During my lunch hour I revised *One Sister Left the Gun*. If the chapter I worked on before Thanksgiving break and the one I edited today are any indication of what is to come, then I think I hit my stride in the first draft. The edit went smoothly and only took about half my lunch period. I was very pleased with the results.

I hoped to visit with the lead counselor about the library store, but she was busy with a college event. I'll check with her tomorrow.

Following today's long afterschool meeting, I would normally feel tired. However, I arrived home still excited that I could observe my mind wanting to fret over this morning's stressors without feeling any urge to indulge it.

"How'd your day go?" Jerry asked.

"Things took some interesting twists, but overall it was spiritually enlightening."

"What happened?"

"The details aren't that interesting," I told him, "Another of the literary analysis groups disbanded, so I'm in the process of regrouping. Literally."

"Sorry you had a bad day."

"I didn't have a bad day. I had a . . . unique day."

"Sorry you had a unique day."

Jerry's a funny guy.

After dinner I searched for Christmas books to give away. How interesting, during this period of building my prosperity, to find treasures I didn't remember. In one book I found a postcard of a Detroit skyscraper behind a majestic decorated Christmas tree. Perhaps 20 years ago I used to display the postcard and had forgotten about it. The treasures increased as I shifted more books from personal possessions to magic-makers for someone else this holiday.

In one Santa Claus coloring book I found pages that I had colored with my nieces, Anna and Caroline, when they were toddlers. In some novels I found Christmas wishes from people I barely knew, but who knew I love reading. Most interesting, in a small book called *Christmas Tidings*, I found an inscription dated 1986. I bought this book the month after we received the results of our AIDS tests. Below the date I wrote, "To a Brand New Life."

On the anniversary of that holy experience, I was again focusing my energy on living minute-by-minute with presence, awareness, and gratitude. *Christmas Tidings*, which I had not opened since that year I bought and read it, provided a holy moment for me.

I felt so moved I took it to the den to show Jerry. A brief wave of emotion swept through both of us. We hadn't even reached December, and already this was one of the most heart-touching Christmases of my life.

I learned again the value of acting on inspiration. If an idea sparks, don't let it become a fleeting thought that flickers and fades. Take it to action, and step back because the flames are going to brighten your life like you've never seen before.

Later that evening Jerry and I watched an interview with Reverend Ed Bacon on *Super Soul Sunday*. I had heard the interview previously on Oprah radio, but it was a nice refresher. I especially appreciated his suggestion to take an hour to 90 minutes every day to meditate. I went to bed early with the intent of waking up about 5:15 to meditate for 45 minutes.

I woke just before 5:00, so I took the opportunity to meditate the entire hour. I was surprised by how much my mind raced for the first several minutes. Not long ago I had increased my morning meditation time from 15 minutes to half an hour. Today during that first half hour my mind bounced around with myriad commitments I had to complete, projects I had going, and random thoughts my mind dribbled all around my mustard seed soul. When I finally latched onto the image of my soul waiting patiently for the thoughts to settle so I could get to what really mattered, my mind flatlined in surrender. My heartbeat steadied as my body relaxed. My mind wasn't sleeping; it had just curled into the nape of my spirit and didn't need to stir to feel noticed. When I finished my meditation, I looked at the clock—I had meditated 67 minutes. It seemed to last the length of one comforting breath.

Jerry awoke riled from a sleepless night. He's infuriated that his school's administration is ignoring a bullying incident. During our conversation, my calm was rattled by the intensity of Jerry's upset. At first I encouraged Jerry to do what he's been thinking about for months—get out. But as we spoke, I realized that he may be his students' only hope. I encouraged him to prayerfully explore whether he was already where God needed him to be, or if his gifts of spiritual counsel could be better used somewhere else. We prayed for Jerry to be a light for the bully and her mother during their meeting that afternoon. I promised Jerry I'd continue the prayers we'd begun together.

Flashes of insight came during that prayerful commute. According to Jerry, his school administrators don't resolve issues because no one takes responsibility for the problem. The assistant principal doesn't act because she believes that decision belongs to the principal. He isn't acting because he has delegated disciplinary actions to his assistants. That leaves Jerry feeling disempowered because, as counselor, he doesn't have authority to expel the bully. Meantime, the girl being harassed is so depressed she's afraid to go to school. Her brother and sister visited the campus yesterday to learn why no one is helping their little sister by disciplining the bully or moving her to an alternative campus.

The scenario reminded me of a district board meeting I attended earlier this semester. A citizen from the community issued a complaint that students' loitering at a nearby drug store after school is turning away older patrons. As I heard his plea, I grew defensive. I noticed how bloated the responsibilities of educators have become. Not only are parents and community members expecting educators to provide support, guidance, and general parenting to their children during the school day, but now they're also expecting us to take responsibility for making sure their children are behaving off campus after school hours. My blood boiled as I thought, why should the school even be addressing this issue? Where are these kids' parents? Why aren't they setting ground rules for how their children behave and where they go after school?

Listening to Jerry's frustration this morning reminded me that, although I didn't say anything at the board meeting, my thinking was no better than how the administration at his school was acting. I was merely passing the responsibility to someone else, thereby excusing myself of accountability. I pictured a race that never finishes because one runner merely passes the baton to someone else, then lies down and divorces himself completely from the competition. It gave me a new spiritual insight. It does no good to pass the baton and expect someone else to run the race alone. If I am in the race, either because I have voluntarily joined or because as a conscious Spirit I am morally compelled to acknowledge that I am indeed in the race, then I cannot pass the baton. Instead, I must hold it until my part of the race is complete, and I will run with all my partners in the race. Our coordinated effort will increase the velocity that will press us forward, make swifter our feet, and keep clearer the path before us.

Day 19: November 30

I went to bed at 8:00 last night excited about getting up at 4:00 to do my hour meditation. When I woke eight minutes before the alarm sounded, I felt enthusiastic about the great meditation sure to follow. That didn't happen.

I stretched, as always, went to my prayer chair, as always, and meditated, as always, with the intent of extending the meditation as I had the day before. Similar to my experience the previous morning, the meditation started with thoughts racing haphazardly around my head. This time, however, I struggled to reach serenity. I focused on my breathing, but upcoming obligations kept interrupting my focus.

Last night Jerry and I watched the next segment of *Super Soul Sunday*, this one with Mark Nepo. Among other insights, he described what we would do if we only had a little while left to live. Jerry and I looked at each other; he was addressing what I had begun with *My First Last Year*. Nepo said (I'm paraphrasing the idea as my mind took it in) that when we are confronted with having little time left, the items on the lists of things we think we need to do start vanishing, and we're left with the very few things that really matter.

During my meditation, I was confronted with all the projects that I have going. Each one came from a spiritual inspiration, so I am confident they are mine to do, and I'm even excited about doing them. All my writing endeavors invigorate me by stretching my talent. The other major projects—shipping Christmas gifts to relatives I won't see this holiday, sending the antique photos to my distant aunt, gathering items for students to shop free—are activities that bless others. For me, these inspirations are not dissolving. But one of my greatest natural skills is the ability to organize. I can certainly prioritize my to-do lists so that I work each day on only what really matters right then. By doing so, I can remain present with each moment. In that presence, I can live fully because I am there—in that moment, with that moment—mentally, emotionally, and spiritually. That's the experience I'm after with this exercise of faith I've entitled *My First Last Year*.

As had happened the previous morning, the second half of the meditation became clearer and more focused. Yet I had an insight that surprised me. I started envisioning myself as coral at the bottom of the sea. I like the metaphor because coral is beautiful, and I want to experience beauty during this life. I saw the coral as strong yet porous, so the energy of Spirit, represented by water, could easily penetrate it. Because it is entirely immersed, the coral is never separated from God-energy, but is eternally engulfed in it.

While feeling excited about this new image, God interrupted. This was a strange experience for me, as I have grown to perceive God as an energy of which I am a part. After graduating from old concepts of an anthropomorphic God outside of me, I have sensed only occasional forays into communing with God as if God were an entity separate from me that I could talk to. God interrupted my self-satisfied coral metaphor with a new thought. "Coral is rigid, breakable, and stationary," the God-thought said. "Why imagine yourself surrounded by water when you can *be* the water?"

Still in meditation, my mind didn't rush to embrace the thought, but took it in gradually. At first I imagined myself like a bloom on the coral, my petals swaying to the motion of the water. Then I pictured myself as strands of petals and leaves breaking free of a stem, drifting languidly in the layers of surf. Finally, the long strands disappeared and I was the water. The water was God, and I was indistinguishably part of that. It was beautiful, in the way I imagined the coral to be beautiful. But now I was unbreakable and free-flowing. In constant motion, the water distilled me into omnipresence. I wasn't just a drop in the ocean. The "I" had dissipated and surrendered to the water, becoming it and finally embracing all its magnificence. The energy of the "I" still existed and was more powerful than ever. But the "I" alone was just a memory, one that I suspected would fade in time.

I now think this is what death will be. The energy continues, the "I" still exists, as I always existed, but it will no longer be the "I" physically unique and independent of God's "I am."

For the past few days I've felt inspired to again email the administrator removed from our campus. More details came out in the news about what he did. His actions, though personally damaging, did not involve the school or district. He didn't hurt a child, didn't embezzle money, and wasn't accused of abusing his wife or child. But he was caught with someone in private, ensuring that he was unlikely to work in a school again.

I emailed him:

Hi Mr. _____,

For the past few weeks, I have been thinking about you and sending good thoughts your way. I don't know what you're experiencing right now, but I want you to know that you are not alone. I, and I am sure many, many others who know you, are holding you up in spirit and seeing bright outcomes for whatever you may be going through, growing through, and heading toward.

I do have some cursory information now about the circumstances that changed your work situation, and I want to reassure you that having that new knowledge does not color my perception of you at all. In brotherhood, I wish for you only the best and see you always in the most positive light. As you move forward on your journey through this life, I support you in spirit and see you proceeding confidently and hopefully toward your highest good.

During this season of preparation and hope, I send you loving thoughts and offer a hand in friendship. I am not a counselor, but I am a good listener and an excellent friend. If you're inspired to connect with someone, know that I am here if you need me. (*Then I added my cell phone number because I suspected he wouldn't feel comfortable calling me at school.*)

Much love,

Roger

As I wrote and since I sent the email, I have been immersed in the loving energy of God. Unlike the coral, I am not a stationary object being embraced by the water which is God. I took action and acted as the water. Through that email, my spirit disappeared into the energy of God, and I've been floating freely through that vast space ever since.

I have work ahead as I set up for an annual faculty event I host in my library. Embarking on this activity, I don't feel frazzled, and no list of to-do's is lords-a-leaping across my brain. I have already done the most important work of my day—I have written to you, dear reader. Now I will set out the displays and bless each with an inviting energy. I will imagine The New Book Preview as Aunt Kate and Aunt Julia's Feast of the Epiphany party in one of my favorite stories, James Joyce's "The Dead." It ended as a night of great insight for the protagonist, Gabriel. With the journey I'm on now, I think each day will provide a new epiphany for me.

At breakfast this morning I told Jerry that today is the last day of the month I started my first last year. Over coffee and eggs, we reviewed highlights of the past 18 days, recognizing as standouts times with each other, our families, and friends at church and the Renaissance wedding. I'm excited anticipating the next 11½ months. I want to stay spiritually awake so I don't miss a minute.

6

In the Midst of Spiritual Magic

Day 20: December 1

Our New Book Preview is my secretary Lori's and my favorite event of the semester. One day each year, we host a special event for faculty. I display all the new acquisitions on tables and atop bookshelves and have a generous spread of breakfast foods in the morning and snacks in the afternoon. Teachers come to the library, peruse the new books, tag any they want to check out, and visit with colleagues. Lori and I decorate the library for the holidays, play Christmas music to set a joyful tone, and dress more formally that usual.

  This morning I arose at my usual time, but skipped my meditation to arrive early enough to ensure that the custodian had coffee brewing and to complete touches that must be done the day of the event. Mine was the first car in the faculty parking lot.

  For Lori and me, this event puts the holidays in full swing. Throughout the day I mingled with colleagues. One young teacher, whom I got to know a little better when Jerry and I went to a restaurant for dinner and discovered her moonlighting as a server, asked what I was up to. I told her about some of my writing projects. Although I hadn't mentioned it to anyone else before, I told her that I was working on being really present and living every day this year. I didn't go into any more detail about *My First Last Year*, but she lit up when I shared with her just the germ of the idea. I could feel her enthusiasm rising.

"What a great idea!" she confirmed. It was one of the most spiritual moments of the day.

Another came while visiting with two other teachers. Both have dreamed of writing a book. One woman I had previously offered to give a free coaching session to start her writing endeavor. The other, a vibrant young visionary, started her book after much encouragement from her husband and me, but abandoned that project to start a cosmetics business.

I inquired how that venture was going. She told me that a renowned makeup artist had invited her to join the staff in New York. Although her eyes widened when she shared news of the invitation, no light glimmered in them.

"You are considering it, aren't you?"

"Dr. Leslie, it's just not possible. I have a young son, and my husband likes his job here." The words weighed so heavily that her shoulders slumped and curled forward. "I have other obligations. I don't think I can have this."

"Quit thinking," I told her. "What is your heart telling you?"

"What?"

"Stop thinking long enough to *feel* what this opportunity is bringing to you, and potentially to your family. What is your heart saying?"

She stood more erect.

"I don't know what you believe spiritually," I said, "but stop thinking about the obstacles long enough to feel what could happen if you entertain the possibilities of this opportunity working for you."

"But to go all the way to New York . . ."

"Who says you have to go to New York? Be creative. Ask the owner if she'd consider opening a branch of her salon in Houston. We are the fourth largest city in the U.S."

Then a spark flashed in her eyes. "You know, it's funny you say that. During our conversation she did mention something about creating franchisers in other cities. But I forgot she said that when

I started feeling sad about the fact that this New York opportunity couldn't happen for me."

"With every opportunity, there's always a creative alternative somewhere in the mix. Sometimes it's obvious; sometimes it's hidden. Look for it."

"Yeah . . ." she pondered.

"I think you found it."

She beamed. "Yeah!"

"And you know what?" the ideas continued. "Since you wanted to be a writer and you love your makeup business, I bet you could marry the two ideas." I thought about writing this book as I'm living the experience. "Why not write about starting your own makeup business, whether or not this new opportunity develops into anything? You became an entrepreneur without any background in business and you've been doing so well on your own that someone in the big leagues wants to take you on. Even if you don't accept any form of her offer, you have so much to share. Let other young businesswomen learn from your experiences—the mistakes as well as the triumphs."

"Yeah!" she repeated.

"That way you can make both of your dreams come true—you'll own your own business and be a published writer. Think of how many other young people with dreams of starting a business—of any kind—would benefit from your sharing what you did to get where you are. You don't even have to make it a formal manuscript yet. Just journal about your everyday experiences. Before you know it you'll have a book that can help so many other people who had a dream like yours."

She turned to the other woman still standing with us. "That's why we need to come in here more often. Every time I leave this library I start believing in things I didn't even think were possible."

Those responses always resonate with me and remind me of the gift of inspiration that I came to this life to share. It was a good day.

Day 21: December 2

With so many irons in the fire, if I work exclusively on one project for a day, my mind gets clogged with worries about how to catch up with others. I slept well last night, but woke feeling anxious about so much to do. Yet, as I mentioned in a recent entry, I have reached a new plateau, and my heart, soul, and body don't respond to my mind's concerns the way they used to. As my conscious mind started fretting, my superconscious remained my predominant influence, and I moved leisurely through the morning. It was Friday, I told myself, and so this would be a fine time to tie up loose ends and not juggle everything simultaneously.

The first major task at work was donating all the Christmas decorations, books, toys, games, clothes, and household items that I'd gathered to give away to needy students at school. I sent an email inviting other faculty members to participate, and the response has been gratifying. One teacher emailed me to say she had bundles of clothes in her classroom closet to donate immediately. Another called to say she could give boxes of stuffed animals that her children had outgrown. Even though I had sent the email only the previous afternoon as school was ending, by the time I brought in three more large boxes of items to donate, the room in the counseling office where students could "shop" discretely already contained a rack of clothes, some neatly folded sweaters on a table, and a few books.

I felt the hope of giving some students and their families a Christmas they wouldn't otherwise have. It also helped me realize that generosity doesn't require money. I can give away treasures that I already have and also be the conduit for others to give. By inviting colleagues to join me in creating a Christmas for students in need, I generated prosperity without a single dollar leaving anyone's wallet.

Years ago, I dined with a small group of people, one of whom was a monk. During a discussion about Biblical events, he said something with which I agreed then and appreciate more now. Regarding Moses parting the Red Sea, he said that he had read a historical geography book confirming that, over some spans of time, the Red Sea recedes so much that it becomes passable, and then later the tide rises and the area that had been dry is immersed again. He reasoned, "Whether the Red Sea parted in one spontaneous motion or if it ebbed over time, the Israelites crossed it, and the water returned before the Egyptian soldiers arrived at the same spot makes no difference. Happening in natural time as we know it makes it no less a miracle."

I thought the same now regarding prosperity. I could have acquired impressive wealth and bought gifts for students and their families. Or I could have acted on one inspiration to give away treasures I already had, and then another inspiration to invite faculty members to do the same. Either approach would have filled a room on my campus with what can become Christmas magic for families in my school community. The inspiration is no less a miracle of prosperity, and the invitation allowed more people to bless others with their generosity.

Beyond giving away items from home, I also had to shop for my family and my student library aides. Being among shoppers on my lunch hour, and finding the gifts I sought, filled my heart. The nagging voice that worries when I veer from my daily writing goals quieted long enough to share the experience with my soul.

Another little prosperity miracle occurred that evening. As usual, Jerry and I headed to our favorite Friday night Mexican restaurant. On the way, Jerry discovered he didn't bring the coupon we had for a free meal. Rather than return home, we continued to the restaurant, already packed with guests waiting for tables to clear. As we stepped in, we heard, "Jerry! Roger!" Our friends Dennis and Ann Marie, to whom we gave the Jim Brickman Christmas CD the previous week, were seated at a table for four. They invited us to join them.

We enjoyed engaging conversation—literally, because I asked them how they met and got engaged. When the check arrived after dinner, Dennis and Ann Marie insisted on paying. Grateful, I thought again about prosperity. Gifts were coming our way as fluidly as they had been going out through my purchasing and sending presents to distant relatives and through my donating treasures I had around the house. As we left the restaurant I still had in my wallet the money that we were planning to spend for dinner. As yet prosperity wasn't abounding as I'd been praying, but I was seeing prosperity in action.

Day 22: December 3

Jerry left early in the day to attend a football game with our daughter and daughter-in-law, Becca and Lindsey, and I stayed home to edit a manuscript for a client. He had not made too many changes from my last edit several months earlier, but enough to require my rereading the entire manuscript to find minor differences that needed polishing. That afternoon I completed the edit and brought my client the revised draft. As the meeting ended, we signed the invoices and he paid me.

During the transaction, he told me he had read my novel, *Drowning in Secret* (www.RogerLeslie.com). "I know from the work you've done for me that you're a great editor. I didn't realize your quality of writing. I'm even more confident in you now."

Sometimes when people talk to me, I sense that their words are coming directly from God. I felt it when he said that. Two inspirations swept through me as we had the simultaneous financial transaction and his comment about my own fiction writing. In my writing career, which entails writing, editing, coaching, and book reviewing, I earn most of my income from editing. My dream has always been to prosper so much from my own writing that I can relinquish the other side jobs. When I edited my client's manuscript this morning, I felt very confident in my skills and knew I was doing an excellent job for him. At the same time, I regretted time working on someone else's books when I'd rather be working on my own.

I have long struggled with this conflict. But last summer I felt the first inspiration to start my own publishing house, which would combine all of my writing-related jobs for the single purpose of producing published works. If Spirit continues to inspire me, I could launch Paradise Publishing with one of my own books, and all the independent aspects of my writing career can meaningfully merge. I see the avenue for generating immediate income by continuing to edit others' manuscripts, whether I publish them or not. But with the client's words about my novel, I felt a tug to continue being as disciplined as I have been in the past about my writing schedule. I want to realign my planning so that I scatter the completion dates of all five works I'm writing right now, but that plan will come when I set new goals with the new year. Meantime, I will steadily and steadfastly pursue the works now in process.

The cash I earned today gave me the money I needed to pay for Jerry's birthday brunch tomorrow. Prosperity was flowing both physically and spiritually. Yesterday I had no idea how I'd pay for Jerry's birthday meal. Now I had the money in hand. Even better, I know that God spoke through this client to encourage me to keep writing my fiction and fulfill my purpose in this life.

Day 23: December 4

With my first last year goal in mind as we drove to Jerry's birthday brunch, I told Jerry to devise any plan for his actual birthday on Thursday, and I'd make it happen. Living as if I cannot leave anything for tomorrow made small ideas grow. Originally I considered taking Jerry to breakfast early enough for us both to make it to work on time. Then I realized we could go to breakfast and get to work whatever time we showed up. The idea expanded to the thought, why not take the entire day to do something exceptional, or spend it at home relaxing with each other and the dogs. I offered all these options to Jerry, then promised to create any experience he wanted.

That positive expectancy flowed throughout Jerry's brunch making the whole experience magical. We traditionally treat the other to Sunday brunch the weekend nearest our birthday at a restaurant we haven't tried before. Although we'd eaten at Brennan's years ago, I picked it for two reasons. First, it would be a new experience because Brennan's had been redesigned after a massive fire. Second, the last time we were there, Jerry was experiencing head and tooth pain so excruciating that he could not eat.

When we arrived the hostess led us to a room lined with mirrors on one side and windows leading to a courtyard on the other. Seated at one of the first tables were some longtime friends, Romie and Ted sharing a meal with another couple. We visited momentarily, and after Jerry and I were seated at our own table, Ted had the waiter bring us Bellinis. Our prosperity was continuing.

Over soups, shrimp appetizers and Eggs Brennan's, Jerry noted how interesting it was to run into old friends as we arrived. As he spoke, I looked up and at a distance saw Bonita, one of our closest friends with whom we celebrated her husband Manuel's birthday last week. As always, she looked beautiful; her hair wafted behind her as she rushed to say hello. She had just finished brunch with a friend and asked what we were doing there. When Jerry said we were celebrating his forthcoming birthday, she insisted we make a plan to get together on Jerry's actual birthday as we did for Manuel.

A few minutes after she left, Bonita returned. She told us that she spoke to Manuel, found out he was working the night of Jerry's birthday, but was available the night before it. She had already decided that when we came to their house they'd treat us to Chinese food from their favorite restaurant. When Bonita walked away this second time, we marveled how everything we could want keeps coming to us without our doing anything beyond declaring the intention.

Day 24: December 5

I meditated for a minimal 15 minutes this morning and dove right into my day. I did not realize what a whirlwind I was entering at work, but the day was tornadic with activities pulling me in various directions. I managed to stay true to my goal of revising one chapter of *One Sister Left the Gun* and am still feeling pleased with how the plot is developing in this section. Several classes came in to research, some double-booked without realizing it, requiring me to renegotiate with teachers and find creative ways to get access for every student who needed a computer. It's nearing the end of the semester, and senior research papers are due. As a result, students who've not paced themselves are panicking and making foolish errors. More than one student came in to print their essay from their flash drive, only to discover that they forgot to save the essay to it, or, in the case of one student, saved an empty document he'd given the title of his research paper.

    Seeing what my students were going through was a spiritual wake-up call for me. I have been working furiously on multiple projects and myriad goals. Although I am making progress on all of them, some have become so demanding that I feel the quality of my focus diminishing. An even clearer sign came from my body, which always signals through pain when I am spiritually or emotionally off. I have felt tightness around my heart. I know it's because I have let myself get out of balance. The unique aspect of this phenomenon is that my soul remains clear and vibrant as ever. While bombarded by recent demands, I have only a faint memory of how overwhelmed I used to feel. Because living my first last year has raised me to a new spiritual plateau, I can maintain positive neutrality as I am pummeled by outward demands. The worldly me dominates my existence less and less. Even in chaos, the spiritual me can watch what the physical me is going through and feel at peace.

    I worked late analyzing one of the longest novels for *Teach Me SUCCESS*, a ready-reference resource for character education that emphasizes the seven traits successful people master. When finally ready to head home, I called Jerry.

"You okay?" he asked, noting the fatigue in my voice.

"I'm really tired."

My body slumped wearily, but on the way home my mind and my soul both felt indefatigable. By the time I arrived home almost an hour later, I was chipper and joyful as ever.

I know the value of spiritual practices. Based on spiritual wisdom from many disciplines, including the Tao, I know the quality of my life will increase if I do less. Until this past week, I have developed the habit of slowing down enough to receive spiritual inspirations, and then I've been taking them all into immediate action. I've discovered one caveat: I've expended equal energy on each inspiration instead of prioritizing and negotiating a manageable schedule. Most time-consuming has been the SUCCESS research study where teachers and I have been identifying models of success in children's literature because I am leading six reading and analysis groups. My entire Monday was consumed by demands to email and visit teachers to reschedule consensus meetings. Additionally, every new group I have taken over has added seven more books for me to analyze.

Reflecting on this project now, I am invigorated by the challenge of making everyone feel appreciated and affirmed for their contribution. But it is more exhausting than my usual independent writing projects. I work very well alone. As a person who has studied using both sides of the brain to develop and teach dynamic goal-setting techniques for almost 30 years, I know how to achieve what I'm after.

Working with so many people is educational. Although I have helped douse a few fires among members of groups that I eventually interceded for or took over, I have learned much about others' work and interaction styles. As I prayerfully consider starting my own publishing business, it's been helpful to see how some people's good intentions implode with poor work habits, unresolved personality issues, and even unrelated obstacles in their lives. I am learning. Best of all, when I write to you about the experiences, I draw ideas from my soul. Through the writing process I can look from a vantage point that lets me see the blessing in it all.

In one writing workshop I teach, "From Inspiration to Publication," I have often described how writers live two concurrent lives: the conscious life, and the subconscious world of creativity. If one world isn't captivating me, my mind is drawn to the characters residing in the other. As I write to you, I see another facet of the prism. Even if experiences seem so overwhelming I don't recognize their blessing in the moment, writing about them gives me objectivity I don't otherwise have. Reflective writing pulls me far enough from the intensity to show me the value of every life experience. That thought opens another circuit surging with soul energy.

Day 25: December 6

I didn't think this work day could be more explosive than yesterday's, but it was. Before 6:00 a.m., my secretary called in sick, so I would be on my own to run the library. Though I'd woken early, I didn't meditate. Not a good idea. I see more than ever that meditation grounds me and emphasizes for my conscious mind that my soul is in charge of everything.

Although the work day was frantic, it was soul-nurturing as well. I had sent another email to teachers thanking them for donating personal goods for needy students and their families. I went to the counselor's office to add items that someone at church had given me, but the room was so packed I could barely open the door. I asked the counselors' secretaries if any students had come by for items, and they told me not one student had taken advantage of this opportunity.

I visited again with the lead counselor, and we decided to revive our original idea of displaying the donations in my library.

We started transferring the goods immediately, and I was awed by how much kept barreling in. I had cleared the library study carrels to make room for games and toys and puzzles and household items. We filled all six carrels and a large table. Meantime, the other counselors wheeled in a half dozen clothing racks. Initially we thought six was too many, but by the time we emptied every box, we had to squeeze the last items onto the racks.

In addition to gently used dresses, shirts, slacks, shawls, and ties, someone donated dozens of brand new jeans and khaki slacks, knit caps and blouses all with the store tags still attached. When we realized all that had been donated, the counselors and I stilled momentarily to acknowledge such immense generosity. A box of donated shoes helped keep our sentimentality from growing maudlin. One counselor pulled out a pair of men's black work shoes. She turned them one way, then another. They were flattened from being near the bottom of the box, so she pulled the tops to stretch them back out. No matter what she did, it was clear someone had donated two left shoes. Puzzled, we stared at them and laughed.

Once we had everything set out, we had enough merchandise to brighten at least a block-full of families' homes at Christmas. I have six students who assisted in the library this year either as an aide or a volunteer. I know for certain that two are either struggling financially themselves (one lost a job and has actively been looking—unsuccessfully—for another since the semester began) or are part of an extended family living together and scrambling to make ends meet. I was especially excited to inform these two students about the donations and encourage them to shop. Their response staggered me. When I told each privately about our "store," intending to give them an opportunity to take anything home they wanted, both responded immediately by saying, "Are you still taking donations? I'm sure I have some things that could help somebody." How lucky we are, and how abundant is the spirit of giving in all of us!

As the day ended, I was still feeling pressure around my heart. On the way home, I talked to my body, assuring it I had not forgotten about it and that I heard it calling out for my attention. Jerry had a dinner meeting with the new music director at church, so I was on my own for dinner. I didn't go to the gym because I'd promised Jerry I'd go straight home to let the dogs out, but I did swing by the drive-through and bought a salad. I chose the healthiest menu item to take care of my body. I also ordered a seasonal peppermint chocolate chip milkshake. I did that to take care of the little boy in me. Both were very happy!

At home I ate my salad, blessing my body with every bite by reminding my organs, cells, and atoms that I was nourishing them with healthy food and promising them I would resume my swimming workouts next week. I then relished the delicious shake while analyzing the last book I need to have done by Monday. Although it had been a busy day, I wanted to analyze the books early in the week because the rest of my evenings would be filled with Jerry's birthday celebrations, and then a road trip this weekend to Jerry's parents' house in East Texas on Friday then up to Arkansas for the Roberts' family reunion on Saturday.

The dogs sat beside me on the couch as I read and recorded my literary analysis. I never turned on the television, didn't play any Christmas music, but in the silence felt the dogs beside me and enjoyed looking up from the book to see the room decked out for the holidays with red lights on the silk plant in the corner, flashing multicolored lights on the rotund Christmas tree, and strings of orange dachshund lights around the small tabletop tree beside me. I analyzed the first 100 pages of the book, fighting fatigue during the last several pages. When I reached the end of the chapter, I let the book rest on my lap, dropped my head back, and slept soundly until Jerry returned. This evening was a vast departure from my frenetic work day. Staying present and aware throughout both filled my heart with vibrant gratitude. My chest wasn't hurting now.

Day 26: December 7

I've learned an important lesson about creating a productive work day: don't start by answering emails. Instead I begin with meditation, and then work on projects that resonate spiritually before diving into the more tedious details that also need my attention. When I made the mistake of answering emails first these past few days, I've felt disjointed until I worked on what's more important to me—the books I feel spiritually guided to complete. After I write *My First Last Year* or *One Sister Left the Gun*, my spirit affirms, "You've just done the most important work of the day."

It's exciting to try new approaches to familiar tasks. By experimenting we can learn for ourselves how we work best. It's also important to conduct the same or new tests periodically because sometimes what doesn't work at one stage of our lives works brilliantly in another. So I don't regret having started my day addressing the concerns presented to me through the emails I've received. It re-taught me how to sustain my own physical and spiritual power. First I should do what is most soul-expanding. Afterward I can take care of smaller details.

At midday, the interim principal brought our new superintendent into my library to show her the "store" we set up. Seeing the huge volume of donated goods staggered her.

"Oh, Roger," she began, then couldn't speak.

I described the generosity from teachers and anonymous donors, and shared the story of the students who offered to share rather than accept donations. Her heart-touched silence sent a spiritual wave cascading over me. "Something greater will come of this," the feeling implied. I don't know what that is, but I shared the feeling with Jerry that evening, and he seemed to sense it, too. We are onto something big when we open to inspiration, listen to it, and then act on it immediately.

"Keep doing this," something told us. Spiritual magic was happening, and we loved feeling its immediacy and promise.

7

Flying, Growing, and Seeing Signs along the Journey

Day 27: December 8

Today is Jerry's birthday. Yea! That fact alone makes it joyous. I expected to get ready alone for an early morning meeting and wake Jerry as I left for the day. Instead, Jerry arose early too and we spent the first part of the day together. Having left in plenty of time, I felt no stress when an accident left me sitting in traffic behind the jam and demanded I detour to a longer route to school.

I rode in silence for awhile, then listened to Maureen McGovern's Christmas CD, one of my favorites. I hadn't traveled the roads of that detour in so long I soaked up the views of all the new businesses and stores along the beltway. A tall bridge arches high over the ship channel on that route. I enjoyed the ascent and glided back down toward my campus. The sky glowed with a soft rose tint, as a cold front that moved in last Sunday had cleared away the thicker clouds. Crisp, clear, and colorful—that's the Christmas season in Houston. I stayed present with it all the way to work, arrived on time, and accomplished everything during the meeting we'd intended.

In the evening Jerry and I met Becca and Lindsey for burgers, fries, and pies at a popular new diner near their house. It's so easy to tell them how much we love them, and they tell us often, too. Since our kids were very young, Jerry has always created a safe space for them to feel loved and to be loving. Because Jerry didn't come out to the kids until they were teens, I had to tread around that space of intimacy until Cory and Rebecca both knew I was not just their father's friend, but a dad to them as well. That relationship has evolved over the years, and was strengthened exponentially when Jerry and I were married in 2007.

Rebecca was the first to boldly embrace me as a dad. One Father's Day she gave us a photo of her wearing an "I love my two dads" T-shirt. It's one of the most touching gifts I've ever received. She's a powerful Spirit still finding her way professionally, but actively seeking work that feeds her soul. She talked about that some during dinner, and is even considering teaching. She'd make a great teacher. Children of all ages love her because she's willing to relate to everyone. She has that "cool aunt" personality that kids love. Although I didn't mention my first last year, I told her that, despite having only a vague awareness of it in her early 30s, she needs to go 100% toward whatever she wants from life.

Jerry reinforced my point by mentioning a coworker in her early 40s who was diagnosed with MS less than a year ago, and just found out she also has cancer. In an unrelated event, last week a lifelong friend of Jerry's youngest brother, Jeff, lost her husband in a fiery car crash.

"We don't know what tomorrow holds," I offered. "So whatever your heart is telling you to do, do it now. You don't have to dig yourself into a financial hole doing it, but as best you can, figure out what matters to you and act on that inspiration without hesitation. If you want to go somewhere, or do, become, or learn something, then listen to that inspiration and act on it. That's what will give your life meaning." I think she and Lindsey absorbed the message.

I've recently had a new revelation concerning prosperity. In the past, I have set and pursued monetary goals with the same goal-setting techniques that work in every other area of my life. Somehow, my finances haven't revealed the same positive results. Lack of success has led to experimenting and observing, and finally discovering that I draw prosperity by holding fast to a vision rather than pursuing wealth. The lesson came with coffee!

Almost two years ago, I saw a Keurig coffeemaker in Jerry's parents' kitchen and then at my older brother's house and thought, I'd like one of those. I enjoy flavored coffee, I like not having to prepare a pot of coffee every night for the next morning, and I'd appreciate the freedom of making a single cup whenever I wanted one. The Keurig became my symbol for wealth, as I think of Jerry's parents as the richest people in his family, and my brother and his wife, Sue as the richest in ours.

On one visit to my brother's large, lovely home in Michigan, which they remodel or redecorate portions of every year, I ruefully realized that I literally could not imagine what it would be like to have enough money to update our house so regularly. The thought saddened me because I believe that to create abundance requires being able to hold a faith-filled vision for it to manifest. I have done that in every other aspect of my life I can think of right now: my spirituality, my marriage, my family relationships, my friendships, my creative output as a writer. The one way I am not manifesting abundance to the level I dream is financially.

So I decided owning a Keurig symbolized having learned a breakthrough lesson on prosperity. First I held the vision for getting one. Jerry and I went to the store and priced them. Even with a 20% coupon, I couldn't justify paying $200.00 for a coffee maker. For several months, I continued to hold the vision and infused it with faith that somehow this symbol of abundance would be ours.

Interestingly, every year some of my immediate family members have an after-Christmas celebration that includes exchanging gifts. Last year, Jerry and I received a rack of individual flavored coffees for a Keurig. We were never asked if we had a Keurig, and we never told those who gave us the gift that we didn't—yet. But the gift convinced me that my vision was manifesting.

At home I displayed the coffee rack on our kitchen counter as a consistent reminder of the goal to get the coffeemaker. Sometimes friends would come over, see the rack of flavored coffees, and ask where our Keurig was.

"We don't have one yet," I would say, and then explain that we received the coffees as a gift.

"How strange," was the usual reply. "Why would someone buy you these coffees when they didn't even know if you had the coffeemaker to use them?"

I didn't say what I thought, but I knew it was because I had put forth a prayer for having one, and the gift was a response to that vision.

When we never came up with an extra $200 any month to buy the Keurig, I tried a new strategy. I took an envelope, wrote "Keurig" on it, even drew a picture of a Keurig, and started a fund. I put a Bed Bath & Beyond 20% coupon in the envelope, and then whenever I had an extra dollar or two, I'd drop it in the envelope to start building the collection.

Every time it built up a bit, some unexpended expense arose, like the dogs getting sick, which prompted me to take the cash I needed at the time to pay for something else. After a few months of never building anything toward the goal, I finally threw away the envelope. Even later, we ran out of regular coffee, so I started filling our Mr. Coffee with the individual cups of grounds. Eventually they were gone, too. When the rack was empty, I stowed it in a cabinet.

Nevertheless, I didn't give up on the hope of one day having a Keurig. But I did stop actively pursuing it.

Then today, I received a voice message from our friend Manuel. We had brought him a present at his birthday dinner, but they did not give Jerry a gift when we celebrated his birthday yesterday. We didn't think anything of it until Manuel left me a message to call him about an idea he had for a special Christmas gift for us.

When I returned his call he said, "I remembered that you guys had those flavored coffees on the kitchen counter a while back but didn't have the coffeemaker. Do you still want it?"

"Yes," I said, "But that's a *very* generous gift." We exchange something small on birthdays and Christmas, but never in that price range.

"What kind do you guys want?"

I described the large capacity model I'd envisioned. "But, Manuel," I told him, "That's about $200."

"Let me look into it."

I asked him to do me a favor. "If you end up getting it, please let me know before Christmas." I didn't want them to give us a Keurig and we bring them a bottle of wine from the grocery store.

Not an hour later Manuel called back. "You've got yourself a Keurig. I ordered it online and it'll show up in a few days."

"That's *so* generous of you!"

"We'll consider this your birthday present, Jerry's birthday present, your Christmas gift, and your graduation gift for getting your Ph.D."

I hung up and thought, Wow! I didn't have to do anything but decide I wanted the Keurig and continue to keep the faith that I would one day have one. Just declaring what I wanted, and only to myself and to Jerry, set something in motion that moved people to make it happen. How else could I explain what prompted our loved ones to buy us the rack of flavored coffees for Christmas, for me to keep it and display it on the counter, for Manuel to see it months ago, and then for him to remember it so long after and feel inspired to buy it for us?

This spiritually active but physically passive approach to pursuing a goal differs from how I've achieved almost everything else in my life. It also feels a bit counterintuitive. Yet it seems to align directly with the Taoist "if you want to accomplish more, do less" theory.

I think to myself how silly it seems that I never just went and paid the $200 to buy the coffeemaker. I do have $200 many times over. But as I've budgeted my money in this stage of my life, I couldn't access that amount without dipping into the savings account I am committed never to touch until my retirement.

So I tried a different tack. Unlike the past, when I would withdraw money from my savings in response to a desire, I held off. I was creative in my approach, starting mini-savings with the envelope strategy and placing the coffee rack on the counter for inspiration.

Although I didn't know it until now, it was feeding the inspiration, and not the coffer, that manifested my symbolic dream of prosperity.

The lesson I learned, and the one I want to share with you, is to be bold about creating a vision for what you want, and then be steadfast in feeding the faith for it to arrive. In other goals, I believe in being consistently active by doing, doing, doing. In this case, the only action required was to remain undeterred in faith. Experimenting with the vision helped, for Manuel only caught his inspiration by seeing the rack of coffees I'd set on our counter. But ultimately sustaining a single vision brought the result. Now, without spending a penny, I will have the coffeemaker as well as the rack to hold the flavored coffees.

At the beginning of this dream, I imagined waking in the morning and immediately savoring a cup of flavored coffee. As I infused my vision with sensory splendor, I imagined that enjoying the experience would confirm how it felt to be rich. As a man of even greater faith than when I declared my intent, I am certain that the physical experience will match or exceed the spiritual vision I've held so long.

Day 28: December 9

Writing five books during this most intense work period of my life, I've begun experimenting with different ways to juggle the projects. Starting at the new year, I could keep the momentum of writing *My First Last Year* and *One Sister Left the Gun*, but designate each month to only one other project. For example, because January 31 is the deadline for the groups to submit their literary analysis, I could dedicate January to *Teach Me SUCCESS*. In February I could commit my energies to compiling all the data and writing the introductory chapters of that same book. The Oscars will telecast at the end of February, giving me all the newest information to include in *Actors and the Academy Awards*. So I could spend March on that work.

Continuing to start each day writing *One Sister Left the Gun* feels right to me. In the past I've set goals for when I would finish novels, but I am now more inclined to give my soul as long as it needs to make it excellent. I have many author role models to inspire me. At one end of the spectrum is Joyce Carol Oates, who generates a brilliant novel or two almost annually, covering various topics and writing for both adults and young adults. At the other end of that continuum is Harper Lee, who wrote and refined *To Kill a Mockingbird* for 17 years and then never published another major work. The inspiration between both extremes gives me an entire gamut of options for letting the *One Sister Left* series evolve. Consistent work on my rewrites gives my vision momentum.

Jerry mailed all gifts to my extended family on Monday, so they should be receiving the packages today. Throughout the week I've been imagining elated responses of each relative receiving a delivery. Whether or not it happens as I imagine, I cannot know. However, the act of giving has filled me with joyful anticipation, which has done my soul so much good—especially during a week where my work commitments have pulled me in divergent directions.

The inspiration to give has sustained a spirit of joy and gratitude even when my mind sometimes thrashes in the whirlpool of projects I pursue. Over this swirling waterway is a lifeline anchored to my first last year. Every writing project I pursue came as a spiritual inspiration, so I want to honor each. But working on them all demands so much of my attention and energy I lose focus of the present moment so essential to living fully aware. Keeping my first last year foremost in my daily thoughts has been essential to knowing I am alive and appreciating the life I have.

At one time I believed my conscious mind was in the physical world and my superconscious in the spiritual. By simultaneously pursuing myriad work projects and acting on inspirations as Spirit provides them, I find both states of consciousness melding. The division between them is no longer as distinct as it used to be. My physical experiences feel more spiritual, and my spirituality grows more comfortable expressing itself in everyday physical encounters.

The phenomenon feels both grounded and freeing. For the first time, instead of trudging or trotting or sprinting along my spiritual path, I feel as though my feet have lifted just a little off the ground, and I have begun to fly. Exhilarating!

Day 29: December 10

Today we attended the annual reunion for Jerry's dad's side of the family in Texarkana. This gathering felt a little solemn because of comparatively low attendance. Jerry's dad and his brother Jake are the only family members from that generation still living. Jerry's Aunt Donna, who usually co-hosts the event, was in the hospital. His cousin, Patty, whom we usually spend the day with because she's so fun, was home recovering from a series of heart attacks. The deaths and decline of loved ones served as a stark reminder of why I set my first last year goal. Live while you can, it implored me.

Remembering how vibrant I felt letting my light shine at the last reunion energized me. I recommitted to my goal of being clear, present, and loving.

As I watched the trees on our drive from Arkansas to Jerry's parents' house, living my first last year burgeoned into life lessons. So far south, we don't have much fall color. If we do see any, it occurs this time of year. Some of the rich reds of the trees were breathtaking. I noticed different kinds of trees, and I thought about how the biggest obstacle most people share in my personal growth and goal setting workshops is their inability to identify their passion. Once people realize their passion, they can take concrete action toward achieving it. Until then, many vacillate or remain stagnant, often discouraged and unfulfilled. Seeing each tree, I thought about how not one started as a seed wondering what it would be. It simply burrowed into the ground and did what came naturally until it burst forth to become what its genetic makeup had ordained from the start. People often spend so much time trying to figure out what kind of tree they want to become, that they don't let the seed of who they could be flourish. Better to immediately plant ourselves and start the process of blooming.

We all have natural inclinations toward certain interests. If we capitalize on those interests by actively pursuing them, then we become increasingly adept at talents which become our trademarks. Those trademarks show us who we are, teach us what we can do, and lean us toward perfecting the skills for becoming who we would love to be.

One of the best, and briefest, bits of advice I ever received: Don't compare. I applied that advice to the trees I passed on this ride. One tree wasn't inherently more beautiful or majestic or fruitful than the others. To see any that way required projecting my own judgment on them. My subjective observations of beauty did not affect any tree. They didn't need my approval to be perfect expressions of themselves. If I am fool enough to compare trees—especially unlike genera—then I am the one who misses seeing the brilliance of all.

I thought about how some people define their self-worth by comparing themselves to others and wondering how others perceive them. Such a perspective might naturally evolve from our desire to feel a part of something bigger than ourselves. As souls, we already know we're connected, and cannot be separated from the wholeness of which we have always been a part. As physical beings, we often reconfirm that connection to remind ourselves we are not alone and our lives matter. In so doing, however, we may compare ourselves to others. The result is almost always inequity, which only distracts us from boldly and vigorously pursuing our destiny.

Some of us will be oak, some willow, some elm. It doesn't matter what you are, only that you are. Be who you are, came the lesson from these trees, and don't detract from giving full energy to that expression of yourself. If you spend your time as a cherry tree wondering if you'd be happier as a pear tree, that time not being you is wasted. The goal is always to become the fullest expression of yourself that you can be. Don't judge who you are, and don't compare yourself to anyone. If you do and deem yourself better than another, then your ego blocks the light your soul is shining on your path to full expression. If you do and deem yourself less than another, then you're standing in the shadows when you could be in the light.

When we find what we love and do it, regularly, we evolve toward more perfect expression of who we were always meant to be.

From the swift car, I noticed the natural alignment of trees in rows and clusters. Like these, our path is no better or worse than another's. We were not meant to walk someone else's path, but to focus on our own. From that perspective we know our own soul. There lies fulfillment and the wisdom that we are doing what is most meaningful to us, to the others our work touches, and to the universe at large.

Day 30: December 11

A little note on perspective. We left Jerry's parents' house early because they wanted to attend church for the annual cantata. Jerry and I packed first thing in the morning, hit the road hours before we usually do, and were home by early afternoon. At home, Jerry turned the heat on and discovered it wasn't working. Rather than give into the anxiety of having to spend money we didn't have on hand, we instead thought how perfect it was to be home early. We called a friend who owns an air conditioning business. He arrived at our house within the hour and fixed the problem for only a few hundred dollars.

If we'd arrived home at our usual time, our friend might not have even been available to respond immediately to our request. I had planned to pay with my credit card, but it turned out that Jerry had enough money in his checking account to pay the bill. Our civic association fees are due this month, and I always cover that payment. So if Jerry pays for a few more incidentals—like our dog Joey's next prescriptions—then we'll both spend about the same without either of us using a credit card.

Prosperity abounds. We see it through the eyes of gratitude and a willingness to recognize it as it appears.

Day 31: December 12

Last night I dreamed that I was seated in a restaurant with many of Jerry's and my family members. *Along a far wall were several gift cards from the restaurant. I stared at the cards wondering how to purchase one for my sister-in-law, who was with us at the table, without her noticing and give it to her as a gift. Lost in that thought for a long time, I finally refocused my attention on the dinner only to discover everyone else was done eating while I had soup and a salad in front of me that I had not even touched. Everyone else stood to leave, telling me to eat and catch up with them later.*

This dream was encouraging me to be more present. Although my distraction was prompted by a loving intent (buying a gift card), my drifting mind kept me from sharing the meal with loved ones. My first last year is reminding me to shift my focus from the distant wall to the banquet in front of me.

On the way to work today I learned that just beyond my immediate vicinity are signs, literal and metaphoric, to help me fulfill my life's purpose. Driving around Loop 610 this morning, I saw a billboard advertising a radio personality who has been popular for many years. The few times I heard him speak convinced me that my life's mission doesn't find support from his message. There are many celebrities whose appeal I gratefully do not understand. But on the way to work, I considered that his appeal might be that he vicariously voices opinions or vents emotion for listeners.

Reminded of other speakers I find motivating and spiritually uplifting, my mind categorized speakers as either empowering or disempowering. My body jolted with the falseness of that thought. First, don't compare. Second, any speaker can be empowering or disempowering, depending on what we are choosing to hear and understand from the message. As I seek to create harmony and unity among people, I do so by working first on myself. That is my process for personal empowerment.

Yet I admire people who start from the outside and work their way in. Some people are transformed by first making changes around them. Further, I realized how naïve my judgment that speakers I perceive as negative or angry or destructive cannot impact the world positively. After all, seeing the billboard of a speaker I don't admire reinforced my desire to promote my own message of peace and spiritual evolvement. I'm learning not to dismiss anything. Everything—even ideas I don't agree with and usually ignore or avoid—can propel me along my journey of self-discovery and toward my goal to empower others.

Contrasting the person on the billboard with speakers who inspire me taught another lesson in empowerment. Passive listeners of any message, uplifting or destructive, cannot move us beyond where we are until they, too take action and live out the message that moves them. Inspiring messages may enrich the soil, but we remain a dormant seed until we not only hear a message, but also act on it. We are all surrounded by plants sprouting, growing, and reaching toward the sky. We become one the moment we burrow into the soil and start the process of active growth.

Those who never do take root by living the life they dream become seeds that dry up and die. But even this prospect is not hopeless. Nothing ever is. The molecules of the dead seeds give rise to other life forces born with the same potential to take root and flourish.

At every moment messages come to us directly and indirectly. On a cold December morning, I noticed a billboard that may have loomed beside the freeway for months. Rather than allow the seed of my observation to be windswept, I burrowed it into the soil of spiritual insight and recognized how all opinions can have value, but only if we put them into action.

I'm creating balance in life. The weight of ideas we don't act upon can tilt our even path. Consistent, fearless action levels it again. Don't just watch an inspiring show. Act upon it. Don't just listen to an uplifting message. Test it with action. Don't just hear your highest self think through an observation about what you know and how you can grow. Process the thought and use it for yourself and for others.

In many of the children's novels I've been reading for my current book study for *Teach Me SUCCESS*, a theme recurs. Toys remain lifeless objects until a child projects onto them personal attributes which make them come alive. Ideas are our spiritual toys. All concepts are inert bundles of potential that we bring to life through our dreams, desires, and actions. Like a child's world of imagination, our dreams reveal the door to the spiritual realm. Only acting on our dreams opens that door.

When I was about eight, I went with a cousin to her friend's house, where we played in her basement. After a while I was ready to return to my cousin's house, but she wanted to stay with her friend. So I said I could find my way on my own and headed up the stairs and back through the main floor of the friend's house. In a moment, my cousin's friend walked up behind me. "Our house is kind of big," she said. "I know it can be confusing."

"Yeah," I smiled and kept heading in the same direction, not catching what she meant.

She stopped me again with, "Where are you going?"

Her question snapped my brain into realizing that she meant I was going the wrong way. I thought I knew the way back. Even after she subtly corrected me so I wouldn't be embarrassed, I didn't catch it. Oblivious to her intent and her help, I had turned to continue, without noticing I was being guided through someplace unfamiliar.

Life works that same way. The billboard on the freeway was advertising someone I didn't think would help me on my own journey. But once I changed my thinking and learned rather than judged, I found a first last year lesson: everything, *everything* along our journey can guide us along our spiritual path.

Guidance appears—as people, as billboards, as dreams—to move us forward. I must pay active attention to those signposts that seem important now. Those I need later will be there when I'm ready.

8

Creating Beauty

Day 32: December 13

This is the busiest my life has ever been. Pursuing this goal to live fully and richly every minute of every day, working on five books, running a library, sharing my life with Jerry, and acting on inspirations that come to me in meditation and in passing throughout my day, I have been more active and felt more vibrant than ever. During this last week of school before Christmas break, I usually slow from a sprint to a trot. By week's end I saunter through the day, feeling alert and alive and aware of my surroundings and myself as Spirit. Being so busy, I almost missed the blessing of that experience. When I arrived on campus today, I didn't rush to start working. Instead I wanted to live in the moment by doing exactly what I felt like doing.

I began by writing Christmas cards to colleagues on my faculty. Feeling connected to everyone I wrote, I languished in the activity. This is the pace I love in the middle of the Christmas season. Once I finish decorating the house, and buying and sending presents and cards, I slow down and savor.

The seasonal joy is seeping into our after-school literary analysis meetings. To say one group member wasn't crazy about the book we analyzed today would be like describing a catastrophic illness as a minor inconvenience. She hated the book, dismissing it as "such a boy book."

She confessed to making her reading tolerable by imagining how much better the story would be with a female protagonist. Further she created her own backstory for characters, determining that the father's meanness could be excused if he had a drug problem, and that the compassionate old neighbor kept putting his hand on the protagonist's shoulder not because he was egalitarian, but because he was drunk and trying to steady himself so he wouldn't fall over. Her caustic comments were only marginally tongue-in-cheek (yes, she hated the book that much), but they made the meeting riotously funny.

Another group member apologized for running late because she had bus duty and had to watch every student board a bus or get picked up by a parent.

My colleague and I laughed about how different it is with older students. When the final bell rings in high school, it's, "Bye, everybody. See you around."

"I guess you can't just leave a first grader at the curb?" my colleague quipped.

I arrived home by 7:00. Over sushi, Jerry recounted his visit with the Texas Teacher Retirement representative in Austin. Jerry is on the verge of creating the next professional stage of his life, and I couldn't be happier for him. He's primed to find meaningful work helping people. Teaching did that for both of us, and counseling did it for him until recently. He's hungry for something more, and taking action as he is will bring it to him in no time.

When he finished listing his retirement options and explored what he might pursue next, I quoted a line from Doris Day on my secretary's desk: "Enjoy each day—it's not coming back again!"

Though I'm living my first last year, we're not focusing on death or on getting old. But this journey has sensitized us to how precious the current moment is, and how fleeting this physical life can seem. Jerry affirmed that he's reached the age where, if he's going to do something big, he'd better do it now. I'm excited to see him immersed in this process and to discover what arises for both of us.

Day 33: December 14

Every day, life continually reminds me of why I'm here and what's most important. I get the message when I'm paying attention. On the way to work this morning I turned on SeriusXM Broadway near the beginning of a version of a song that has resonated with me for almost two decades.

Playing was the song "Sunday" from Stephen Sondheim and James Lapine's Pulitzer Prize-winning *Sunday in the Park with George*. At the end of Act I, the cast recreates Georges Seurat's painting *A Sunday Afternoon on the Island of Grande Jatte* while singing:

> Sunday, by the blue purple yellow red water
> on the green purple yellow red grass
> Let us pass through our perfect park
> pausing on a Sunday . . .

I have known the song for years, had seen it performed in a local production of the play, and had listened often to my favorite version, led by Bernadette Peters, on a two-volume Sondheim tribute cassette Jerry and I bought 20 years ago. But it was back in 1997 when the song "Sunday" struck a chord in my heart that has forever reminded me how it feels to be alive.

In 1996 I finished a demanding independent studies Master's degree program in creative writing. Almost immediately after finishing that work, I took the job as high school librarian on the campus where I'd been teaching. Accepting the new position required me to return to school for 27 more hours of graduate work, this time in library science. On emergency certification as librarian, I was doing the job that I was going to school to learn. As the only librarian in my building, I discovered almost everything through trial-and-error, which made for an especially rigorous first few semesters. I would finish my work day and hurry to the University of Houston-Clear Lake nearly an hour away, take evening courses, and then head home to get some sleep and repeat the process the next day.

By my third semester at UHCL, I was exhausted and emotionally spent. I held it together until late one night driving down a barren strip of Red Bluff Road. It was a Thursday night after 10:00 p.m. I'd been running myself ragged for so long, always hanging on to excel for one more day, in one more class, on one more assignment. Driving home that black night, I felt the tenderness of Bernadette Peters' delivery of the introductory words "order, design, tension, balance." When she ended by saying "harmony" with an inflection that seemed to come through the patient smile of a loving mother, I lost it. As the strings glided in and then the song crescendoed to the climactic "on an ordinary Sunday, Sunday, Sunday" I wept in stony, absolving bursts. The stress mounting in my body for three years found release through the soaring rhythms of a single, rousing song. The fact that the song was about a work of art, and the play from which it came was about the struggle of the artist, made it even more meaningful to me. Even before I completed a single book that proved to me I did indeed have the heart of an artist, I knew that desire was in me.

My dream of being a writer has always been fueled by wanting to create something beautiful. My soul recognizes beauty in various forms, even those for which I don't believe I have any talent. Long ago I learned from sources who know music that I do not carry a tune well, yet my soul still soars when I hear beauty created through instruments, including the human voice. That night in my car alone on a lonely stretch of road in 1997, I felt cleansed and transformed by the song "Sunday." Since then, whenever I hear it, I am taken back to that experience and remember why I have always wanted to be a writer.

Hearing "Sunday" on the way to work this morning reminded me of working on *One Sister Left the Gun* yesterday. To me, writing fiction is my ultimate effort to create beauty. The theme resonates with me always. Even in this novel, a central character seeks meaning in life by learning to create something beautiful. Interestingly, she attempts it by learning to play music.

I have a natural propensity to set and achieve goals. Having focused on goal setting my entire adult life, I have written books about the topic, and have taught the concept to adults, young adults, and children for decades. I know goal-setting so well, I am known as "The Goal Guy" and am sought after for my expertise. So even when part of me doesn't feel like following through on a goal, the wiser side of me perseveres. Yesterday, although I was immersed in other projects, I stopped what I was doing in mid-task to make sure I fulfilled my commitment to revise at least a few pages of *One Sister Left the Gun*.

This morning, thanks to "Sunday," it struck me. The purpose of writing my fiction is to create beauty. I aspire to write novels that stir hearts with the same impact that I experience when I read great writing, like *The Great Gatsby*, or see a masterpiece painting, like Rubens' *Samson and Delilah*, or hear a song as exalting as "Sunday." But it is not just the final outcome I am seeking. While the result is what I want for others, I realize that as an artist whose medium is words, I want to immerse myself in the process of creating that beauty. When I am writing, I am living a spiritual experience I do not get from any other stimulus. In an effort to leave a legacy of beauty that I hope will inspire others long after I am done with my journey through this life, I must not only dig even deeper inside myself to discover the source of that beauty for me, but I must also build a spiritual sanctuary where I can sit with God, and with my characters, and live in the nurturing insulation of my own soul. From there, I believe beauty will emerge through my writing, connecting my soul to the souls of those touched by what I write.

At this moment my heart feels content. Writing today's entry has invited me to find comfort in the home I've built inside my soul. By sharing this with you, I've invited you in. In linear time, you will be experiencing this entry months or years from now. But spirit is timeless. So even if on a conscious level you take in these words through your eyes and brain on some other calendar date than when I'm writing this entry, it is only because we've already shared it as I'm writing it. I picture you as I write, and I'm there with you as you read.

To me no words express love more than the reassurance of "You're not alone. I'm right here with you." As a spiritual man, I believe that message does not end with physical death. When I hear that message, I am immersed in the pool of eternity where I lose my physical form and become the water. I am part of what loves me, and at the same time, I am the love that sustains me whenever my mind thinks I'm alone.

Beauty sustains. That is why, every time I hear "Sunday" or read a favorite passage of *The Great Gatsby*, I am emotionally moved, spiritually fed, and intellectually challenged to create something of beauty that does not yet exist. In that beauty are order, design, tension, balance, and, if the product matches the vision, harmony.

Day 34: December 15

Today was the last day that students could select items for themselves or their families from the library "store." Few things remain. On one study carrel some books are scattered. From three of the clothing racks hang slacks, shirts, and a few blouses. Everything else has been taken.

As I worked in my office, one of our special ed teachers called to me. "Dr. Leslie, are you there?"

"Here I am." Before I could leap from my chair to greet her by the circulation desk, the teacher appeared in my office doorway guiding by the shoulders one of our most mentally handicapped students who was holding two bulging bags of clothes. A broad gap spread like a tiny teepee between her front teeth and her eyes veered sidelong even as her face was directed toward me.

"What do you say?" the teacher asked the student.

"Thank you, Dr. Leslie, for my Christmas."

I choked out, "Oh, you're welcome" and sat immobile in my office for several long seconds after they disappeared. The sweetness of her thank-you brought tears. I flushed with gratitude for being spiritually invited to participate in a process that gave someone as helpless and innocent as that child something special this Christmas. For my part, it only took slowing down enough to hear the voice of inspiration, and then acting on it. My wish this Christmas had been to do something meaningful. I acted on several inspirations and had received positive feedback for many of the actions. But none touched me as much as that little girl with the faraway corner glance but very present smile. I intend to hold dear the image of that sweet student standing in my doorway to remind me how dynamic and healing even the simplest acts of kindness can be.

Day 35: December 16

For the past several days I have been trying to devise a creative way to pay our civic association dues without dipping into my savings. I prayed and watched for inspiration, but none has appeared.

The bank with my savings accounts is near my campus, far from home. Because school let out today for Christmas break, I wanted to decide before the end of the school day whether to take money out of my savings to pay the dues. I had to generate the money, as the dues could only be paid by check. I knew I didn't have that much extra cash in my checking account, so I had to come up with something.

No royalty checks arrived these past few days, and no new clients have requested a manuscript edit. However, a new friend from church, who is also a public speaker, emailed me to confirm a meeting we'd set to present a series of goal setting workshops after the new year. To review what I wanted to share with him at the meeting, I looked over the goal sheets I had composed earlier this year. I consistently complete planned activity columns in my goal charts so I am always in the process of achieving something regarding my writing, health, spirituality, and financial prosperity.

When I looked over my financial goal statement, I realized that I had specified that I would complete my financial commitment by not touching only some of my savings accounts. Earlier in the year I had determined that I could withdraw money from one account if I needed to meet specific financial obligations such as car insurance and the civic association dues.

As I read the goal statement, I felt immediately freer. I knew I could withdraw the money from my savings to pay the dues while remaining true to the goal. On the way home from work that day, I made three stops: to the credit union for a withdrawal, to my bank for a deposit, and to the post office where I mailed my payment for the civic association dues two weeks before the deadline.

Even though right now I don't see signs of wealth that match my vision, this experience reminded me that I am prosperous. My systematic savings plan left me enough money to cover the homeowner dues. This example may reveal miniscule progress, but it's progress I acknowledge with gratitude while hoping for monumental growth in this area in coming years.

While this advanced planning may seem to flow upstream from my first last year commitment, it actually indicates to me the immediacy of miracles perpetually streaming through my life. By finding the old goal sheet, I demonstrated that I already have what I sought. Life is not about acquiring what I don't have, but realizing that I already possess everything I need and desire. What a dynamic lesson to remind me to stay present and grateful, and to live only for now.

Day 36: December 17

I realize as we begin our Christmas break that I have been utilizing my right brain more. Usually I'm a very left-brained, concrete sequential thinker when completing tasks. Early in my career, I only wrote one book at a time. More recently, I've been writing two books simultaneously, one work of fiction and one work of nonfiction. As I pursued my doctorate, two books turned into two books and a dissertation.

After earning my Ph.D., new inspirations detonated. I responded by acting on them all. Starting so many writing projects has required personal growth. In the past I would feel overwhelmed by new demands on my time beyond the goals I'd set with structured plans of action and concrete deadlines. Now I am juggling many projects and not reaching closure on any of them. Yet I am doing and achieving more than I think I ever have in my life.

Besides my writing, I'm also doing other tasks more sporadically rather than systematically, as I usually do. For example, Jerry and I had intended to clean house together once we had time off for the holidays. But today Jerry started writing his Christmas cards while I cleaned the den and kitchen nook. It was a start to getting the house together, and a switch from our more common routine of setting aside a day and working until we had the entire house in shape.

The spontaneity that keeps me focused on the present continued later in the day. When I finished the den and kitchen nook, I was ready to get cleaned up myself. Before stepping into the shower, I noticed tinges of gray between the white tiles. So I scoured the shower, even though I usually do that when I clean the whole bathroom.

My left-brained personality doesn't usually pursue activities so reflexively or find it so easy to live with half-cleaned bathrooms or spottily completed work of any kind. But doing that now isn't bothering the more regimented side of me. When it feels right, we'll clean the rest of the house together. We have to—all my family is coming over Christmas Eve. As inspiration stirs, we'll respond. Fewer plans invite more alertness to the present moment. I'm awake and vibrant . . . and grateful.

Day 37: December 18

I no longer create many experiences where someone else has control over my success. I have relative autonomy as the only librarian on my campus, and ultimate freedom to write what inspires me. But my subconscious must be working through some constraint because last night my two dreams had me answering to someone else.

DREAM 1:

I was traveling in each dream. In the first I sat near the front of a plane one row behind a young woman who kept interrupting work on her computer to go to the restroom. As I watched her activity, it occurred to me that she might be doing something illegal, like ingesting capsules full of drugs like the protagonist in Maria Full of Grace.

Whenever my fellow traveler went to the restroom, I glanced at her computer screen and saw that she was looking up and writing about a war-torn Middle Eastern country, which also led me to wonder if she were involved in terrorist activity. I had my laptop, too, so I looked up the site she was on to get a better idea what she might be doing. I watched her activities to see if she did anything more suspicious, but she didn't. I even visited with her, conversing with her about nothing in particular, but she never said anything threatening. However, I did sense that she had some politically radical ideas and might be working on a plot to act on them.

We landed safely and she went ahead of me through customs. They didn't check any of her baggage very closely, not even her computer. When she cleared customs, I watched her shoulders relax. Then I went through customs where they checked me thoroughly. The entire time they looked through my baggage, I wondered if I should have said something about the young woman to a steward during the flight. The customs officer opened my laptop, turned it on and searched the sites I most recently visited. Of course, the last one was the terrorist activity site. I explained that I was a writer, and apparently they recognized me because they did not seem concerned about what they found. But interestingly, instead of reprimanding me, one officer said, "I think someone needs to go back and grab the young woman we just let through. I don't think we're done with her yet."

DREAM 2:

  I was cruising with relatives as we often do. While passing through customs at one port, I was with a cousin who in the dream was still in her teens, and another cousin who in the dream was just a toddler I was watching. I had my passport and ID, but they didn't have theirs. I couldn't find their parents or anyone in their immediate family who would have their ID, so I had to prove that they were really with me and that I could be responsible for them. I had a bag full of writing materials with me, and as I explained to the customs officer how these two children from different generations were indeed related to me, I said, "We're connected through my grandmother. She and this teen's grandmother were sisters, and she is this toddler's great-grandmother."
  I dug through my bag and pulled out a photo album. Flipping through the pages in search of a photo of my grandmother and her sisters, I found another of the teen cousin. I showed it to the customs officer to prove that they really belonged with me and that I could vouch for them being in my party.

  Although I didn't feel helpless in either dream, I sensed an undercurrent of powerlessness. Though I had done nothing wrong,

I had to prove my integrity and my relationships to someone who controlled whether I continued to my destination.

I believe we create our own opportunities, challenges, and roadblocks to success. These dreams seem to suggest it's time to overcome some limiting belief or fear because Spirit is ready to move forward.

Day 38: December 19

Jerry and I spent the day getting the rest of the house together. Not only did I clean my rooms in record time, but I also organized the office where we have been haphazardly storing excess items for months. I condensed piles of Jerry's belongings into five boxes I stored in a bedroom closet. I'm sure it'll take him a while to sort through all his music and tax papers and school counseling materials when he finally gets to it, but for now the office is dazzling. I'm relieved every time I walk down the hall and see the office looking roomy and organized.

So pieces of my life are as they have always been. I like being organized, and I like my environment clean, uncluttered, and spacious. But internally I have more tolerance for a little chaos. For now, it's okay not to work on one book at a time. Instead of feeling frustrated, I can enjoy juggling and renegotiating meetings with six different literary analysis groups. I don't have my financial quandaries answered yet, and Jerry and I are both occasionally discouraged that we're not making better financial headway with the projects we've already set in motion.

Even though I'm living this experiment of packing in all the richness of life in a 12-month period, I have the patience to know that persistence is the key to most success. I have the diligence and patience to remain undeterred even when results don't materialize as quickly as I sometimes wish they would.

Right now I'm looking forward to much but, in the meantime, I am loving and feeling grateful for what I have, even if some of it feels unfamiliar. I am growing. I am changing. I am becoming who I have long dreamed of being.

9

A Gift Fit for Angels

Day 39: December 20

On a news program this morning, a revered scholar described the books he loved reading most this year. Later in the hour a long established pop star sat at the piano singing a Christmas song from a new holiday CD. The camera cut to the scholar reveling in the song. That image sent a flush of empowerment through me. I feel magic and universality in moments, however fleeting, when one person who has aspired to greatness touches the heart of another who has done the same.

Later my mom and I resumed our annual Christmas outing. Because malls demand more walking than my mom can handle any more, we took in a movie. Afterward we spent an hour browsing through an antique mart then ate a light dinner. By 9:00 we returned to my parents' home where we visited with Dad.

During our conversation I secretly studied my parents, appreciating how relatively healthy and vibrant they seemed. Both of them, especially my mother, have had numerous health challenges recently. At different times this year both were hospitalized, but they have done well in recent months. I took the time to acknowledge their recovery and appreciate that tonight, they both seemed happy.

As another year draws to a close, I imagine many people take stock of what they still have and what has gone away. I know I do. I always feel grateful that I still have my parents, and Jerry and I both comment regularly about how fortunate we are to be our ages and have parents still living and independent. It's a rare blessing we don't take for granted. It felt especially comforting to bask in gratitude of that knowledge as I sat alone with my mom and dad in their family room just visiting, talking, and laughing.

When anything feels challenging or gets frustrating in life, Jerry and I remind ourselves that we know what's most important to us: the opportunity to share time with our loved ones. It's an incomparable blessing we continually appreciate while we have it. I can't know how either of us will respond when our parents die, but recognizing my gratitude while I'm with my parents fills my soul. I believe that our continued spiritual connection after death will remain richer for my having appreciated their physical presence while it was still here.

Day 40: December 21

Last night I had an interesting dream which I will only highlight here. *As an adult, I was watching children play baseball on the cul-de-sac of my childhood home. While retrieving something for one of the players, I saw that whoever was living in my childhood home had left the front door open. From my distant proximity I tried to peer in to see the entrance hall. Looking closer I saw an "open house" sign on the front lawn. It was 9:00 a.m., and the open house wouldn't begin until 1:00.*

I became very excited about seeing my old home. Because I had not been in the house for over 35 years, I knew much would be changed, but I didn't mind. I still wanted to go back inside and explore what is there now and reminisce about what was there in my childhood. I awoke feeling the anticipatory exhilaration of having the chance to tour my old home later that day.

Like my house in the dream, I can reexamine where and who I was when I first started this journey through life. This first last year has made me especially sentimental. I'm pleased that the opportunity to revisit those earliest memories excited me. The prospect of culling those old thoughts and emotions feels empowering. I'm not surprised that this dream came the week of Christmas. It's a time I'm traditionally nostalgic, gladly reviving memories of my formative years.

Any life rich in detail, thought, and emotion is lived in balance between current experience and reflective examination. As a spiritual explorer, I live both in the physical world and the inner chambers of my soul. Besides being parallel, the two worlds mirror each other, creating a multidimensional existence that would be flat and comparatively lifeless otherwise. I believe, no matter what our professions, creative endeavors, or spiritual inclinations, this dual dimension of life infuses our experiences with meaning. We must live life and then reflect on it regularly in order to know who we are, what we value, where we've been and where we're going. Living my first last year, and writing about it now, is making that meaning especially profound.

Day 51: January 1

During the rest of my Christmas break I took a sabbatical from journaling daily. Instead, I kept in mind pivotal moments and general observations to determine if writing from a broader perspective would highlight more vividly only what was most important during this first last year.

In addition to not writing, I also took a break from my regular meditation and prayer work. The result, as you might guess, was disappointing. Although I loved the time we shared with family and friends throughout the holiday season, something felt missing when I wasn't consistently activating the spiritual aspect of my life.

During the days leading up to Christmas Eve, when Jerry and I host my family's gathering, I made a conscious effort to slow down and savor my familiar holiday rituals. Every December I assemble a Christmas jigsaw puzzle. This year I chose my favorite, a shadowy blue street scene called Christmastown USA while playing favorite Christmas music. During this and other traditions I've developed, such as decorating the house or wrapping gifts, I realized I spend most of these activities alone. Yet I don't feel lonely, as I am nurturing my soul—or more accurately, my soul is nurturing me. Enjoying each activity I feel profoundly content, and aware and grateful that I am alive.

Some recent memories from this holiday remain vivid. Joy pervaded our Christmas Eve celebration with my family. Jerry served spaghetti and meatballs, everyone had at least one present to open, and my nieces Maycee and Charlee, as always, brightened the festivities with youthful energy. The moment stirring most in my heart came at night's end as I watched my mother and father walk to the car. A rush of gratitude surged through me as I noted how vibrant they seemed.

During recent Christmases my mother has been ill at home or in the hospital and therefore hadn't attended the gatherings. But this time she was here, as were my sister and her spouse, and my younger brother, his wife, and three of their daughters. The unity of having several immediate family members together lingered as I watched my parents take sturdy strides down the path from my front porch, across the sidewalk, and up the driveway to the car.

Next morning, Jerry conducted the Christmas Day church service. Because our church is an hour north of our home, we loaded the car and took our two dachshunds with us so we could head directly to Jerry's parents' house after service. There's a prayer room at the church adjoining the sanctuary, so during the service I sat with just the two dogs in that cozy room. I couldn't distinguish any of Jerry's words, but I heard all the music through the wall separating me from the congregation. Back straight and eyes closed in meditation, I sat in the plush wingback chair with Joey, our black dachshund, against my left thigh and Rex, our red dachshund, draped across my lap. It was a unique and moving spiritual experience to be there in physical solitude yet there in spiritual connection with people I have grown close to in the years since Jerry became their minister.

Although I didn't get to see it, the most memorable moment of the day occurred right after the service. During the closing affirmation, the volunteer prayer leader for the day goes to the prayer room, where the dogs and I were cloistered, to be available for congregants wanting prayer support. A few seconds after the final strain of the peace song that concludes the service, that day's prayer leader opened my door. I grabbed Joey but Rex darted out of the room. Jerry told me later that he looked up from speaking with a church member right after the service to see Rex dashing between rows of chairs in the middle of the sanctuary. He said it was the cutest thing seeing our chubby red dachshund scamper about, sniffing and exploring this new wonderland.

Between Christmas and New Years, we enjoy watching *Kennedy Center Honors*. My own desire for excellence is always stirred by the talent and dedication of artists who have achieved so much. The retrospective about jazz musician Sonny Rollins highlighted detours in his career including a self-imposed exile that he took to hone his craft. The details reminded me of an old commercial featuring a saxophonist playing on a bridge as a voiceover explained how he stopped performing until he reached a level of excellence to which he aspired, but, until then, had not reached. Although I was still in my teens when I first saw that commercial, the message always remained with me. Over the past few months I even thought of it while revising *One Sister Left the Gun* and feeling that the writing still isn't as strong as I want it to be to honor my grandmother and her sisters.

As I watched the tribute to Sonny Rollins, I wondered if he were the man highlighted in the commercial. I looked him up online and indeed he was. This time, instead of feeling just generally inspired by it, the special felt more personal. I love my work and I love my grandmother and her sisters. I no longer feel a sense of urgency to publish the novel *One Sister Left the Gun*, and I have released the fear that planning a four-volume fiction series is too daunting a task. If I haven't developed the talent I need to make the books what I envision them to be, then I will do whatever it takes to hone my skills until the manuscript is a gift fit for the angels that generation of women in my family are to me.

Breaking from the routine of writing five books simultaneously has shed new light on productivity and quality of work. The approach has slowed progress on all of the books and fractured my mental and emotional energy so that I don't build enough momentum to get swept along by the work and finish it with gusto. For example, when I wrote *Film Stars and Their Awards* (www.RogerLeslie.com), I was taking Ph.D. classes but had not yet begun my dissertation. That movie reference book took four years from idea to publication. But my enthusiasm for the project filled me with such zeal that I couldn't wait to return to the manuscript every morning, as if it were a friend I missed each time I was away.

I had that feeling about *One Sister Left the Gun* until I started working on so many other books. Even when I felt overwhelmed trying to write the first draft while also working on my dissertation, the novel compelled me to continue writing. Interrupting the multitask approach made clear that I need to give each work its individual due. To honor each I must prioritize my commitments and work on them one at a time. Deep within I feel a tug to discover a more effective use for my talent. Like Sonny Rollins, I must hone my skills to honor the works that Spirit has so graciously given me the inspirations to write.

Speaking of talent, Jerry sang at two New Year's Eve services at a large church where he solos annually. I dropped him off at the church about 4:30, picked up some dinner for my mom and dad, and spent the evening with them before returning for the final service where Jerry performed. I was joined by our lifelong friend, Constance, and her sister, Kelly, who sat beside me. Jerry concluded his musical interlude with a rendition of "Auld Lang Syne" so tender and gentle that I felt his spirit sweep across the sanctuary. I was so overcome I reached for Kelly's hand, and we clasped each other throughout the song until our fingers trembled.

I know I am biased about Jerry's singing voice, but my opinion is continually reinforced by others who come up to him, or me, or both of us and marvel at the sweetness of his delivery. I know Jerry's heart, and I am as certain as I am grateful that when Jerry sings he is drawing from the pool of divine energy of which we are all a part. I know that feeling as a writer, and I experience it whenever I do for others anything inspired by Spirit.

That divinity is also clear to me in Jerry through the messages he gives at church and even more powerfully in his meditations. But when Jerry sings I feel God resonating through me and I believe wholly that he draws from the divine in some of his greatest songs, especially those that he appears to deliver effortlessly. As I have with "O Holy Night," I have now reserved a special sanctuary in my heart for his "Auld Lang Syne" and will return to the memory of his singing it this New Year's Eve often to remind me how beautifully God works through us if we just use our natural talents.

This revelation reminds me to edit *One Sister Left the Gun* using the same spiritual practices as the initial composition. The first draft unfolded briskly because my meditations opened the creative channels to allow spiritual energy to flow. I've been editing with my conscious mind, believing that drafting is a right-brained intuitive act and editing a left-brained chore. At every writing stage, most of the energy and power must be spiritual. That same philosophy could improve everything I experience. Coming from Spirit can make every human experience divine.

I have answered the call to write the series. My limiting conscious self has sometimes entertained doubts about my skills, much like Moses wondered why God would choose him to lead his people when he didn't have a gift for speech. But God told Moses He would give him the words. I recall how often during the most daunting months of writing both the first draft of *One Sister Left the Gun* and my dissertation, I didn't know how I could keep writing the novel. But I started each writing session in meditation where I would summon into my superconscious my grandmother and her sisters, who consistently reassured me that I needed to do only one thing:

show up. All I had to do was sit at the computer willing to write, and Spirit would give me the words.

In that sense, my writing seems as effortless as Jerry's singing when it touches me the most. My conscious mind doubts, but my superconscious sits at the computer and is willing to be led by whatever force I am a part of—we all are a part of—and show up to do the work. From there, if I let go and allow myself to be led, and then have the courage to follow and the fortitude to follow through to completion, then I will have lived, and I will have fulfilled my purpose in this life.

As I write these lines I am wondering about you, the reader, right now. What is it you're called to do? What touches your heart? What continues to tweak your subconscious in such a way that reminds you, "That's what it is. That's what I'm called to do. Why do I keep putting it off, or why do I not resume that activity? *That* would be fulfilling. *That* would be rewarding. *That* would be challenging enough to scare me just a little. When I'm just a little scared, I'm forced to engage my own courage. When I do, I know I'm alive."

You may believe that it's not fear holding you back from pursuing your dreams, but perhaps fear is just manifesting in another form. Fear can appear as procrastination, as laziness, as busyness doing something irrelevant. It might disguise itself through a focus on the needs of others to the neglect or exclusion of your own dreams.

Oh the joy of stepping into the line of fire! How courageous we are when we simply answer the call tugging at our hearts. Seated near Sonny Rollins at *Kennedy Center Honors* was honoree cellist Yo-Yo Ma. During his segment, he addressed this issue profoundly by admitting, "I'm not brave. I'm actually pretty scared a lot of the time. But I must like being scared because I keep doing things that scare me."

What scares you? Don't gloss over the question. Consider it. What have you longed to do that scares you? Breathe and think. You know. You know that you know because it's always been yours to do. Yes. That. Do that. Start.

Where do you begin? Just show up. Arrive where you need to be to do what you feel called to do. Bring with you one thing: willingness. Everything else will appear. The tools. The support. The people who can guide you. The courage you need to move one step, then another, then another.

When you stop reading this entry, I urge you to take one of two actions. Either begin right now doing what your heart longs for, or write down what you're thinking and feeling right now with the intention of taking action on your dream within the next 24 hours. Before you pick up this book again, you will have begun and your life, before your mind can even fathom it, will be transformed. It won't be different or strange or new. It will finally be familiar because you'll be doing what you've always known you were here to do. Ready to begin creating your gift fit for angels, you will know that you are home.

10

The Truth is Below the Surface

Day 53: January 3

At the New Year's Day service, Jerry led the congregation through an extended peace meditation. So long in that spiritual state, I realized that my first last year has already moved me to another spiritual plane. Now I want my everyday experiences to bring authentic satisfaction that keeps me always in tune with my soul. I feel that harmony in meditation and strive to sustain that spiritual undercurrent throughout each day. It can be as profound while I'm interacting with individuals, speaking to groups large or small, or spending this time writing, where I am physically alone, but spiritually connecting to everyone who will read this work long after my first last year has lapsed.

Day 59: January 9

Opening to Spirit has rejuvenated me this new year. Since returning to work last week, I resumed editing *One Sister Left the Gun* and am captivated by its evolution. Some expressions seem beyond me, as though I've tapped into something greater than my conscious mind could write. I know my love of writing has always come from this phenomenon: writing books demands cultivating ideas from a deeper, bigger, and greater realm than the world of conscious thought.

This activity is a metaphor for how I believe all of life works. We can cruise through our day-to-day life on spiritual autopilot and survive just fine. The universe keeps working, we continue living, and we can even be quite happy. But there exists a richness experienced only by our awakened soul, and the abstract rewards of that awareness reveal a dimension to life that changes everything. Some religions call it being born again or attaining enlightenment. Some psychologists and educators call it self-actualization. However it is labeled, I believe spiritual awareness is evident when we act beyond our simple selves, moving through life in accordance with the energy and dynamism of something greater.

The other day I noticed my perspective shift because of my first last year. While thinking about travel plans Jerry and I want to make before November, I envisioned the months constricting and dissolving. Making the most of limited time requires setting priorities. If I only have this year, my future plans can't rest on the promise of *someday*. I must choose now what is essential and do that, and only that, to ensure that I fulfill my destiny. Having such an overarching life goal fuels my creative energy to write, teach, and share insights like the one I describe now.

Until recently, I thought it was enough to feel and act on individual inspirations. But empowerment builds momentum when we remain in the flow of the energy that first inspired us. Inspirations are not isolated spiritual messages we alone bring to the three-dimensional world to work with independently. We co-create divine ideas by staying attuned to our higher power and acting only from the source.

Putting that idea into practice made me an instant helper. Arriving at work I took a moment to meditate. After the meditation, I checked on some students and one was in a panic because she just lost her new cell phone. I spent the entire period helping her retrace her steps and consider all possibilities. She worried that the girl who had been sitting at the computer next to her took it. As soon as she had remembered leaving her cell phone beside the keyboard, she ran back to that area of the library only to discover that both the girl and her phone were gone. I continuously reassured her that we would find it, and each time I did another idea for where we could check and how we might secure more help finding it came to me. We acted on each idea and before the period had ended, we tracked down a friend of hers who had also been in the library and took the phone for her, but couldn't get out of her next class to return it.

I have moved through the day at a leisurely pace. I feel as though I am not on my own turbo-propelled schedule, but on Spirit's. I check in, do what I feel inspired to do, and then go back to Spirit. I've never approached a work day quite like this before and I find it fascinating and comforting to surrender my plans to something greater than I.

Winter is whisking through Houston with torrential rains. Every time I look outside I think how lucky I am to have a job indoors. Some people have complained about the weather, saying we've gone from drought to drowning. But more often I've encountered people appreciating the rain. For every person who has come in and complained that she had fixed her hair so beautifully this morning and now it's wet and stringy, I have had an encounter like one during lunch when I saw a student staring out the window. She sat so immobile that I inquired if she were sick or depressed.

"No," she gazed at me with eyes softened by joy. "I'm more than fine. It's so soothing to watch the rain."

Her message touched me. I'm not in charge anyway, so quit trying to grab the controls. Following our inner guidance, we discover that our journey is set with our original intention expressed as a dream, a wish, or a goal. Once we embark on our personal quest, we'll see how the universe takes us past any obstacle, placing us along the same journey as others who remind us that nothing is ever lost. The most calming, grounded ecstasy comes from noticing and appreciating what is right in front of us.

11

Say "Yes" to Every Inspiration

Day 68: January 18

I have expanded the scope of my first last year goal. I used to shun any feelings and experiences I perceived as negative. My life's mission was to find a way to stay happy no matter what circumstances I faced. But I have redefined happiness. To live fully, I now believe I need to honor the entire spectrum of emotions and recognize that every feeling has merit. Living fully every day means living everything—disappointments, grief, frustrations, conflicts—with as much enthusiasm as the joys and triumphs.

Keeping my promise to be bold and brave this year, I believe I can face any situation and embrace any emotion. So long as I'm spiritually awake, I can sustain a grounded happiness even if my surface feelings contradict the accelerated happiness I so often emanate. Don't get me wrong. I still think that dazzling joy is my natural state. But it's the largest facet on a gem with multiple nuances. Each is beautiful in its own way. Together they create a metaphoric parade of lights more captivating than any flat surface.

My soul—the real me when everything else is stripped away—knows true contentment and understands that nothing can diminish spiritual joy. With that knowledge, every other emotion is just temporary.

Through early stages of life, I had isolated glimpses of what it meant to be deeply happy, but that awareness took root gradually. One Easter when I was a boy, my grandmother was in a uniquely vibrant mood—funny, playful with several of us grandchildren, and, particularly rare for her, demonstrative in her affection. I recall looking up at her in the kitchen, an isolated moment when she was so cheerful and open to us, and I thought, *This is what happiness looks like.* I knew it for awhile, but in time it faded.

As a teen, I was watching *Guess Who's Coming to Dinner* when a single line of dialogue touched me. Watching their grown daughter from a distance, Katharine Hepburn tells Spencer Tracy, "She's always been a happy human being." Her words washed over me like a baptismal wave. In that moment I committed to a lifelong quest of making sure others could always say the same of me. Nearing adulthood, I had a little better grasp of the wheel that steered my fate. But I would still drift at times and forget the promise that line of dialogue fed my soul.

In my early twenties I attended a church service where four men sang an upbeat hymn. During the song, one man embodied joy. His expression, body language, even the energy around him glowed with pure elation. I watched him and thought, *I want that for me,* and now I know it really is attainable.

Who can say if he was feeling the profound joy I projected onto him? I know now that the insight I had was not about his ecstasy or energy, but mine. In that observation I projected onto him what was happening in my own heart. That moment, I recommitted to live my life with joy. Although during several subsequent stages of my life I have taken detours from the path of unalterable, faith-filled happiness, I set my feet firmly on the path I wanted in those three incidents during my formative years and have never wavered from that ideal. I see now that the goal of this book is not a new quest, just a re-commitment to those inspirations I embraced many years ago.

Day 80: January 30

During Christmas break, I committed to write only one book at a time when I returned to work. My first day back on campus, many prior commitments I made earlier swept me into the same overloaded schedule I didn't plan to recreate. My anchor project remained *One Sister Left the Gun*. Writing every day filled my soul.

But other demands circled around my head like drooling vultures. As the deadline for all literary analysis of the children's chapter books loomed, some groups didn't do their work, while others did it incorrectly. To get it to the publisher as promised, I spent days reformatting rubrics, rewriting text, and transposing then recalculating statistics. Further, I'm planning a thank-you reception for the 50 teachers who helped with this research.

For upcoming workshops and speaking engagements I accepted, I've had to prepare presentations, write speeches, and then deliver them. Further, some former editing clients returned for me to provide feedback on their newest drafts. I am exhausted.

Last night I dreamed that, in the middle of the school day, I thought I was sick and wanted to go home. With three classes left in the day, I calculated how much I would miss, and how much I would later have to make up, if I went home.

The idea felt so good, I considered calling in sick to work today. But already scheduled were my trip to pick up gift cards for the reception and a final literary analysis meeting.

Right now I am living proof that too much of a good thing, even if it is my passion and it is fulfilling my life's purpose, erodes the spirit. My emotional reservoir feels so empty the hairline fracture in the drain is visible. I need refueling.

As I drove to work wondering how I'd generate the energy to present a great workshop this weekend, I caught part of a Gary Zukov interview on Oprah Radio. His message about intention invigorated me. Instead of thinking about my own exhaustion as the workshop nears, I need to focus on its purpose: to inspire people to discover and live their passion.

I felt spiritually called to speak and I answered that call. To reach my workshop attendees at a soul level, I need to show up spiritually, not just physically. That requires nurturing my spirit this week so that I repair that hairline crack before it becomes a gaping hole. The idea of it prompted a refreshing exhalation.

What is life without transformative joy? Pause. I took a deep breath. Pause. I took another deep breath. Even committed to my first last year, I became so busy I stopped reflecting enough to know I'm alive. As Socrates said, "The unexamined life is not worth living." By reexamining my life, urgency has given way to hope.

I loved TV as a boy. At the end of summer 1971, commercials advertising ABC's upcoming season flashed floating scenes from their new fall lineup to a tune with lyrics that said, "This is the place to be. This is the place to be. This is the place to be with ABC." Anticipating new episodes of my favorite shows tickled my throat and sent tingles up my back. I'm feeling that way now. To me, this is the sensation of hope, of anticipation, of soul-emerging joy. One sincere meditation re-routed my energy.

Although my body is tired, my spirit feels revived from just having been acknowledged again. How patient the soul is to wait until I finish the quickstep to nowhere and notice that the song has changed. I start back on my journey again. As I sit here and pause, I breathe and am conscious of my breath. I realize how unaware of my thoughts I have been lately. Although I am still too tired to exalt in my revitalized spirit, I sense my spark reignited. Right now, in this moment, I feel grateful to be alive.

Day 87: February 6

Before my body could match the recovery of my spirit, I had more lessons to learn. Totally spent, I had three major events that impacted other people. Despite exhaustion so palpable my body ached from breathing, I prepared for and hosted a reception for all the educators who contributed to the literary analysis for *Teach Me SUCCESS*. The reception was well attended and much appreciated, but I was in a fog. I glided through my interactions like a depressed actor portraying a gracious host.

After school the next day I went to Bayou Publishing to pick up copies of *Success Express for Teens* to sell at my next goal setting workshop. En route I realized I had not received a royalty check from that publisher for some time. At Bayou, the publisher handed me my books and an envelope containing a royalty check. As we met briefly, exhaustion steamrolled me. I held my own, but I sensed my energy fading toward oblivion.

On the verge of a deluge, the sky was a menacing charcoal gray. It was the perfect setting for my barely-staying-on-the-edge-of-the-abyss physical state. Before I pulled out of my parking space, I pulled from the envelope a check for one of the biggest royalties I'd ever received. It wasn't New York Times best seller sized, but it was generous enough to trigger some rousing "Thank You, God" shout-outs loud enough to drown out the raindrops pummeling my car.

Jerry and I went out to eat that evening with two close friends. You might be wondering, "Why would you go out to dinner with friends when you're so exhausted and you have to get up early to do a 3-hour workshop the next morning?" I knew Jerry and I would go out to dinner anyway, and the friends agreed to meet early, so the plan didn't veer far from how the evening would have transpired anyhow.

Fortunately, Jerry carried our part of the conversation the entire dinner. I participated a little, but mostly focused on eating a healthy meal in hopes of reviving myself. I can't ever remember being more exhausted than I was that evening. When I felt that tired before, I had a clear schedule and anticipation of relief. This time, I felt close to comatose wondering how I would motivate people to create the life they dream during my goal setting workshop the next morning, and then inspire people spiritually the one after that.

Jerry and I were home a little after 7:00. My body ached, and my digestion was a mess. I didn't feel as though I was coming down with anything, I just think my body was screaming for relief. I took two ibuprofen and two Imodium and was asleep by 7:30. That night I slept 11 hours and the next morning felt somewhat revived.

Upon awakening we turned on the news to check the weather: torrential rains were falling all over Houston. Not many people had pre-registered for the workshop anyway, so now we wondered if we'd have any participants. Jerry, who would be attending the workshop, and I got ready and headed out through pounding rain. By the time we reached the workshop site, the storm had diminished to an intermittent drizzle.

Though only ten people attended the workshop, it went well. My introductory PowerPoint to the inspirational song lifted the energy in the room. It remained steady despite drab weather, sparse attendance, and my fatigue. Working to stay enthusiastic and motivating the entire three hours, I gave participants concrete steps toward living the life they dreamed.

That afternoon Jerry rehearsed for an upcoming show while I went home and napped. My goal was to recover and get back into physical, emotional, and spiritual balance. I slept a little over an hour, then awoke fully alert. I did a few tasks around the house before Jerry returned in time for us to attend a friend's birthday party.

I had a good night's sleep and woke early enough to go over my message one more time before heading to church. I gave the speech, paying special attention to my pacing and articulation. As I spoke I felt a powerful wave that assured me that I was doing good work.

Shelley Winters once said: Every now and then, when you're on stage, you hear the best sound a player can hear. It's a sound you can't get in movies or in television. It is the sound of a wonderful, deep silence that means you've hit them where they live.

I experienced that silence during my message. It was reinforced by expressions on congregants' faces, as well as that silence being interrupted by audible grunts of insight or realization. The second time I do anything, I wonder about a sophomore slump. The first time something goes really well, it might be all Spirit and beginner's luck. The second time often determines whether I have the mettle required to do something well, or if my first success was a fortunate accident. This second time speaking here felt even better than the first.

On the way home, I listened to the CD of my message. I had written it a week-and-a-half ago while feeling physically and mentally depleted. As I heard some ideas I shared and some poetic turns of a phrase I used, it hit me. Even when I didn't intentionally strive to reach that deeper spiritual reservoir I draw from when writing my fiction, that spiritual source rises to reach me. I composed the message with my creative faculties deadened, yet it included the same organization and abundance of supporting quotations that I usually spend hours researching.

My favorite inspirational quotation is generally attributed to 18th century German writer Johann Wolfgang von Goethe: *The moment one definitely commits oneself, then Providence moves as well. All sorts of things occur to help one that would never otherwise have occurred. A stream of events issues from the decision, raising in one's favor all manner of unforeseen accidents, meetings and material assistance that no one could have dreamed would come their way. Whatever you can do or dream you can do, begin it. Boldness has genius, power and magic in it. Begin it now.*

My work on this message confirmed the truth of his statement. I had said "yes" to giving the church message. Somehow, in the fog of being overworked, overwhelmed, and overcommitted to more projects than my conscious mind could do justice to, Providence came through to create everything I needed to help me succeed.

I think I've been so exhausted not because I've said "Yes" to so much, but because I haven't stayed in the flow of my source of real strength.

Thinking on a conscious level about what it takes to complete everything I have been doing lately has worn me down. All the while, I could have ridden the wave of Spirit that simultaneously provided the inspiration and the means to achieve it.

Thank God we all can access a power much greater than ourselves. I have known and used this energy for most of my adult life. But recently I mistakenly thought I had to access it properly in order to use it. I see now that, as Goethe assured, when I say "Yes" to a project and begin it, Providence steps in to create magic. I am proud of the message and its impact on the congregation. I am even more excited to learn that Spirit intervenes on my behalf much more than I ever realized. Its monumental power is driving my dreams to make a positive impact during this lifetime.

I told a friend at a Super Bowl party last night what I've learned: saying "yes" to every inspiration overwhelms me only when I try to pursue goals unaided by Spirit. After receiving a soul inspiration, I mistakenly stepped out of Spirit's continued flow and found myself fighting currents that were actually spiritual waters lifting me to my next level of enlightenment. From the source of all inspiration comes unlimited energy to move us boldly but naturally toward success.

"I'm finally learning!" I marveled. "And it's helping me achieve my life's mission."

"Which is?" she asked.

"To help reveal to people their soul and empower them to live from it so the entire world becomes a more loving, supportive, encouraging, and inspiring place for ALL people."

She smiled, "You're living your dream."

Until my mind fully embraces the lesson about staying in the flow, I may still become overwhelmed or tired. But growing spiritually requires accessing divine energy and being continuously enlivened by it. I am not a singular entity divided from the whole or depleted by overuse. I am a conduit of divine power. This realization reinvigorated my desire to fulfill my life's mission.

During the Super Bowl halftime show, I stared transfixed at the performer. Thinking how much energy it took for me to host a reception for 50 people on Thursday, lead a workshop for only 10 yesterday, and then speak to 100 people at church this morning, I felt awed by the courage and stamina required for her to step out midfield and entertain millions of people worldwide.

Her massive work on that performance helped me appreciate my tiny steps this week to motivate and inspire people. As I shared in my church message, any small step by an individual with the pure intent of blessing others is a giant leap for the spiritual evolution of humankind.

We live to bring to conscious awareness what our souls always know—that we are part of the one source of all power. Tap into it, tap into it, tap into it, then watch where it takes us. What a journey!

12

Narrowing My Focus

Day 111: March 2

On my trek to work this morning, I listened to Gary Zukov explain to Oprah how the universe gives us tiny wakeup calls to keep us spiritually alert. As I thrilled at the spiritual insight, I looked up to see a police officer aiming a laser speed gun directly at my car.

The sight dropkicked my heart into my stomach. My eyes shot toward my speedometer, which indicated that I was going nearly 75 in a 60 mile an hour speed zone. Within seconds the officer pulled me over and stepped up my car. I turned the radio volume to a whisper and let down my window. "Hi."

Instead of responding to my greeting, he shot, "License and registration."

I handed them to him.

As he looked at my identification instead of me, he asked, "Are you aware that you were going 73 in a 60 mile an hour zone?"

"I'm sorry," I confessed, "I was so engrossed listening to Oprah I didn't even notice my speed."

He ducked his head in the car to listen. Sure enough, Oprah was talking. I couldn't tell whether it was my sincerity, my contrition, or the fact that I was listening to Oprah that eased his aggression, but from then on he matched my pleasant delivery with every response.

He returned with a ticket and instructions for getting it dismissed by taking a defensive driving course.

"How much is the ticket?"

"Too much," he assured. "It gives the amount on the back of one of those sheets. But if you just pay it, you get points added to your record. Get enough points in a six month period and they'll revoke your license."

I wasn't worried about that. "This is the first ticket I ever got," I confessed. "But thank you," I smiled.

He smiled back. "You have a good day."

As I resumed my ride to work, I marveled at God's clear instructions: "Slow down, Rog. You can be more present and more alive when you take it easy and stay aware of each moment. There's no hurry to do or have or be anything because, as a soul, you already do and have and are everything you need to fulfill your mission in this world." How much more obvious can a message be than, after 34 years of driving, to get my first speeding ticket as Gary Zukov describes the universe's little wakeup calls?

I thought about the fact that my moving violation didn't hurt anybody. I didn't run over anyone, I wasn't texting or talking on the phone while driving. Everything else I was supposed to have or do, such as a carrying a current license and proof of insurance and wearing my seatbelt, I was doing. But this experience seemed the perfect metaphor for my life since the new year began. I have been doing most everything as right as I know how to honor my spiritual path, but I wasn't noticing the obvious spiritual wakeup call of feeling overwhelmed instead of inspired. I am learning to focus on what is working, how I am growing, and how the universe is helping me.

13

Rewiring Thoughts

Day 115: March 6

Jerry and I invited my brother and our two nieces to join us on the midway at the Houston Livestock Show and Rodeo to play games, ride rides, and eat carnival junk food. Standing in line to buy our tickets as Jerry made a phone call, I felt inspired to buy tickets for the family behind me. I glanced at the ticket prices, calculated how much it would cost to buy tickets for the couple and their young son, and then found in my wallet the right amount of cash to treat them. I purchased all our tickets, then turned around and said, "Hi. I just bought your tickets. Enjoy the rodeo on us!"

I handed the tickets to the woman and, after her initial surprise, her face lit up. She thanked me as I walked away. Jerry saw what I had done and acknowledged the gesture. As we approached the turnstile to enter the rodeo, we again saw the family. This time the man smiled and thanked us. Jerry replied by suggesting they pay it forward, and we went to the rodeo and never saw the family again.

This act of kindness turned out better than some in the past because I let one gesture, prompted by inspiration, be only one gesture. Then I went on my way and enjoyed the time with Jerry, my brother, and nieces. Previously when I've responded to an inspirational nudge, I felt so happy that I continued seeking opportunities to give until I exhausted my resources. Continuing the effort moved me from responding to God's urgings to forcing my own hand. This morning, by no accident, the next page in the Tao book I am reading suggested responding only to Spirit instead of busying ourselves as if doing and achieving could bring us fulfillment.

It occurs to me that my spiritual inspiration to buy their tickets may not have come to me randomly, but as a direct response to that family's prayers. Maybe I was the instrument of a miracle of sorts for them, an answered prayer that not only let them eat a little more or play a few more games, but also reinforced, revived, or even gave them a glimpse of Spirit at work in their lives. It's just as possible that I was merely a generous stranger who saved them twenty dollars. But as I imagine various spiritual possibilities, I love that I will never know which is true. Not knowing makes the memory of the act even more exciting. It feels freeing not to be in charge.

When I started my first last year, I listed several things I wanted to do because I thought I had to boldly press forward on my spiritual journey. But that energy is misspent if Spirit is drawing me along the path. Receiving inspirations seems to indicate it does. In that case, perhaps my only goal for my first last year should be to stay fully awake for when Spirit calls. To venture out on a self-imposed quest requires stamina; to progress along a Spiritual journey requires boldness to press forward and, more meaningfully, inward to discover ourselves on the path we're taking.

Day 118: March 9

It's fascinating to realize that there really is nothing new to learn. Instead, we spend our lives rediscovering or seeing from a different vantage point what our hearts have always known as our minds find new ways to grasp and use it. Sometimes that rediscovery comes from making a life change. Other times it requires only a change in perspective.

After several years of disenchantment with his job as a middle school counselor, Jerry feels he must change careers. If he stays at his job any longer, he believes it would literally kill him. The school climate is similarly affecting coworkers he loves. One woman has developed welts all over her beautiful face; her doctor told her the cause was stress. Another disheartened colleague has been diagnosed with multiple sclerosis and cancer.

In contrast to these disconcerting red flags are Jerry's experiences as part-time minister at a church of genuinely loving spiritual explorers. Recently he paid a hospital visit to a congregant battling leukemia. He described afterward how natural and on purpose he felt comforting the patient. The menace of cancer did not have the same toxic effect on him as the disheartening atmosphere of his middle school.

I told Jerry to seek a better fit for his life's mission. With his attention on what he wants rather than what's causing pain, he'll either get a new perspective on what's happening at his school, circumstances will change, or most likely, he'll be drawn to a better job.

"Step through your fear of change," I encouraged. "You don't need to know what you'll do next. You don't even have to take a leap of faith and leave this job before something else appears. Once you shift your focus from what's bothering you to what you'll create next, the fear will become hope."

As Jerry works through the process of building courage enough to leave education and seek fulltime work in another field, ideally the ministry, I ask myself, *Where could I be braver? How could I more directly live my mission to be the author whose works reveal to people their souls?* It may also require a career change. As likely, a small shift in perspective will bring life-changing results.

Day 129: March 20

I listened to an interview with Jill Bolte Taylor, the neuroanatomist who suffered a stroke that destroyed much of the left hemisphere of her brain, temporarily wiping out the limited thoughts of her ego. Since recovering, she said she doesn't meditate because her mind instantly distinguishes egoic thoughts from expansive ideas of peace and presence. This concept stretched my imagination. While meditating I reach states of great peace and receive life-changing inspirations. To be in that state every waking moment would be paradise.

As I aspire to develop the skill of being that spiritually attuned, I will continue meditating with the intention of sustaining that spiritual euphoria longer and longer throughout my day. It will help to be even more selective about the thoughts I entertain and the feelings that arise. The thoughts and feelings are interrelated. I am not my thoughts, so I may change them at will. To monitor my thinking, I gauge the feelings triggered by those thoughts. If I am feeling a way I don't wish to feel, I can change my thoughts, and the feelings will shift accordingly.

I had some great inspirations during the spring break Jerry and I shared last week. It stormed mightily the Friday our break began. We had previously made plans to take my parents to dinner that night, and my dad had wondered if we would call and cancel our outing because of the downpour during rush hour traffic. Because we're living my first last year, we dismissed that option and just got in the car and drove. We had a fun and ultimately very sweet encounter with my parents, and with my sister who joined us at dinner. Jerry grew sentimental at one point in the evening and told my parents how much we loved them. He also assured them that they had nothing to worry about concerning their future because they had us to take care of them. It was a beautiful moment. My parents are not emotional people, and they don't respond much to pure, sincere sentiment, but they took in and appreciated what Jerry said.

We've been busy achieving the travel goals we listed the morning I started my first last year. We had wanted to vacation with Jerry's parents in Arkansas and take our dream Mediterranean cruise. We spent this spring break in Arkansas with Jerry's mom and dad. While on the road, we told Jerry's folks that we put down a deposit for a Mediterranean cruise leaving from Barcelona this June. "You should go with us," we shared as an afterthought.

Jerry's dad lit up immediately. "Okay." He turned to Jerry's mom. "Mother?"

She considered for only seconds, asked a few logistical questions, and then she beamed, "I say let's do it!"

I love his parents. To both Jerry and me, they are outstanding role models for savoring life. They are almost always willing to say "Yes" and go and do. Perhaps one of the most valuable examples they have set for us is to never consider an idea long enough to talk ourselves out of it.

An opportunity to live that lesson came yesterday. We returned from our Arkansas trip with renewed motivation to help Jerry make a career change. We reasoned that if Unity Circle of Light wasn't ready to take Jerry on full-time once this school year ended, he might need to find another church. Because he wasn't scheduled to speak at Unity this Sunday, we planned to visit another church he thought might be a good fit.

When a virus infected our home computer, Jerry called the repairman. Forgetting our plan to check out another church, he accepted the only time slot the repairman had available for the next few weeks: Sunday morning.

As we wondered if we'd made a mistake by changing our original church plans, the repairman called back and asked if he could reschedule for Saturday. Our Sunday opportunity re-opened. Interestingly, when Sunday morning came, Jerry vacillated about what to do. I think the fear of changing careers was stalling him. So I said, "Let's go."

I have learned to say "Yes" to going anywhere by thinking, if I stay home, I know what I'm going to get. But I don't know what

I might experience if I get out and go, especially somewhere I haven't been before. With unexpected traffic and a detour that seemed endless, we thought we'd be late for the service. Thanks to an alternate route on Mapquest, we arrived at the church five minutes before it began.

We liked the message and music, and the positive atmosphere. We especially enjoyed receiving communion together, a ritual not part of a Unity service. After church we found a diner with great omelets and fruit pancakes and waffles we loved. Dining out in fun surroundings is one of my first last year ideals. I always feel vibrant amid people enjoying life.

As we neared home, we passed a huge house for sale that we wanted to tour whenever the realtor had an open house. It was 2:00 and the sign on the lawn read "Open house today, 2:00-4:00."

Everything has felt so spiritually aligned lately. I know it's because we have been recognizing that we are in the flow of Spirit and are responding to inspirations as they appear. The reciprocal nature of being in that flow touched us on Saturday. As we sat with our margaritas and enchiladas at our favorite Mexican restaurant, a woman came up to our table and asked if we were with the Houston police department, as she was certain she recognized us, perhaps as former coworkers. We said no, but then asked her where she patrolled, as Jerry works in Spring Branch and I in Galena Park.

Once we established that she recognized me from Galena Park, we enjoyed a warm visit and the woman resumed her seat in the booth beside ours.

When our second round of margaritas arrived, she called to our server, "I'll take care of those."

We expressed our gratitude for her generosity, and immediately I remembered the family at the rodeo whose tickets I purchased. We thought about recording the policewoman's name with the intent of returning the favor one day, but then I remembered my lesson from the rodeo. Don't take the reins from God.

In the flow of grace, we were blessed with a thoughtful, friendly gift. Accumulating debts to others for their acts of generosity would only clog the light, gentle flow of Spirit. The stream of grace extended from the rodeo tickets to the margaritas. Seeing how it's all connected made me happy.

Creating happiness is not about doing, knowing, or having more. It comes from the awareness that we choose our thoughts, and our thoughts create our emotions, including happiness. That chain reaction keeps us in tune with the spiritual current flowing though us in every experience we create and accept. I believe that basic wisdom is my guiding principle for my first last year.

14

Spiritual Millionaires

Day 132: March 23

I'm pulsating with such euphoria that I hope writing about my current state etches a defining imprint on my soul. For the first time in two months, I resumed work on *One Sister Left the Gun*.

Recently I have felt tiny nudges from the universe to resume novel writing, one of my most spiritual experiences—ever. Seeing a student who did some research for the novel for me last semester reignited the spark. Moments later encountering a teacher who provided information about guns for a pivotal scene in the novel fanned the flames of inspiration.

Yesterday, that inspiration became a burning desire. Since setting it aside last fall, I resumed reading *Think and Grow Rich* at breakfast. The chapter where I left off concerned Napoleon Hill creating a spiritual committee of great men he admired, some living and many dead, who could advise him about what to do. Reading that chapter reminded me of my pre-writing meditations with my grandmother and her four sisters, two of whom are still living. I missed that experience and wanted time with them again.

I also revisited some exercises from *Think and Grow Rich*. Several responses about who I am and what I want to contribute to this world referenced the multiple-volume *One Sister Left* novel series.

This morning I arrived at school early to meditate and resume rewrites of *One Sister Left the Gun* before work. I keep my favorite photo of my grandmother and her sisters in front of me on my desk beneath my computer monitor. As always, I held the 3½ x 3½ silver framed photo in my hand and gazed at each sister, then closed my eyes and meditated. In stillness I waited. Nothing happened at first, but after a few minutes I called out in my mind "Baka" (the variation of the Polish term *Babcia* that we grandchildren called her), and she and her sisters appeared.

I promised them I had not given up on the novel. Baka assured me that she, her sisters, and even I know this work is evolving in its perfect time. They never doubted we would continue the work. The presence of God caressed us all as we prayed. In my office sanctuary I revised Chapter 47, where Helen takes Honey with her to church. When finished, I felt my familiar rush of ecstasy for doing what I came to this life to do.

Learning that Jill Bolte Taylor has mastered staying present and in gratitude has motivated me to recognize and savor sensory experiences. Usually I like being disciplined about what and how much I eat. Thinking I was eating something healthy made even bland food more palatable. Lately, however, the present-moment pleasure of savoring delicious food has begun to mean more to me than the long-term perceived benefits of having made a healthy choice. At a restaurant with Jerry and his parents recently, I ordered baked snapper and grilled vegetables; everyone else had fried catfish and shrimp. My snapper was stale as a frontier sermon, and the vegetables as tough and wrinkly as the old preacher delivering it. But the one bite of batter-dipped shrimp that Jerry's mom gave me plunged my senses into a saliva-drenched dance. Even its tangy-sweet aroma as I brought the morsel to my lips left me rocking from waves of delectable pleasure.

This week I've eaten so much I told Jerry I must have a tapeworm. Like a deprived child, I eat and want to keep eating. Although the indulgence ebbs occasionally, I believe I formed this habit at the Renaissance wedding as my first last year began. Normally

I only indulge on vacations and during holidays. Now I'm finding pleasure in so many treats I used to deny myself.

I've relaxed my workout routine as well. I still lift weights most mornings, but since my first last year I've only intermittently gone to the gym to do cardio or to swim. In the past I would have felt proud of sustaining my strict routine, aware of the immediate and long-term benefits. By eliminating the long-term concern, the new me enjoys eating more and working out less. I'm certain I'll find a balance between extremes, but right now I'm savoring present moments, especially those sweetened with a rich dessert.

Last night Jerry called as I approached the gym and asked if I would skip my workout so we could go out to eat.

"Yes!" I said without hesitation.

An earlier rainstorm washed away the dense pollen and dropped temperatures to a comfortable 65 degrees. So Jerry and I picked a restaurant with an outdoor patio and had a glorious, leisurely meal. As we sat there, on a Wednesday evening, eating cheese-drenched enchiladas and sipping happy hour margaritas, I told Jerry, "This is the life I dream. We're living it now." Jerry agreed.

Thanks to my first last year, I'm doing more of what brings me pleasure and feeling more confident in my faith. Now I regularly acknowledge being spiritually grounded, grateful, and happy. I continue to pursue my goals, but without thinking I need something else to occur to achieve them. It has happened. I am living the life I dream. When I think only about my first last year, I no longer worry. I've even stopped wondering when some of my financial dreams will manifest to the degree I previously anticipated.

I am satisfyingly immersed in the abundance of love, creative expression through my writing, and prosperity. I claim it and take responsibility for using my gifts and passing along the joy they bring to me in an unending spiritual flow. Yes, this is the life I've always dreamed. One of the best aspects of being in this space is knowing that I have always had everything I needed and wanted, even when I wasn't aware of it. All that matters to us is in our immediate grasp. How freeing, empowering, and uplifting to see life from this vantage point.

I'm floating in the blessings of eternal light, and I know it. No wonder I'm such a happy man.

Day 133: March 24

Jerry is more ready than ever to discover what God has in store for him to fulfill his mission in this life, which he knows involves being a minister and singer. Earlier this year he visited with the board of the church where he is sole minister, officially in a part-time capacity, to tell them of his plans to leave education and his need to generate enough income to at least match what he brings home from both his full-time counseling job and his part-time ministerial position. When he presented his idea to the board, they responded, "Tell us how much you need and we'll see how we can make it work."

Right now our small church is re-securing its financial stability after investing all of our previous savings in the independent facility we now lease. When Jerry spoke to me about what the board asked of him, I told him to tell them exactly what he needed. "Don't lowball it," I warned, for I suspected that, as with most business negotiations, the board would hear Jerry's requested amount and either counter with a lower offer or work to reach Jerry's desired total incrementally as the church grew.

At their next meeting Jerry told the board what he needed to net the same amount he's earning from both jobs now. But we held to the vision of that amount or something greater, and boy did God ever deliver something greater!

Within days of his meeting with the board, an anonymous donation was promised to the church in the amount of $1,000,000. Only one specific request came with the donation: amply compensate the minister for the great work he is doing.

Though the money will go to the church and not Jerry, we recognized that his work prompted the generous gift. We are overcome to see Jerry's vision and faith producing tangible results. His breakthrough even reinvigorated my dreams about my new publishing house.

I fell asleep easily thanks to a great swim yesterday, but woke in the middle of the night. Rather than lie in bed tossing or turning, I went to my prayer chair and meditated. God came to me clearly and said something big was about to happen today. I tested that thought, wanting to make sure I wasn't putting pressure on myself to deliver something grand now that Jerry had made such a huge stride in his dream. I was reminded during my meditation not to create stress by taking the reins from God, but to be ready for what I am spiritually asked to do.

Excitement about my dream of starting Paradise Publishing flourished. I have been wondering about one of my publishers lately. He not only runs his publishing house, but also purchased all the machinery to produce his authors' works on site. A few years ago he tried to sell that equipment to the publisher of another of my books. For the first time, I realized that the publishing house with all the equipment is in Spring, the town adjacent to The Woodlands, where our church is located. Although I haven't shared this idea with anyone before I'm telling you, I had thought in the past that an opportunity could come when the publisher might sell his entire publishing house, and I could create my own on that site. We shall see.

The overwhelm I once felt about running a publishing house ceased. I will do what I am called to do: foremost, write to inspire others. As the visions I've sought that have also been seeking me come to life, people whose dreams align with mine will show up so we make our dreams come true together. I envision marketing experts, work assistants and business partners, graphic designers and editors coming into my life to fulfill their dreams through Paradise Publishing. I won't have to do it all, but I will continue to write and bring to life the works that I have been inspired to develop. I am thrilled!

Anticipating future plans distracted me from my first last year only until I acknowledged how instantaneously life can evolve in God-time. Although I cannot see publishing every work I have in progress during my first last year, I can launch Paradise Publishing and initiate plans for all the books I've begun. That way new works can continue leaving my legacy after my first last year.

Meantime, I have much living to do. Jerry and I agreed to celebrate this great spiritual leap his quest for a new career has brought. It doesn't matter that the money doesn't belong to the church yet, or that only a portion of the money will go toward Jerry's salary. Spiritually Jerry manifested his vision and we want to thank God that it has happened by honoring it now.

Spiritually I see that we are already living the life I dreamed. This is it. I am here. I have always been at the point of true fulfillment, but didn't always know it. We all are. We have nothing to do but follow the guidance of Spirit or God or intuition or whatever you named it or however you frame it. It simply is, and when we open to it and get our minimizing, worrying selves out of the way, the gates of heaven open to let us step into achieving the quest that is our life's purpose. In the process, we draw to us others on their quest whose dreams we can help come to life because they complement our own. This is how I believe life works. All of life is a joyful blessing if only we have the courage to let go of old fears and claim it. For most of my life I have dreaded the death of loved ones and feared my own demise. I see now that conquering the fear of death requires acknowledging its inevitability so I can get on with really living. The space beyond fear is joy. That's where living my first last year has taken me. Although as a spiritual being I'm not surprised to find joy beyond fear, I am no less awed by its bliss.

Continuing my human experience leads me to suspect I may not stay in this state of euphoria. But I do know that life exists only in the now. Keeping in mind my first last year encourages me to remain present. Perhaps that's the key to eternal life—recognizing that infinity's bliss is always at hand, never waiting beyond some future achievement. While basking fully in today, we aren't distracted by fear of losing tomorrow.

I thought of God's promise in my middle of the night meditation. Something big indeed happened today. I discovered that eternity resides in each moment.

15

Awakening to Enlightenment

Day 136: March 27

On Saturday evening, Jerry and I had our first millionaire dinner! We know we do not yet possess a million dollars, even though being a multimillionaire author has been part of my personal vision for more than 20 years. But I once heard a man include Mother Teresa in his talk about the richest, most influential people in the world.

Another speaker argued that she lived in near squalor, broiling in the heat of India's ghettos without air conditioning and other comforts.

"She may not have a quarter in her pocket," the man said, "but her actions stimulate millions of dollars in donations annually. Without touching a single coin, she can move money the way Jesus said we could move mountains. So don't tell me she's not rich!"

Jerry and I appreciated that perspective even more after he came home the other evening with the news about how the ministry he is creating at our Unity church attracted a million dollar donation.

One interesting observation I made about our dinner: nothing about the experience was new except my perspective. We still self-parked our car, as we normally would. We ate at a restaurant we'd frequented before. We ordered what we would have ordered in the past. I even mentioned to Jerry during dinner that nothing on the physical plane was different, but a shift had occurred within me. I felt as though we were in a mighty flow of energy, of which we'd always been a part, but now we were contributing more directly. We didn't need anything more than we already had. What brought elation that night—the comfortable atmosphere, the delectable food, the stirring conversation—we'd enjoyed most of our lives. What I had left behind this time was the claustrophobic sense that I only had so many resources at my disposal, and that if I exceeded my budget it would take time and extra effort to ultimately pay for dinner.

Learning not to take the reins from God helped in this situation, too. As I charged the meal, I genuinely trusted, as opposed to fearfully hoping, that when the credit card bill came due, I would have the resources to pay it. Without a worry, I signed the receipt immersed in the emotional space of enjoying every aspect of our first millionaire dinner.

I can't call this our first millionaire dinner in general. Often we have shared meals with millionaire friends and relatives. But this time, Jerry and I went to dinner in possession of our own millionaire mentality. That made all the difference.

In other ways, Jerry and I are really feeling Spirit move us. On Saturday I was assembling a jigsaw puzzle while listening to a random selection of CDs of 20th century standards covered by Maureen McGovern, Tony Bennett, and Carly Simon. Jerry walked into the den as Carly Simon's version of "Moonlight Serenade" began to play, and Jerry remarked, "Aw! This is dancing music." We danced in the den until the song ended. Since my first last year began we've created many similar small moments that have provided a mental scrapbook of loving memories.

On Sunday I took my current draft of *One Sister Left the Gun* to church with me to pray about what to do next with it. Dixie, one of my favorite friends from church, was the day's prayer volunteer. When the service ended, I brought the manuscript to the prayer room. The timing was perfect; no one else was there and I entered immediately.

"What is this?!" she asked, looking at the 4" binder overstuffed with 726 pages.

"The newest draft of my most recent novel." I asked her to pray that I continue doing what I am called to do with it, especially in honoring the people who inspired some of the characters and in reaching the people who can be touched by the message.

We sat to pray so I could rest the manuscript on my lap. She led us in a moving prayer honoring the people who would read the novel, but focusing primarily on those who inspired the characters.

After the prayer I confessed, "I'm really more the stenographer than author of the work."

"The people who inspired the characters are dictating it to you?"

I nodded yes.

She smiled knowingly.

I am amused now that I thought it was so revelatory to admit in a previous entry that I meditate until my grandmother and her sisters show up to lead me through the writing. In *Think and Grow Rich*, which was published in 1937, Napoleon Hill discusses doing the same with his spiritual mentors. I thought it might surprise or confuse someone who's not a writer to tell her that I am merely recording the ideas that my inspirations give me, yet Dixie knew.

This weekend I meditated about what to do next with the novel and had one of the most fascinating meditations of my life. I had had a quick flash of inspiration to share the manuscript with two friends from church, both retired literature professors. When I mentioned it to Jerry, he asked if he couldn't read it first. To ensure that I would do what was best for it next, I meditated about what action to take. Interestingly, in such meditations I usually visit alone with God, or a visual representation of God stored in my subconscious.

This time, God appeared, as always, but this time accompanied by my grandmother and the four sisters. They, in turn, were accompanied by other characters from the book, an experience that hasn't happened in meditation since one of my earliest, still unpublished novels from the 1980s. But it didn't stop there. In the 1990s I used to meditate by seeking guidance from not only God, but also various male angels who each were self-actualized in an aspect of life I was working on, such as faith, prosperity, or love. They all appeared, too, as though old parts of my psyche and new elements of my creative Spirit were meeting.

Usually in my meditations I experience very calm and intimate dialogues with God, or equally gentle advice from the angels or loved ones who enter my inner sanctuary. This time the atmosphere felt jovial. As my angels and God and the characters from my latest novel mingled, who should breeze in but F. Scott Fitzgerald and then Harper Lee, the respective authors of *The Great Gatsby* and *To Kill a Mockingbird*, the two novels I most wished I'd written. For the first time in a meditation, nobody gave me advice or helped me surrender my physical limitations through metaphoric imaginings of merging back into the ocean of Spirit energy. Instead, it was a party.

My "I" disappeared in the milieu of revelers, and so "I" had no observations or reactions about what occurred. But in this brief, unique meditation, I became part of all energy, or what I've labeled the Allsoul. From it I emerged refreshed, knowing I was to pray about my manuscript, which I did at church, and then leave this hard copy for Jerry to read as I began the next revision.

Day 139: March 30

Lately I've wanted to reach closure on some of the career projects I've been juggling. Progress has been fascinating. For example, as I imagine completing some of my books, I can feel myself floating through more spiritual breathing space.

The other night I woke feeling frustrated because three teachers are now two months late in submitting their SUCCESS data identifying models of success traits in award-winning children's chapter books. Although their tardiness sparked my discontent, I knew the real source: me. I gave teachers the deadline as we began the project, but haven't followed through on keeping them accountable. My mind argued that I shouldn't have to keep professional adults accountable for what they agreed to do. But my soul knew that every experience is a mirror. I was projecting onto the teachers frustration with myself for not knowing how to be assertive, yet still loving, and ask them for what I really needed.

As always, my solution came before I recognized the problem. Three similar messages surfaced this week emphasizing kindness. Wayne Dyer listed it as one of four essential qualities in an interview on *Super Soul Sunday*. One of my Notes from the Universe this week centered on kindness. On a CD I've been listening to, Pema Chödrön referred to being kind in our meditations and during our dark periods.

To reach closure on the research phase of this book and learn my spiritual lesson required that I wrap my request in kindness. At first I focused so much on being kind that I didn't communicate the urgency of needing the work completed. But creating an atmosphere of kindness made asserting myself easy. With clarity but no annoyance, I made clear my need to receive all data within the next five days. One teacher thanked me for being flexible, and promised to have everything in this week. Thanks to my kind approach, the other two felt safe enough to admit that they couldn't get the work done. Clarity from them made it easy for me to take up where they left off and form a new group to complete the work.

When I teach goal setting, I emphasize the impact of a deadline. If you set a goal without one, then you can always put off until "someday" fulfilling your heart's desire. This research deadline forced me to make clear what I needed. My first last year taught me that there's no greater deadline than death. It's forcing me to step through my fears and do what must be done to achieve what I came here to do. Like a wise and loving parent, it insists, for my own good, that I not leave till "someday" the inspirations to complete the work that is my legacy.

I'm making swift progress on *One Sister Left the Gun*. I finished the second revision last week and began a new revision on Monday. It's going smoothly and I'm already 117 pages through this new draft. Despite the speed, I am unlikely to reach closure with a final, polished draft of *One Sister Left the Gun* before my first last year ends. For me novel writing concludes with getting feedback from an editor and revising again until the work is ready for the public. So I learned another lesson about deadlines: some projects demand them; others require only a commitment to consistent action. If this novel is to be excellent, then it will need the spiritual energy and physical effort required to make it so. Forcing a deadline on this creative process feels counterproductive. I commit to giving this work my full creative attention, and letting it evolve in its own time. Leaving a legacy taps into eternity. To fulfill my greatest desire as a writer means my works will outlive me. Until my first last year, I never fully grasped that concept. Our lives may end, but our contributions live on as long as they're remembered and passed on by others.

More interesting insights have come about closure. Besides writing many books at one time, I'm also reading many books. I finished Napoleon Hill's *Think and Grow Rich* last week, and went back to another prosperity book I had been highlighting, Dr. Maria Nemeth's *The Energy of Money*. I found my bookmark in a middle chapter and decided first to reread only the passages I'd highlighted before continuing from the page I'd bookmarked. Over the past two days I reviewed all the previous chapters and continued reading from there this morning. I read about ten pages before discovering another highlighted section.

That's strange, I thought. I then flipped through the rest of the book and found highlighted passages through the very last chapter. I had finished this book months ago and didn't even remember it. I now realize that I must have left the book with my unread or unfinished collection because I wanted to take notes and interact with the highlighted passages, as I often do with my books.

Like every other spiritual lesson, this one is about perspective. When I decided to get closure on some projects and took action, everything aligned. Some projects demanded new action to reach the end. Another convinced me that consistent action was more important than a deadline. Others I'd already finished. Once I stepped back for a spiritual perspective, I discovered that what I wanted already manifested.

Again I learned there's nothing we have to do and nowhere else we need to be to realize we are already whole. Everything we need for happiness is already in our possession if only we'd wake up and acknowledge it. We don't find enlightenment; we *claim* it once we realize it has always been ours.

Day 139: March 30 (Back for more thoughts)

I expanded my thoughts on enlightenment while listening to a Pema Chödrön interview. She seemed to imply that we are all reaching toward enlightenment, and that some people have reached it but most of us have not.

"That's not true," I said aloud in my car.

We are all enlightened. Everything we need to know we are already processing. Our truth is unfolding layers of new wisdom all the time. All of that *is* enlightenment.

Chödrön reinforced my perspective when describing two people she considered enlightened. Despite being enlightened, one suffered frequent depression and another lashed out with frightening wrath if challenged or frustrated. The old me would have thought those behaviors proved those gurus couldn't be enlightened. In the past I believed enlightened people were always grounded, gentle, kind, and wise.

Now I believe differently. I think we are all enlightened, and we all stay awake to that truth at different intervals and to different degrees throughout our lives. My goal is to be consistently and perpetually awake to enlightenment. When frustrated, I am not unenlightened. My awareness is just sleeping, and I have the power to rouse it and return to full expression of my spiritual wholeness.

My need to awaken is evident when I compare myself unfavorably to others, or when I feel emotions inconsistent with love, peace, and inner strength. Just because we have thoughts that don't seem enlightened, doesn't mean we are not. I am awake enough to know that I am not my thoughts. Thoughts are not truths. When they surface, I never have to claim them. Instead, I can see them as illuminated balls of energy that guide me to a better grasp of faith.

Our willingness to grow makes us full spiritual expressions of all we can be up to this point. As souls, that's who we are. To me, that's enlightenment. As we evolve, we may pass through different dimensions of spiritual awareness, but we are never not enlightened. We may act less than enlightened when we mistake the physical world for reality. At dinner last night, my dad and I talked politics. He said that he'll read some political perspectives online and get sucked back into the debate, the "us" against "them," the anger or injustice or rant, and then feel upset and find fault with the world. My dad concluded that the media slants things in such a way to get people riled, or they report information to divide people.

I disagreed. Any time we blame someone else for our perspectives, we're handing the responsibility of it, and the power to change it, to someone else. The media wouldn't report what it does, how it does if people wouldn't buy into it. "When enough of us quit listening, the news as it's presented will end," I assured him. "When we let go of old beliefs that are anything less than godly, contentious behavior will stop. The change comes when we choose better."

I told him that's why I don't dwell on news. I learn enough to have a general sense of what's going on with social and political issues, but I don't feed off it because I find no nourishment there. The more I immerse myself in spirituality and away from the physical plane, the less I am drawn into political debate.

I'm especially sensitive to spirituality and harmony as I live my first last year. Knowing that this is the only March 30 of this year that I will live, I only want to say and do what reinforces my connection to others. That's what feeds my soul. I am seeking harmony, as I believe death will ultimately confirm that we are all one. Just seven months from the end of this journey, I cannot create hurt or dissent that I may not have time to repair.

16

True Prosperity

Day 151: April 11

Jerry and I have both had the flu for nearly a week. Besides wanting to get physically well, I'm ready for a spiritual breakthrough concerning money. When I told my sister that we were finally taking our dream Mediterranean cruise this summer, she asked, "How are you going to pay for it?"

I replied, "I'm praying about that," which I am. But remembering how excited and hopeful I felt about past financial goals, I realized I have been worrying as much as praying about how to pay off the charges for our cruise and plane fare.

Money has been a threshold of faith in the past for me. Once again, I am determined to live in faith more fully by trusting God to provide. I know to begin with gratitude. That idea is reinforced as Jerry and I read Rhonda Byrne's *The Magic*.

Today Jerry met with the million dollar benefactor hoping to get a clearer idea of how the money will be used at the church, and what portion will pay his salary as Unity's full-time minister. I awaited his return thrilled for Jerry and hopeful that his journey would teach me something about prosperity.

He returned disheartened. Nothing from the meeting secured an exact income for him, as anticipated. The donation, divided into monthly installments of a few thousand dollars, will help cover Jerry's salary. But Jerry has no concrete figure to determine his monthly income before he has to select a package from Teacher Retirement System.

Nevertheless, we moved forward in faith, discussed Jerry's retirement options and chose the best one for his immediate needs and long-term goals. Besides not feeling well, Jerry has begun to descend from the high he felt since he decided to leave education and then learned of the million dollar donation to the ministry. I felt disappointed for Jerry not getting his clear financial plan, and for me not seeing a spiritual message that could answer my prosperity prayer. It seemed we had spiritually aligned with a plan that was manifesting now. Jerry and I still believe it's manifesting, but not in the time or the exact way it seemed it would.

Though I dragged through the workdays thanks to steady doses of DayQuil, my spiritual disciplines kept my heart buoyed. Jerry and I are doing the exercises from *The Magic*. Each morning I'm reading a passage from Wayne Dyer's *Living the Wisdom of the Tao* and rereading my highlighted notes from *The Rules of Money*. Most soul-enhancing of all, I am writing this book, which is as therapeutic as my usual journaling where I dialog with God. These practices keep me focused on my soul.

The most valuable lesson I'm learning is to stop thinking I need to learn something about prosperity that has previously eluded me. Nothing is missing. Jerry's meeting with the benefactor did reinforce a lesson: stay the course I'm on, communicate consistently with God, and take immediate action on every inspiration.

I live prosperously, even if money is not currently flowing enough to cover all expenses. I am a rich man because I love and am loved by a husband with a beautiful heart, and family and friends I cherish. Every time I sit at my computer I am living the writer's life I dreamed since I was twelve. That's abundance. By beginning every writing session in meditation, I reap my richest reward: I know my soul, I feel connected with God, and I experience eternity each time I'm visited by my grandmother and her sisters. I love that I will continue, not revive, all those relationships when my actual last year ends.

17

Live from Your Soul

Day 162: April 22

I am learning much from my feelings and thoughts. After four invigorating days when I presented a workshop on the seven success traits at the Texas Library Association conference, I received an email reminder that all faculty at my school had to work a Saturday tutorial blitz for students. My gut sank.

To turn disappointment into optimism, I determined to make the day meaningful by writing or building on the dream to touch people's souls. At work, I was crestfallen to learn that I was assigned several menial duties, such as directing 10th graders to their tutorial rooms, and setting up and monitoring lunch. Rather than indulge the thought that these mundane tasks were meaningless, I resolved to stay positive. That resolve was instantly tested when an assistant principal told me I also had to attend a training today for a state test she needed me to proctor all day Wednesday, Thursday, and Friday. Now I had four potentially wasted days looming ahead.

Undeterred, I focused on my goal to touch souls today. After directing 10th graders to their tutorial rooms, I saw the young teacher who is building a cosmetics business. Whenever I see her I give her a little pep talk and bless her silently to succeed. Today I approached her with, "Tell me some exciting news about your business." In our conversation, I offered marketing ideas that seemed to inspire her.

At lunch I was assigned to help the teachers passing out pizza. I stood behind them and took the empty cartons as the pizza disappeared. At one point, a teacher turned to me and said, "I'll give a dollar to the first student who thanks me. It's so frustrating. I've given away at least 500 slices already and not one kid has said, 'Thank you.'"

The inspirer in me came forward with, "We're educators. If they're not doing what we think would be valuable, then let's teach them." I stepped up to the table beside hers and started passing out juice boxes. I began by looking at students and saying "hello." They said "hi" back, took a juice box, and said "thank you" without my even having to prompt them. Immediately thereafter I started complimenting students, as I often do in the library, on their cool eyeglasses, great shirts, or pretty highlights in their hair. They would smile and say "thank you" for the compliment and then another "thank you" for the juice box. When one boy just took a juice box I handed him and started to walk away, I prompted, "Be sure to say 'thank you.'" And then I continued encouragingly. "Try it a lot. You would not believe the power that a simple 'thank you' can have. I'm not exaggerating when I say it can change your life!"

I started the process with no more than 10 to 20 students. After the trend began, nearly every student, without being prompted or complimented, said "thank you" not only to me for the juice, but also to the teachers handing out pizza.

That teachable moment taught me as well. I dreaded lunch duty because I thought it would render that time useless. Instead it gave me a chance to live from my soul, share a simple concept of gratitude, and watch Spirit spark a chain reaction that touched nearly every student who went through the lunch line. I started my day committed to touching people's lives. Wanting to do it through my writing, I initially perceived my menial assignments as deterrents to my goal. Instead, they proved the ideal context for me to watch Spirit in action.

Had I not learned this lesson, I might have dreaded Wednesday, Thursday, and Friday because proctoring a state test demands that teachers do nothing all day but read the directions to start the test and then watch students testing. For someone as goal- and action-oriented as me, proctoring is excruciating.

However, to think of proctoring as a waste of my day was counterproductive, as it would set me up to think time was slipping away without my achieving anything. So I came up with creative ways to spend the hours I would normally have identified as "doing nothing." As students tested, I focused on each, one at a time, and prayed for their success not only on the exam, but also through their spiritual journey. I imagined them discovering their purpose, living their passion, and fulfilling their soul's destiny. With nearly 30 testers in the room, all that praying and envisioning took time. On Thursday I memorized all their names. Friday I silently identified them by name and then attributed to each student one admirable trait I'd learned, observed, or inferred about them.

One way to live life with meaning is to choose what we'll do and follow through with action. But school experiences this week proved we can live the life we dream in everyday experiences we wouldn't choose. Spiritual insights don't have to come to us in stereotypic ways like visions or serendipitous encounters. By living from our souls in whatever we do, we find spiritual opportunities in any context, no matter how deceptively familiar or mundane it may seem.

Day 173: May 3

Occurrences in our physical world are a mirror for us to see what we need to do spiritually. When I'm physically ill, I know it's time to check in to see what's unsettling in my soul.

I think I'm stopped up spiritually and need another breakthrough. I realized this yesterday when I was home sick again with new symptoms from the same malady that has plagued me, to varying degrees, since Easter (talk about symbolic). Hit with the flu full throttle on Easter Monday, I slept the entire day. The rest of the week I felt persistent head congestion and intermittent achiness and fever, but I never felt so bad that I needed to see the doctor.

The following week I woke each morning feeling less energy and strength than normal, but never had a relapse. Since then I have been getting better but am still not fully myself. Then Monday the air conditioning was out on campus and I ended the school day feeling as though whatever illness has been lingering in me was back, this time the congestion having moved from my head to my chest.

As I did Easter Monday, I slept through yesterday. In the night I lay awake, my mind fretting over incompletes in my life. One of my greatest natural abilities is organization. Lately, however, I have had an unattended pile of mail in the breakfast nook, and now even a bag full of more mail and papers that I need to tackle. At work I have had two piles of unfinished projects on my desk for so long I don't notice them anymore.

I see my current sleeplessness as a metaphor of the illness my body has been carrying, even only lightly most of the time, for weeks now. I apparently forgot my New Year's resolve to pare down my commitments because again I'm doing so many different projects I'm not reaching closure on any of them. The congestion in my body is an obvious sign of needing to eliminate clutter I've let accumulate. The fact that it started in my head and moved to my chest tells me when I change my thinking, I will feel better emotionally. With this new awareness, I have sought spiritual guidance.

Beyond the metaphor of my health, I know that help and counsel appear as signs in the world around me. As I drove to school this morning my mind was consumed by all I had to do until a mockingbird flew in front of my car. I can't recognize most species of birds on sight, but I knew this one had wings and a tail shaped exactly like the illustration on the cover of *To Kill a Mockingbird*. Immediately I grasped the spiritual message. I know that Harper Lee took 17 years to make *To Kill a Mockingbird* her masterpiece. I can let go of my re-surfaced eagerness to complete *One Sister Left the Gun* and let it evolve in Godtime.

Without realizing, I had committed to a self-imposed deadline of finishing it by the end of my first last year. I had learned this lesson about my fiction before. Why or how I forgot, I didn't know. But I felt relieved to learn it again, and I planned to take it to heart. "Thanks," I said aloud to the mockingbird that crossed my path.

I love spiritual signs because they come from our own creation. They are Spirit's way of showing us what we need in a way that has obvious meaning to us. Signs don't have to be unusual to capture our attention. For example, there was nothing unique about seeing a mockingbird fly over my car this morning. It is the state bird of Texas, and we are in the middle of spring. Surely there are thousands of mockingbirds flying all over Houston. Crossing paths with one is not extraordinary.

Furthermore, I don't believe God sent me that mockingbird to advise and reassure me. I think the mockingbird was soaring across the sky, and would have if I weren't driving at that exact spot this morning, or even if I was driving at that exact spot but didn't notice it. The impact comes from being spiritually awake and deciding to create meaning from what is happening around me at any time of any day.

The mockingbird passed, but it was I who chose to notice it, recognize the wingspan as a mockingbird from a copy of *To Kill a Mockingbird*, connect that image with prior knowledge (I knew that Harper Lee took 17 years to complete the work), and then relate it to a spiritual need I have right now (I wanted an answer to the struggle of how to fulfill my dream of completing all the books I am currently writing).

I believe all spiritual messages appear this way. Things occur all the time. If we choose to ignore them or to perceive them as random, we can. If we choose to infuse them with meaning, we can do that as well. Like everything in life, there is no right or wrong except for the judgment we place upon it. In this case, I chose to see the mockingbird as a reassuring sign that answered a prayer. Uplifted by my interpretation of this spiritual sign, I can keep writing the novel at a steady pace—after all, being undeterred is one of the seven traits

I espouse as essential to success. But I can rest assured that so long as I stay faithful to my quest to complete the work with excellence, not just a piece of fiction I want to have done and behind me, I can continue to write with faith, and I will finish it in Godtime. Letting go of a deadline gives me breathing room and reassurance. By honoring the commitment to keep revising the manuscript until it's polished, I will succeed in creating the work Spirit (and, in this case, the spirits of my grandmother and her sisters whom I love so much) has honored me with the task of writing.

Through illness, my body sent me a spiritual message to slow down, clear my mind, and ease my heart. By seeking a sign, my mind saw the mockingbird and realized I could honor my commitment to my grandmother and her sisters without the restriction of an unnecessary, self-imposed deadline.

Relearning this lesson shows me how integrated my first last year is with the rest of my life. This first last year did not begin my spiritual quest. It is one phase of a lifelong journey of enlightenment. I am not trying to finally align my spiritual life once and for all. Rather, I accelerate my spiritual evolution as I focus on what I value most, stay awake to each moment, and learn, or relearn when necessary, the lessons that infuse my life with meaning.

18

Two Whacks on the Side of the Head

Day 174: May 4

Last night I had another variation on the recurring dream that has given me pause for 30 years.

DREAM:

>Employed at the school where I first started teaching, I can't find the principal's office because the building had been redesigned and the entrance to his office suite was not where it used to be. I took a chance and entered through a door near the old entrance, and inside found the principal's secretary.
>
>She said campus police were running a security check of the parking lots and needed to know what kind of car I drove. Because I couldn't remember, she told me to find my car, write down the make and model, and come back and tell her.
>
>I couldn't find my way out of the suite. Instead of asking directions, I chose a door that I thought might lead to the central hall of the school. I opened it and was right. But because of renovations, the hall was unrecognizable. I exited the building thinking I'd end up where I parked. Instead I was at the opposite side of the building.

No problem, I thought. I'll go back in the school, follow the main corridor, which was a straight shot to the other end of the building, and end up where I'm supposed to be. The corridor became increasingly narrow and dilapidated as I followed it to the far end of the hallway and exited. That exit put me on the grounds of an elementary school blocks from the building I just left.

To get back to my school, I had to cross an expansive grassy area filled with puddles. Cutting diagonally across the field, I found myself among teens and adults playing soccer. As a joke, a player kicked the ball in my direction and hit me on the head. The teens laughed, but the adults ignored me. The expanse of grass ended at the edge of a cliff two or three stories above a beach.

I recognized the coast as my favorite little town in Michigan. The path back to my school was narrow, but I decided I could make it through. As I proceeded onward, I found myself in an inner tube floating high above the water.

Behind me a heavy, middle-aged woman in her own inner tube held a huge boulder. I could tell by the way she handled it that it was a light-weight prop, probably made of styrofoam or sponge. Good-naturedly she tossed it at me to hit me in the head. It bounced back and she caught it.

When I asked her what that was for, she excitedly told me it was a promotional prop to advertise her first published book on the topic of geology. I asked her if she belonged to any of the local writers' groups. She mentioned the leader of one of the groups and asked me if I knew him.

I told her I had presented with him at a conference once, but I didn't know him well. Even though I was having a dream, I knew it was May, so I asked if she was going to be around in July when Jerry and I returned to the small coastal town. She said yes, handed me her business card, and asked for mine.

I dug into my wallet and pulled out a card gnawed as if by moths. I tossed away the gnawed one, pulled out one in better condition, and then paddled the air until I was close enough to hand her my card.

INTERPRETATION:

I woke from the dream feeling anxious, and asked Jerry to help me finally interpret these recurring dreams of being lost. "Am I lost because my passion to be a writer is misguided, and that I was really meant to remain a teacher?" That possibility disappointed me, but it could be plausible, as teaching was a very natural fit for me. I loved the work and students, and was blessed with many awards and a bond with several students that has lasted to this day.

I felt relieved when Jerry thought it meant just the opposite. In school, I'm lost. But floating on air at the Michigan coast, my idyllic place since childhood, I share with an excited fledgling writer my own, broader experience and longer history as a writer.

Jerry found it interesting that in the dream I get hit in the head twice. A motivational book we read and loved years ago is Roger von Oech's *A Whack on the Side of the Head*. Its message, as I interpret it, is that life is always guiding me, gently at first. If I miss life's cues, I'll get a tap on the shoulder. If I keep missing cues for my highest path, life will eventually give me a whack on the side of the head. This dream gave me one—twice.

Jerry's feedback helped me realize that I've been asking myself the wrong questions to interpret this recurring dream. Instead of wondering what the changing hallways of the school mean, I should ask myself, "Why am I trying to get back to the school? It's not what it was when I taught there—the entire place has been remodeled."

Already lost in these recurring dreams, I cannot reach my destination because the school keeps changing, with stairwells that never existed suddenly materializing, or halls disappearing once I reach them. An obvious mistake I make in each dream is never asking directions. Instead, I keep struggling on my own to make my way through a shifting maze.

In earlier versions of the dream I never find my way back to my destination, the classroom. This time, I never found my car, or even the parking lot. This new caveat to the recurring dream makes me think I will unlock the mystery of these dreams if I can answer the question, "What's driving me?"

The car symbolism seems most relevant now. The fact that in the dream I don't know what I drive indicates to me that I am not clear about what's really motivating me. Initially, I know my interest in writing developed around age 13 when I realized I was gay. I didn't want to know the truth myself, let alone have anybody else figure it out. In the final years of grade school, I dropped my friends and withdrew into what quickly became a very lonely existence. As a writer, I could create something that gave me a new identity. In time, I discovered that my writing could impact the world in which, at the time, I felt invisible.

It worked. By the time I graduated high school, I had written my first novel. Although it has never been published, even classmates who didn't know my name referred to me as, "The guy who wrote the book."

From these memories, I know part of my drive to write is self-serving. I found a way to be noticed for something positive at a time when my self-esteem was below ground level and I believed I was non-existent to most everyone. As I continued to write, I created works to help others, which enriched the task. Through my writing, I could leave a legacy.

That came easier and more naturally as a classroom teacher, as I continually received feedback from students, parents, administrators, and the community that my work was touching lives. I knew it, on a soul level, during most days in the classroom with my students. To this day, I still receive affirmations that the motivational work I did with students helped shape their lives. Some I cited on the speaking page of www.RogerLeslie.com. Inspiring students to embrace their dream lives convinced me that as a teacher, I was not living mine.

Writing is challenging. But the challenge of ending every work wanting to find ways to make the next one better fuels the spark and keeps my passion surging. So what's the attachment to teaching that causes the recurring dream? During my last year of teaching I felt so burnt out I had to leave the classroom. When word got out that I wouldn't be teaching any more, many students and colleagues expressed disappointment. One parent lamented that her son would not get from his high school experience what his older sisters had because I would not be there to provide it.

Through angry tears, an honors student from my last graduating class told me that I was leaving my true calling and would be cheating future students of opportunities I had given others in the past.

Part of me agreed: I felt disappointed in myself for not sustaining my passion for teaching. The perfectionist in me wanted to continue being a master teacher and become a stellar, successful writer. By the time I left the classroom, I had only published one book and several articles. It was a start, but, at age 36, I felt far behind in manifesting my writing dreams.

I think the perfectionist in me prompts the recurring dreams. It keeps trying to find a way back to who I was at school in those glorious days. Honestly, my years in the classroom could not have been any happier or more fulfilling. But that wasn't my ultimate dream. To be true to the vision that first gave me an identity I could love and be proud of, I had to risk giving 100% of my creative energy to being a writer.

Do we choose our fate or does our spiritual quest call us? I think ultimately we find fulfillment when both those motivations merge into a single goal. I knew I had to narrow my life's quest to only writing when teaching held up for me a mirror of disappointment. Just as my first last year reminds me to live today, every class period I spent teaching young people how to pursue their dreams became one more hour I was not working on my own.

Twice in the dream I got knocked in the head. First, it was by a ball on a field where I was not playing, but just passing through. That, to me, is the teaching field. The teacher burn-out was the whack on the side of the head that prompted me to live my dream as a writer before I let more time pass and the dream drifted away. During my teaching years I was writing. I had completed two novels, three screenplays, and many shorter works. Except for teaching articles and a local history book, nothing got published until I left the classroom and my fateful detour as a librarian introduced me to colleagues that would be my mentors, co-authors, and liaisons to the world of librarianship and publishing.

In last night's dream, the second whack on the side of the head came from the fledgling writer whom I could teach because of my experience. Although I haven't been in the classroom full-time since 1996, I teach all the time—in my library, as a public speaker, at conferences, as a writing coach and mentor. In the dream, the new writer, though older than I, had the youthful enthusiasm of having finally achieved what I did years ago as a writer, and we shared time together and exchanged business cards while floating high above the coast of the little Michigan town that has represented a mini paradise for me since I was a boy.

Why would I struggle so hard to get back to find a car I can't even remember the make of at a school that no longer resembles where I taught when I could float gently above my own paradise with a writing colleague excited to meet me and learn from my greater experience? Whatever my subconscious thinks I've lost by giving up teaching has not been lost, but completed. It's time for me to let it go, and with it, the recurring dream where I'm lost, frustrated, and seeking something that has been gone from my life and spirit for decades.

With no time to waste in my first last year, it feels good to resolve old issues and remind myself what mission I came to complete. Writing about my life strengthens me and provides a forum to help others find their way. I still teach. As an author, my classroom extends across the world.

19

In Heartbreak, Soul's Beauty

Day 175: May 5

As one could expect in a year designated as one's last and best, much change will occur. After multiple rounds of flu symptoms, I saw a doctor Monday, and made it home earlier than usual. With Jerry working late, I took the opportunity to revise *One Sister Left the Gun* in hopes of completing the current revision by my upcoming birthday.

I skipped the usual meditation with my grandmother and aunts and started this writing session with a quick prayer of gratitude. Plowing through the text, I adjusted story details, shaded in fresh nuances of character, and tied up unraveled plot details. By 8:30 I completed this draft, paused, and said another gratitude prayer to God, my grandmother, and her sisters. Only a few minutes later my mother called with news. Ciocia Honey, my 97-year-old great aunt in Michigan, had died. Ciocia Honey was one of the sisters who comes to me in meditation and after whom I modeled one of the most fun characters in *One Sister Left the Gun*. She had been in declining health for months, so my mother's call was not a complete surprise.

As I ate dinner earlier that evening, I read the birthday cards that had arrived. Arlene, Honey's daughter and caregiver, had signed her card from "Aunt Arlene, Uncle Tom, and Ciocia Honey, too!"

Knowing she was not long for this world, I felt a rush of gratitude that Ciocia Honey's name could still be added to my card. Now I had the news that she was gone.

After hanging up with my mom, I turned down the lights in the den and sat in silence. I closed my eyes and visited with Ciocia Honey in my heart. At one point, I opened my eyes and looked up toward the ceiling to see if, by chance, Ciocia Honey might appear to me as a farewell, as one sister in the novel does. I had never had an apparition materialize in front of me before, and none did this time, either. I can't say I even felt a palpable presence of Ciocia Honey. But I did imagine her joining with the other sisters who'd passed, each thirty years ago or more. A joyful warmth enveloped the sadness of the news.

I waited until Jerry arrived home to tell him of her death. We held each other and cried only momentarily. As we released our embrace, Jerry smiled through his tears and said, "Good for her!" She'd wanted and anticipated death for some time. At birthday celebrations, our family sings "Happy Birthday" and "Sto Lat," a Polish birthday song that translates "May you live to be 100." On her 96th birthday, Ciocia Honey gestured with thumbs down and shook her head no, with a smile, as the family sang "Sto Lat" to her. She never lost her faith-based, joyous spirit. No matter what she faced—losing her eyesight many years ago, being wheelchair-bound this past year, losing her appetite and dwindling to 68 pounds before she died—she would steadfastly affirm, "Things could always be worse."

I told Jerry I was writing *One Sister Left the Gun* the very moment she made her transition. Spiritually, I was with Ciocia Honey and her sisters during this pivotal time in her soul's journey.

Yesterday Jerry checked the old and new messages on our phone machine. Last year on my birthday (one day from being exactly one year ago), Aunt Arlene and Ciocia Honey left me a birthday message where they sang "Happy Birthday" to me. I had saved it. Jerry and I listened to it again. Cioc's voice sounded gravelly with age, but my heart leapt at the opportunity to hear it again.

As you know, I keep my favorite photo of my grandmother and her sisters beneath my computer monitor on my desk. I wondered what it would be like taking a moment to look closely at each sister, as I do every morning before writing *One Sister Left the Gun*, knowing that Ciocia Honey is gone and only Ciocia Stas, the youngest sister, is still here.

This morning as I studied Ciocia Honey in that photo from 1970, my mind contrasted the details of her face with a photo from last summer that I display at home. Although the contours of her skin and the smile and her eyes, now vacant, could have been two different people, the shining countenance that has always inspired me never diminished. It reassured me to note that our exterior may age, but our souls remain vibrant as ever.

When I finished the latest draft of *One Sister Left the Gun*, I felt proud of the results. I can't anticipate readers' reactions, but I hope that my efforts bring joy and pride to the spirit of my grandmother and her sisters. That was my goal when I began the first draft almost four years ago. The biggest blessing for me has been spending time with them through the meditation and writing. How soul-assuring to know that writing this novel has brought me closer to them than I was when they were all still here.

Knowing that someday I will die fuels my desire to make the most of my first last year. It also inspires me to strive even more to live from my soul. I believe Ciocia Honey always did, and from her example I believe more than ever that life is eternal, and loss is the illusion.

Day 183: May 13

Last week I received the call that Ciocia Honey passed away. Yesterday in a private room at the veterinarian's clinic our beloved Rex died on my lap. In that moment I re-learned one of the most meaningful lessons of life: when we exercise the courage to do what love beckons, painful experiences unveil the most radiant spiritual beauty.

On Wednesday, Jerry noticed that Rex's breathing was labored and his heartbeat accelerated. We called the vet, described the symptoms, and set an appointment to take him in the next afternoon. Rex slept well that night, and he made it through the day with Joey, our black dachshund and his brother. After our work days, Jerry and I took Rex and Joey to the vet. We always take them both because, in their eleven years, Rex and Joey have never been apart. Our regular vet wasn't on duty, but we met another doctor who was very compassionate. Reading on Rex's chart that his last checkup revealed a slight heart murmur, she listened to Rex's chest and said the murmur had increased significantly. X-rays showed fluid surrounding his heart until it almost filled his chest cavity.

Another doctor drained some fluid and did an ultrasound that revealed a large tumor. Because the tumor attached to a chamber at the back of the heart, they could not operate. Instead he would drain the rest of the fluid and keep Rex overnight. If fluid did not return by morning, we could take Rex home. He might live weeks or months. But once it filled again, whether immediately or in the near future, his death was imminent.

As we learned all this information, Rex had been in an incubator getting oxygen. The vet let us go in to see him. Approaching him in that glassed-in chamber is an image I will hold in my heart forever. I was awestruck. Drained of the excess fluid around his heart and revived thanks to the incubator, Rex looked again like the vibrant dog of years past, not the one who had been transformed by a slow-developing illness over the past months.

Rex had always been so chubby that our daughter Becca nicknamed him Chubber. Over the past months, he appeared heavier. When I saw him in the incubator, he had resumed his normal body shape. He was still our Chubber, but the bloating that we mistook as weight gain was gone. Those changes had occurred so gradually we barely noticed them. Thanks to the oxygen, he was also much more alert than when we brought him in. When he saw me his head perked up, his tail quivered and its tip fluttered in elation. In those signs I saw not just the puppy-joyful dog he had always remained, but the spirit of Rex that we loved all these years. Rex was such a grounding force in our household. Jerry always said that Rex had great self-esteem because he approached everyone as if he were meeting a new friend who would love him instantly. And they did.

I tapped on the glass of the incubator. He craned his head forward and sniffed at my finger. The doctor let us open the glass and love on Rex. Jerry and I took turns kissing his head, telling him we loved him, and reassuring him that we'd be back tomorrow.

We went home with instructions to return the next morning. In less than an hour, we had gone from not knowing anything was seriously wrong with Rex to facing losing him. The shock it initiated in the doctor's office gave way to immediate grieving. We both cried the night through and held Joey to us closely.

In the morning Jerry called the clinic and learned that our regular vet found 1,500 milliliters of fluid again surrounding his heart. Rex was surviving in the oxygen chamber, but he wouldn't last long, so we needed to get there soon to say goodbye.

As I stood in the shower bawling, I decided that I would hold Rex when the vet euthanized him. Years ago, Jerry and I had had a dachshund named Max that lived to be 17. We had just returned from a trip when we discovered that Max was probably dying. Late that night, we rushed Max to an emergency medical clinic where they told us he was suffering from renal failure and it was time to let him go. Everything happened so fast, we took the doctor's advice, said our tearful goodbyes and watched as the vet took him to the next room to euthanize him. Although Max was so sick and in pain he was almost delirious, I later realized that I could have been there to hold him when he died rather than let him be taken back by a stranger to die.

I told Jerry that I wanted to hold Rex when the doctor gave him his shot.

"Are you sure?" he asked. "I've heard some people say they were glad they did it, but others were haunted by it for long after."

I didn't know what my response would be, but I wanted to do it for Rex. My first last year inspiration told me to be bold. Now was my chance.

With Joey in Jerry's arms, we arrived at the vet and were led to a waiting room with a loveseat and chair. The doctor who did the x-rays brought Rex, wrapped in a lamb's wool blanket. Because he had just come from the oxygen chamber, Rex was breathing well and recognized us all immediately. It was obvious by the way he hung his head and the uncharacteristically sad droop of his eyes that he was sicker than ever. But he perked up just enough to ensure us that he knew we were there and he was glad to see us.

The vet set Rex on the loveseat. I crouched down to kiss his head and to look him right in the eyes and tell him I love him. Rex always gave the sweetest little laps on the tip of my nose in response to my loving on him. This time he didn't lick my nose as he normally would when I loved on him. "One more kiss?" I asked Rex and put my nose right to his mouth. His little tongue sprang out and licked just once. "Thank you, Rexer," I said, then sat on the loveseat beside him.

Immediately Rex crept onto my lap and surrendered his weight to me. I asked the vet if we could be with Rex when he euthanized him, and he said, "Yes, we'll do it right here." He then told us that Rex would not last long without the oxygen, so he would give us a few minutes alone with him and return to administer the injections.

Between agonized cries, we said our goodbyes. "You're our little boy," we reminded him. "We will always, always love you, little guy."

"You've brought us so much joy," we said, and he did. He was always happy and excited to be alive. He modeled for us every day how to wake up joyful and stay that way whatever the day brought.

Just as Jerry did every morning before he left for work, he told Rex, "You're our angel." He brought Joey close so he could get Rex's scent and so that both knew that the other was right there.

When the doctor came in, he knelt in front of me and explained that he would give Rex three injections. The first would flush the catheter, the second would be an anesthetic to put him to sleep, and the third was multiple doses of the anesthetic that would make his heart stop beating.

Rex was tilted on his left side, so as he received the injections, I stroked his right side, watching his little face. In seconds, the vet had administered the injections and I could feel on my thigh that Rex's heart stopped beating. He never flinched, never moved, never whimpered. He had already nestled onto my lap and stayed in the exact same position until he was gone.

The doctor left us alone to take as much time as we wanted. I continued stroking Rex's side, and stared at his coat. Although he was mostly red, his bristled hair was a blend of red and brown and black. I studied the canvas of colors and also looked at his head and face. From my angle, I could see the grey whiskers under his mouth, which was open slightly.

The acute pain of watching Rex go opened me to greater beauty than I ever experienced. He looked so peaceful and sweet that my grief merged with gratitude for the lasting gifts I received from loving Rex, and having him love me. I felt so present and connected to Rex through his transition that my heart seemed weightless. Surrendering to the love that first exploded as tears of grief, I was overcome by the raw purity of attention and emotion. In one of the saddest moments of my life, I felt exalted by love for and from Rex. Gratitude filled me for having acted on the inspiration to hold Rex as he died. This moment could not have been as intense or intimate if I had done anything less. The experience was so beautiful I wondered why I feared it.

How foolish I am to ever fear risking being too vulnerable, too intimate, too close to someone or something I love. In a bolder way than I ever had before, I met the experience of the death of a loved one and realized it didn't take any courage at all. As I stroked Rex's body, it occurred to me for the first time that throughout his life, I focused on how much he enjoyed my petting him. Until I ran my hand along his body resting on my lap in the peace of death, I never realized that petting my dogs had always been one of their great gifts to me. Even as I grieved, this moment of touching him still and realizing that it felt no different than when he was alive was immensely therapeutic for me.

Jerry commented that Rex's eyes were still open.

Rex didn't feel any heavier after he passed than when he was alive. He felt as he did all the years that he sat on my lap as we watched television, or I read, or even when I worked on the computer. We stayed for about fifteen minutes after Rex passed. Finally I lifted him off my lap, we wrapped him in the lamb's wool blanket as instructed, and I watched Rex's little face peering out of it as we closed the door behind us.

Jerry didn't want Rex left alone in the room, so he got two attendants to come in and prepare to take him away as we left. From the hall outside the door, I searched one more time for Rex and caught one final glimpse of his sweet face.

On the way home I thought about the date and told Jerry, "I'm exactly half-way through my first last year." Rex had ushered in the second half for us with new lessons, new insights, and the beginnings, I was sure, of new spiritual growth.

That day we made calls to family and close friends, and received an outpouring of condolences. Mostly from the exhaustion of grief we napped until our daughter and daughter-in-law, Becca and Lindsey, came to our house with take-out from our favorite Mexican restaurant. We toasted Rex and spent most of the evening sharing stories about him.

Jerry and I both remained very attentive to Joey. He seemed fine so far. He ate well and went outside as he normally would. I even played fetch with him, and he wagged his tail and seemed to love the attention as much as he always did when I would play with both him and Rex.

When Jerry left this morning for a church board meeting, I carried Joey to my prayer chair and visited with Rex's spirit. I began the meditation by talking to Rex, which made me bawl all over again. But something told me to stop talking and to listen in case Rex had a message for me. As soon as I did, the most blissful calm came over me. I didn't hear a voice from God or see a vision of Rex, although my mind conjured up plenty. My favorite was seeing Rex rushing toward me with his big barrel chest skimming the ground, his ears flopping, and his muzzle tilting right in a happy expression.

That image dissolved as I pictured Rex's spirit as a tiny ball of light. Then I did hear a message in my head. Whether this was God, or Rex's spirit, or my superconscious revealing spiritual wisdom, I don't know. But Rex's message was clear. He was a tiny ball of light, as was Max, Jerry's and my first dachshund, and as was Bonnie, the pet cockapoo my family had during my childhood. I too am a ball of light. Connected, we all comprise an infinite mass of illuminated orbs that includes everyone and everything that loves. I was seeing only my little section of it, but although we were joined, the balls of light were distinct. Rex told me that we all came from this mass of orbs, and that we would all return to it.

He said that he knew Max and Bonnie even before he came into my life. He assured me that Joey, who knew all this too, would be fine even as he worked through grieving his brother in this plane.

In the vision I noticed Ciocia Honey's ball of light too, and understood that, as balls of spiritual energy, there was no distinction among life species as we know them here on Earth. Just last week, after Ciocia Honey passed, I asked Jerry what he imagined her spirit was doing, where it was, and if it was connecting to the spirits of my grandmother, her other sisters who had passed, and her other loved ones such as her husband and parents.

In accounts of near-death experiences, I knew that, as they leave their bodies, spirits hear their loved ones urging them toward The Light. I always felt conflicted about what form these loving beings took. Do we see our relatives as we remember them in their prime, free of disease and glowing with the vivaciousness of life? At one time I savored that possibility, because I would love to hug my grandmothers again, to feel the soft puckered skin of Baka's chest against my cheek and Grandma's reassuring arms around my back. I would love to hold little Max in my arms with his paws beside my neck, or feel roly-poly Rex surrender to me as he always did, confident that no matter what position he was in, he was safe in my embrace. I would love to feel Bonnie's soft blonde coat just as I did in my tweens when she was my only friend on lonely Friday nights. I held to that hope until in recent years I started imagining that we are really masses of spiritual energy temporarily experiencing an Earthly existence.

But the thought of being energy took away the sense of individual identity for me. For awhile it made me think that in death we shed not only our body but also our individuality. As we die, I thought our spirit merges back into the mass of energy that is God like a drop of water falls back into the ocean and is no longer the drop but merely part of the ocean.

Rex has taught me otherwise. I feel assured right now that Rex is connected to the infinite mass that is God, yet he maintains his individuality. In time I will recognize and merge with him, and Max, and Bonnie, and Ciocia Honey, and my grandmothers, and anyone else that goes before me. Even as nothing separates us, we still emanate the uniqueness that makes us who we are at our best.

In meditation I spoke to Rex and prayed.

"I love you, Rex. You are my baby, as much now as you ever have been. Although I cannot feel you physically, I'm embraced by you spiritually. Through the cracks of my broken heart, I sense as strongly as if God were rocking us in loving arms, that our souls are touching, and I am a complete and grateful man for the gifts you've given me. Thank you, Rex, for the opportunity to love you and for always loving me unconditionally, even when I made human mistakes of impatience and frustration.

"Thank You, God, for the inspiration to hold Rex as his body surrendered, and for the courage to step through the illusion of fear and extend the simple loving gesture of providing a familiar place for Rex to rest as he took his last breath.

"Rex, what I thought was my gift to you turned out to be your gift to me. I am eternally grateful, and I'm excited about continuing our life together as spiritual buddies. Jerry was always right: you're our angel. How blessed I am to love you still."

I embarked on my first last year to become more physically and spiritually alive. Holding Rex as he died, I felt the rawness of living fully from love. Discovering the individual balls of light in my meditation convinced me we maintain our identities and connections after death. In his life, Rex brought joy to each present moment. In death, he showed me a source of eternal hope.

20

Legacies and Signs

Day 185: May 15

In thinking about what I wrote last time, I realized that the memories I have clung to about my grandmothers contradicted my meditation experience about our being balls of light energy. Further, the hugs that I described wanting to re-experience came from a meaningful time for me, not from my grandmothers' prime when they were most vibrantly alive and active in this life. Questions about those contradictions crossed my mind throughout the weekend as both Ciocia Honey and Rex taught me new lessons.

At our Mother's Day get together yesterday, Mom brought a copy of the PowerPoint that scrolled during Ciocia Honey's wake. Watching slide after slide, I realized how little of Ciocia Honey and her life I knew. And yet despite our limited time together, she profoundly impacted my life.

I strive daily to bless others. By living that intention and co-creating my journey in this life with the spiritual force that guides it, I plan to leave my legacy.

Watching highlights of Ciocia Honey's life, I knew that we leave a legacy whether or not we intend to. Ciocia Honey led what I consider a simple, straightforward, and spiritual life. While running a neighborhood bar, she took care of many people. My grandmother told me how Honey invited alcoholic, disenfranchised customers to her home for Christmas Eve so they wouldn't be alone. That altruism, which she demonstrated long before I was born, prompted me to examine my own actions and strive to be more loving. She couldn't have known that sixty years after the act of kindness it would help one of her great nephews make better choices in his life.

Rex is also teaching me valuable lessons. I've thought constantly about him since his death, sometimes joyfully remembering how funny and cute he was, but more often saddened by how much I miss him.

The image of Rex in the incubator stays with me. Until we saw him looking trimmer and more alert, we never recognized his recent physical transformations as signs of illness. Unlike Joey, who only has a few sprigs of gray peeking through the sleek black hair on his head, Rex's head and face grayed quickly. Having only had black dachshunds in the past, we thought red dachshunds must lose their color prematurely.

At Rex's last physical in January, the doctor detected a slight heart murmur. He thought it was a result of Rex's weight, so we never considered exploring the symptom further. (Now that I know the results, I wouldn't have wanted to. Learning that he had an inoperable tumor would have initiated worry and sadness months earlier.)

All his life, Rex had been overweight. At his last regular visit to the vet, he hadn't gained. But after the doctor drained the fluid from him, I realized how much his body shape had changed the past few months. He felt no heavier when we lifted him, but Rex did feel less solid. We thought that too was another sign of his body aging naturally. We didn't realize that his girth was bloating from retained fluid.

Another sign that should have been a clue: when we walked the dogs, sometimes Rex would just stop. Our former dachshund, Max did that only after he got very old. The last time Max stopped, he refused to go on and I carried him back home. When Rex stopped, he could resume his normal gate after a little encouragement.

I know now that we saw the signs of Rex's decline but didn't know how to interpret them. Even if we did, I don't believe they appeared early enough to save him. But they're valuable now as a spiritual metaphor. They remind me that God guides me with signs all the time. Some I recognize and understand so I can take action. Others, like Rex's symptoms, I miss or don't yet have the wisdom to catch their meaning.

Learning from Ciocia Honey that I am leaving a legacy even without writing invites me to slow down and savor present moments more. When I do, I learned from Rex, I can become more adept at recognizing and interpreting signs to guide me along my spiritual journey.

Despite the temporary sorrow of losing loved ones, my first last year is teaching me the value of being more present with every experience, not just the joys and celebrations. I have nothing to fear. As a soul, I am a light, eternal and forever unique.

Day 193: May 23

Jerry and I have grieved all week, but somehow yesterday was the toughest day, and for no particular reason. My secretary called in sick, and the day in the library was slow. I left for work feeling blue and grew more depressed throughout the day. I tried to force myself to write, but I couldn't focus. So I spent the day re-shelving and straightening books.

Such work is tedious but therapeutic. Holding a volume of Emerson's essays, or seeing a book by a Brontë or a James usually ignites a bonfire of new ideas. That didn't happen yesterday. My mind smoldered until it clouded my heart and constricted my throat so I could barely speak.

All day my thoughts bombarded me. "You have nothing relevant to say. What you do say isn't profound or poetic. You've never been as successful an author as you dreamed of being. You don't make much of an impact in this world, as a writer or a person. Your book ideas are not the spiritual inspirations you like to believe they are.

Look how much of your life you've dedicated to what still isn't getting read. And start a publishing house? You?"

As a soul, I know I am not my thoughts, and thinking something does not make it true. But the rampage didn't lift the vice constricting my heart.

Luckily, Jerry's faculty was honoring him and five other retirees with a farewell party at a local restaurant. Being there for Jerry encouraged me to smile and visit with people that Jerry cares about. Even that simple interaction helped lighten my spirits. After the party, he and I had dinner at the home of our dear friends, Manuel and Bonita. They are always a comfort. After we shared the details of Rex's passing, our conversations streamed into vacations and family and summer plans.

This morning I woke feeling better. Meditating reminded me how wise it is to have consistent spiritual practices. Without them, the infected thoughts that engulfed me for a day might have made me doubt who I really am. They taught me how to look at my human experiences, including my thoughts, from the neutral space where Spirit resides. Observing rather than fighting the thoughts invited my heart to begin creating reconciliation out of the upheaval.

On the way to work today I listed in my head the smartest things I've ever done.

1. Love Jerry
2. Do the spiritual work to discover and feed my soul
3. Stay true to my initial inspiration to be a writer.

Then I wondered, what qualities gave me the gifts of my relationships, my spirituality, and my dream career?

Love requires courage. I recall the moment a year after befriending Jerry when I fell in love with him. That awareness put me at the edge of a cliff. I could recoil and maintain my footing on solid ground. Or I could leap and hope to fly. Taking that risk gave me the greatest gift of my life: my marriage. That bond built the trust that enriches every other relationship in my life.

Spiritual growth requires the faith to believe our own wisdom. Knowing our soul frees us from others' rules and gives us an unlimited wellspring of peace. In that space of peace we build our own paradise.

Following a dream demands persistence.

For many years, nothing in the outside world reinforced the idea that I was meant to be a writer. But deep within I had the courage that would bring me love and the faith to trust that still, small voice encouraging me to press forward. The two qualities that introduced me to Jerry and my soul gave me the strength to stay the course of my dream career. Courage and faith made persistence possible. Motivated by the desire to bring the gift of inspiration to others, I found the greatest reward for myself. I discovered that I have and am a soul.

When I write, my soul is speaking to me and connecting me to other souls, much like the spheres of light I recognized as Rex and Ciocia Honey. With courage, faith, and persistence, I can stay the course to fulfill my destiny.

To honor our connection on my first last year journey, I will continue sharing with you my insights, my foibles, my aspirations to help you recognize and live from your own soul. We are connected. Even as I sit here having a conversation of faith with you, I'm grateful for your presence in spirit and the anticipation of your physical presence in my life when this work reaches you.

Day 200: May 30

Thanks to what I keep learning spiritually, I have moved through the grief from Rex's death and am feeling celebratory gratitude for the mounting gifts he and Joey keep giving me. When Rex's ashes arrived in a brown lacquer box, I set him in our bedroom so he could be with Jerry and Joey and me when we sleep.

This week when I've told people about Rex's passing or people have offered their condolences for our loss, I have felt only gratitude.

"Rex gave me one of the best gifts I will ever get in this lifetime," I say, "He showed me how to be joyful and love life every day." I then relate the story I mentioned to you earlier about how, just two days before we realized that Rex was sick, he scurried down the hallway, his paws click-clacking along the hardwoods, excited about starting another day.

Joey has taught me an invaluable lesson as well. Whether or not our taking him to the vet with us and having him present when Rex passed made it easier for him I cannot say, but Joey has not missed a beat since we brought him home after Rex's euthanasia. Joey has been happy and active and even more playful since he's been the only dog in the house.

I know that first weekend he probably devoured the attention we gave him. We loved on him non-stop, as much because we needed to hold him and feel his holy, natural animal presence as to make sure he was getting plenty of attention now that his brother was gone. But even after we left him in the laundry room as we went back to work, and he was alone for the first time in his 11 years, Joey has been fine. Every time I note another way he shows me how accepting he is of Rex's passing, I am reminded how present Joey is. What an empowering example for me to emulate. Instead of feeling empty or missing Rex, I stay in gratitude for the lifetime of memories Rex gave me, and for the fact that right here, right now I have so much in my life that fills it with love.

Spiritually, I have made further headway in my understanding of the vision that came to me in meditation after Rex's body surrendered. As you may recall, I had seen Ciocia Honey, our first dog Max, my family's childhood dog Bonnie, my grandmother who was Ciocia Honey's sister, and Rex all clustered together as orbs of light. From that vision, I realized that in physical death we don't lose our individual identity as a single drop might when it plops back into the ocean. Yesterday, I thought about Plato's Theory of Forms. If I remember it correctly, everything we see on the physical plane is only a representation of the ideal it emulates. So a physical tree is not really an independent and actual entity, but merely a version of manifested "treeness."

Thinking of the vision that came to me in what I now call The Rex Meditation, I realized that Rex was never the little dog I loved to hold and even kiss on his big, barrel chest. The physical Rex was just a mirror of the spiritual orb of light reflecting from the cluster of Allsouls I saw in the meditation. I used to believe that our souls picked a body, entered it and lived this life, and then moved to an eternal elsewhere. I no longer believe that. Instead I think Rex, like every soul, is now and always has remained connected to the Allsoul. He never separated from it to come to this life and manifest temporarily as a physical body. He reflected in the form of a cute and sweet and happy physical entity that another soul, like the one that reflects as me, could love.

I believe now that when I die I'm not going "back" anywhere, because I never *left* where I've always been. I am reflecting in this physical dimension as the me I see in the mirror; but the real energy I am is always connected with my grandmother and Ciocia Honey and Max and Bonnie and Rex and all the angels and saints. Collectively we are Spirit energy, the Allsoul.

Now that I understand this concept, I can't miss Rex because I know we were never separated. We were joined before he expressed into my life as a puppy, and he will remain part of me throughout eternity. In time, I believe I will connect with every expression of Spirit that comprises the Allsoul. During this physical lifetime, I get to learn and remember and know who I am through reflections of many souls. The deadline we call death gives this physical life urgency and relevance. Living a first last year has awakened me to the power of the present moment. When I'm awake to it, I can see eternity.

Day 200: May 30 (Back for more)

My recurring dreams of being lost at school seem to have ended. Last night, I dreamed that I exited the school, stepping out into a clear, fragrant day, and flew!

DREAM:

In the middle of the day, I stepped out of my bustling school and into a warm, tranquil day. With nothing going on, I could do anything and create of this day anything I wanted. In people's yards across the street, I saw signs that read either "Precinct 5" or "Precinct 2." I headed toward the "Precinct 5" sign. Once I could see both signs more clearly, I realized that they were the same sign. Only my earlier vantage point made them appear different.

For the first time, I knew that was I able to do anything. First, I chose to fly. I soared toward the main thoroughfare through town until I saw a building where I wanted to test my new powers. My first thought was to have a great sexual experience. Inside the building, a small factory circa the 1920s, I saw an Asian man working alone. He approached me and we kissed until interrupted by his slender wife. In their midst I knew that I was a healer, and I came to heal their relationship. I moved him close to his wife and headed to the factory's front offices.

Behind this part of the building were hangars with huge doors open to an airfield. A large middle aged man wandered about, looking for someone from his past. I blessed him and told him he would find that person, and he left.

I returned to the front of the building where another middle aged, overweight factory worker asked if he could help me. As he neared, I had a revelation: I had the power to create anything I wanted. The instant I had that thought, without my doing anything, he transformed into a handsome, slender man about my age. We kissed.

"What is it?" I asked, sensing his concern.

"It's my leg." He leaned back for me to lift his pant leg. A large chunk of his left calf was missing, perhaps removed to prevent the spread of cancer. "Help me," he whispered.

I put my hand over his calf and stared into his eyes. As his pupils dilated, I could feel against my palm his leg reforming the tissue that had been lost. His pupils expanded; his calf grew. When his leg resumed its healthy shape, I instructed, "Stop. You don't need to do more because you're healed." To continue beyond healing the leg would have created new damage.

He smiled gratefully. With him healed, I had done what I came to do. I was filled with love for and from him.

I moved on to further explore my new spiritual powers. Outside, I flew, and imagined going very far and seeing much. My flying faltered, which concerned me. I returned to the airplane factory. Now a doctor wearing a lab coat and large tan plastic rimmed glasses, the man I healed looked more handsome than ever. He interrupted treating a patient to give me his full attention. I trusted his love as much as I would God. "I need your help," I told him, afraid I was already losing the spiritual powers I'd just discovered.

He smiled, "I'll be right with you." His reassuring gaze allayed my fears. Everything was fine. He would help me when he finished with his patient.

Reassured and spiritually reignited, I went back outside and flew down the side street with the precinct signs and landed in an empty field. Running across the field, I tried, but failed, to get airborne.

I took off my clothes, knowing I would be invisible and weightless without them. I struggled removing my t-shirt, and while it covered my face I felt suffocated. I removed all my clothes, even my glasses once I decided I didn't need them to see. Taking away the glasses blurred my focus until my mind created clearer vision than I ever achieved with corrective lenses.

As I crossed the street, a car sped toward me. I took a big risk and tested my belief that I was not only invisible, but also penetrable like a ghost. I stopped in the middle of the street, stood firmly on both feet and put my hands on my hips like Superman, then watched the car come right at me.

Before it reached me, the car turned. Another vehicle came toward me, this one large and powerful like a Hummer. I tested my theory again by standing in the middle of the street and watching it speed toward me. At the last second, the vehicle swerved just enough to miss me, but the side-view mirror grazed my arm. When the driver, another middle aged, overweight man, stopped, I asked, "You could see me?"

"Yeah," he replied.

I was still made of physical matter. I looked down and wasn't naked anymore.

The driver stopped at the school to pick up the drill team sponsor, whom he described as a beautiful young female. "Would you ask her to come out?"

Though I couldn't picture this teacher, I agreed. Entering the building, I didn't know where to find her. Before the door closed behind me, the man hollered from his vehicle, "You went in the wrong door!"

As I heard his words I knew, with perfect clarity, that if I went back out and entered another door on that same side of the building, I would find her.

INTERPRETATION:

I am learning to ease the mind chatter (I left the busy school) and focus on my soul (outside I found tranquility and superhuman powers). To me, flying represents spiritual freedom and the ability to manifest in physical form what my soul knows I can do, be, have, and create in this life.

My first thought of using my new spiritual powers to seek a sexual connection represents for me the gateway out of my self-imposed prison. The fact that both kisses led to healings—of a relationship and a leg—confirms the connection between the physical and spiritual. As a young adult, I isolated myself for fear of being recognized as gay. Ironically, sexual desire made my hunger for emotional connection so palpable it pushed me past my fears until I created meaningful bonds with people. Without my sex drive stirring in me the need for human interaction, I might have continued hiding from the world, never discovering the spiritual core from which my life's purpose to inspire others emerged.

Discovering that I can fly then entering a 1920's airplane factory tells me that my powers are not new; I am realizing my spiritual heritage. It's also interesting that the airplane factory is about building something that enables not just the pilot to fly, but passengers as well. In other words, my gift of flight is not meant just for me, but for me to help others fly as well.

I believe the overweight middle aged men I keep encountering represent how I could have ended up if I didn't know I am a soul—unattractive, sluggish, and asking someone else to find the beauty I seek.

The handsome man represents many ideals. Our kiss awakens in me his need for healing. With my touch and direction, he heals himself. Sexual attraction, a primal physical need, drew me out of isolation and into interpersonal connection with him. But during the interaction, my soul sensed a greater purpose, and I knew what to do to achieve it.

I later remedy my flying trouble by finding him transformed into a doctor. In our first encounter, I guided him to the wisdom that could heal his leg. He took that knowledge to become someone who heals others.

I also love this character's physical transformation. He went from representing the unenlightened me I could have been, to a beautiful man who needed my connection for healing, to a healer. He symbolizes my own transformation from the most limiting awareness of me as a physical being to the highest form of Spirit. In the dream, I had the power to help him heal himself. When I needed him, he had become the loving doctor who could help me and made me know again that I could fly.

Shedding my clothes represents starting a new life as a spiritual being. The doctor became Godlike as we gazed at one another through his glasses. Then my vision cleared when I discarded my own.

In the new awareness of my spiritual state, I was still experimenting and learning, but it took bravery, of which I had plenty. To prove I was invisible and penetrable, I stood like Superman as cars raced toward me. Learning I was not invisible or penetrable surprised but didn't disappoint me, or make me believe I was less spiritually evolved than I thought. I simply found it an interesting learning experience.

Then I went back into the school to find the beautiful drill team sponsor for the driver who hit my elbow. Entering the school, I heard the driver's warning and immediately knew which door would lead to her.

The school represents the physical world. In the past, I was lost and anxious as it kept transforming so I couldn't find my classroom. In this dream, I went back into the school to find a beautiful young teacher for someone else. No longer lost or confused, I can better fulfill my quest to help others.

In 2010 Jerry and I attended the Houston film festival that included an audience Q & A with guest star Shirley MacLaine. Before I asked her my question, I told her that I learned a unique fact about her that she might not know. While researching my book, *Film Stars and Their Awards*, I wondered which acting families had the most award nominations and wins from the leading academies and critics' circles. My data revealed this rank of the most award-honored acting families:

4. the Redgraves
3. the Fondas
2. the Hustons

And the most award-honored family is comprised of

1. Shirley MacLaine and her brother, Warren Beatty.

The crowd applauded and murmured with interest. MacLaine's response: "What a curious thing to want to know."

After the Q & A I handed MacLaine a signed copy of *Film Stars and Their Awards*. This weekend, another, shorter dream brought back memories of that encounter.

DREAM:

In an upscale department store, I saw Shirley MacLaine behind a counter promoting a new product. Because the store had so few shoppers, I could approach her immediately. I laid a copy of Film Stars and Their Awards *on the counter and reminded her that I was the author who discovered that she and Warren Beatty were the most award-honored acting family in history.*

She flipped through the book as though she felt an inspiration and asked, "How would you like me to take this on Letterman?"

"On Letterman? You'd do that?"

"I like the book, and I like the fact that you include information in it that I haven't seen in other sources. Yeah, I'm scheduled to be a guest on Late Night with David Letterman. *I'll take this with me. It'll give me something to talk with him about."*

"I'd love it!"

"Consider it done."

"May Jerry and I come to the show?"

"Sure. I'll reserve two seats in the audience for you."

Imagining what her promotion could do for the book thrilled me. Then I thought of her. "Jerry and I have guest bedrooms in our home. Would you like to stay with us for the rest of your Houston visit?"

She thankfully declined, and I left with one last succinct comment. When I walked away, I felt great about how the interaction ended because I had said exactly enough. I didn't go on thanking her to the point I seemed to be begging for her marketing support of the book, and not so little that I seemed indifferent to the kindness she was extending.

Elation turned into anxiety as I thought about the book's 2008 publication date. Away from MacLaine, my mind worried about how I would update the book with current data and get it to the publisher in time for MacLaine's guest spot on Letterman. *As quickly as my mind tore through my confidence after the affirming interaction with MacLaine, it rebounded with the awareness that the book is already exactly as it needs to be.*

INTERPRETATION:

By envisioning prosperity instead of worrying about lack, I see how life manifests new avenues for abundance that I could never think up on my own. Even if my mind sometimes doubts, I know that my works and I are enough.

Day 204: June 3

During two recent doctor visits, my blood pressure registered a little high. In meditation I can feel my heart beating faster than usual. It's the end of the school year, and Jerry and I are exhausted. Spirit is telling me, "Slow down."

I'm still reading one Tao message every morning, and twice this week a line said to stop everything, do nothing, for in stillness the Tao will become clear. One way to honor this spiritual message is to take a break from writing. I may jot down inspirations so I don't have to remember them all, but I won't journal until Spirit prompts me.

Cutting back should force my mind to retain only the most relevant details of this phase of my first last year. When I started this journey, I committed to set priorities, do only what really matters, and let the rest go. I think writing less will help me make strides toward achieving all three goals.

21

The Presence of the Past

Day 240: July 9

I haven't written in over a month. As I've cut back on activities, my mind has slowed down and become more in tune to the present.

Throughout June, I focused on the concept, "In nothing is everything." On one level, the concept is telling me, in stillness I gain clarity. Only unstirred water reveals the bed of the pond. By rustling the water, we create energy but lose the ability to see beyond the surface. On a deeper spiritual level, the concept is teaching me what, until now, I have been afraid to believe. I'm beginning to let go of needing to hold onto my own physical identity and others' (my grandmothers, Ciocia Honey, Max and Rex and Bonnie) in death. Acknowledging that possibility feels huge and scary and freeing all at the same time. My revelation was reinforced by a new insight about Rex: I don't miss Rex because he's always with me spiritually, but I do miss his personality.

This summer Jerry and I realized our dream of cruising the Mediterranean. More than 20 years ago we set the goal after watching an enchanting movie called *Shirley Valentine* about a dismissed housewife who leaves her family behind to take a dream vacation to Greece. She has imagined the trip so long that she has specific expectations of what it will be like, especially a simple moment of sitting at a seaside table watching the sun set. What she finds is different from what she anticipated, mostly because she is not the same woman who first created the vision many years earlier. Ultimately the bittersweet reality of paradise is richer and fuller than the fantasy.

My first last year goals had to include a major trip because vacations stir the vitality and presence I sought when starting this year-long journey. Though we travel extensively, we anticipated this cruise as a trip of a lifetime.

Thanks to my paternal grandmother, I learned as a child to appreciate travel as a blessing. Grandma had a difficult life. In her 30s she divorced and developed such severe rheumatoid arthritis that her two children had to lift her out of bed each morning to start her day as a single mom and factory worker.

Raising two children alone on her blue collar salary limited many aspects of her life, especially the opportunity to travel. Over the years, she took a few bus trips to visit her sisters in northern Michigan or my dad when he was a soldier stationed in Tennessee, but she never had a vacation.

After retiring in her sixties, she and two sisters took a week's vacation to Hawaii. It literally was the one and only trip of her lifetime. Forever after, she displayed a photograph of her and her sisters standing on a tiny bridge amid multicolored flowers in full bloom. Throughout its run in the 1960s and 1970s, Grandma watched *Hawaii Five-0* on Sunday nights, searching for glimpses of places she'd visited. When I watched with her, she would point out familiar landmarks with a gleam in her eyes. Considering all the traveling Jerry and I have enjoyed in our lifetime, I can only imagine how impactful that one trip must have been to her.

Our Mediterranean cruise wouldn't be my only trip like Grandma's in Hawaii. But taking it during my first last year meant I had to enjoy it as if it were my last. That perspective intensified the fun, the newness, and the awareness of how lucky I was for the opportunity to see so much in only two weeks.

Jerry, his parents, and I had a brief layover in Amsterdam before we caught our flight to Barcelona, where the cruise began.

As the four of us waited in the Amsterdam airport, I sat next to a handsome, sandy-haired man with dark whiskers framing his narrow lips. When our eyes met, I said "Hello."

It was immediately clear we didn't speak a common language. In our effort to converse, he seemed as sincere as I in wanting to connect. He told me he was from "Russia . . . Moscow," and he recognized "Michigan" on my open passport. With no more words the other recognized, we fell silent. I extended our encounter by offering him a wintergreen Breathsavers. He took one, then I did, too. Though we only shared eye contact, a few words, and a small mint, I felt united with him. Half way around the world, both thousands of kilometers from home, we found common ground. Starting that trip with a globally spiritual encounter set the stage for my feeling connected with everyone.

Across two weeks and seven countries, that sense of union persisted. As I took in new landscapes and cultures, I felt spiritually filled. I consistently remembered to appreciate how lucky I was to be healthy enough to take such a trip. Everywhere I went—from the places that surprised me because they were run down and graffiti-riddled to those whose vistas were so beautiful I had to stop to catch my breath—provided a glimpse of Eden. What made it paradise? Sharing it with others.

This trip reminded me what matters most: the oneness of all souls. We thrive knowing that all souls are united. Some people focus on differences to affirm their individuality. They compare themselves to or criticize others instead of recognizing that, in what matters, we have no differences. In the lobby of the Hotel Realto in Barcelona where I first wrote this passage in longhand, I was warmed by the beautiful smile of the cute young Spaniard working behind the reservation desk. I sensed the excitement of a Pakistani family all sitting on their luggage waiting for a taxi. I heard my in-laws talking with Jerry in their Arkansas drawl, especially as they laughed together. We were a patchwork of cultures held together with a common spiritual thread.

In my daily life I sometimes feel isolated, thinking I need to be and do more to connect with people. Leaning against a dazzling lobby mural watching a small cross-section of humanity, I knew better. I feel flushed with gratitude and wholeness. None of us is alone—ever. Forgetting this truth used to drag on my heart. How light—both in weight and illumination—that awareness makes me feel now!

The Mediterranean cruise provided many other new first last year lessons. At the solarium bar, I waited to purchase drinks from Pricilla from Manila, the bartender we befriended, when a stocky, mocha skinned man with a buoyant gait stepped beside me and scanned the cocktail menu. The same inspiration to buy tickets for the family at the rodeo told me to buy this man a drink. When Pricilla approached, I ordered Jerry the ship's specialty margarita and me a frozen mudslide.

The man smiled at me. "I was thinking of ordering a mudslide."

How easy Spirit made it to act on my inspiration. "Sounds great," I told Pricilla, "I'll have one margarita and two mudslides." I turned to the other customer. "It's on me."

"No. You don't have to do that," he insisted.

"I'm happy to."

"Really?"

"You'll love it," I assured. "I had one yesterday."

He shook my hand and, with a curious twinkle in his eye, asked, "Who *are* you?" as if this simple act of kindness was somehow exceptional. That moment, I felt like a good ambassador for humanity.

Every day on the cruise, I encountered this man and his family—at the solarium pool, playing cards on deck, at dinner each evening. To repay my generosity, he handed me his card and offered free access to his online library of resources that might help me as a writer. When we returned from the trip, he had already emailed me a friendly note. I responded and hope we maintain our international friendship.

During our tour of Rome, Jerry and I had lunch with a family from Miami. When we learned that the son seated beside me would start high school this fall, we advised him to get to know his librarian, who could help with reading assignments and research, and his counselors, who could find him scholarships. We spent most of the lunch encouraging him to get involved, to volunteer and do community service, and, once we discovered he hoped to attend an out-of-state university, to research scholarships and secure tuition assistance.

I offered to send him a copy of *Success Express for Teens* to help him set goals and, handing him my business card, told him he could he could email me if he needed help with literature or writing assignments. His eyes lit up, and his parents couldn't stop thanking me.

Our vacation reinforced a habit that's grown stronger this first last year. I approach every experience expecting to love it. Anticipating blessings helps my mind focus on the good. It finds it every time. This perspective intensified my awe on cruise stops that exceeded my expectations. My heart leaps remembering a Santorini sun set from the rooftop café where we ate. But even cities to which I'm not eager to return didn't disappoint because my mind was seeking only good. As our tour bus passed graffiti riddled buildings in one city, I didn't rush to judgment. I looked past that detail and found ruins on hilltops steeped with history that made the stop impressive.

For goals, I believe, "Seek and ye shall find." For joy, it's, "What you seek, you find."

Though more familiar, Jerry's and my trip to Michigan later this summer felt just as magical. The highlight was achieving our goal to reunite my mother with her lifelong friend, Barbara. During our road trips, Mom sits in the back seat oblivious to where we are. She never commented when we stopped for the evening only a few hours into our southbound ride back home. She also didn't notice signs indicating we were near the town where her friend Barbara and her husband Larry live.

We pretended the front desk clerk at our motel recommended an elegant restaurant nearby and told Mom we were going to shower and dress up a little better for dinner. Without tipping her off to our plot, we suggested she might do the same. When we picked her up at her room an hour later, she was still wearing her traveling clothes.

"I didn't feel like changing," she said.

Outside the restaurant, she wondered aloud why we chose such a nice restaurant, but it still didn't register that we were up to something.

My mother likes a well-lit table so she can see what she's eating. When the hostess stopped at a table where Barbara and Larry were sitting, their menus hiding their faces, Mom pointed to a better lit booth and said, "Can we sit here instead?"

"I think you want to sit here, Mom," I said as Barb and Larry set down their menus.

Jerry, Barbara, Larry, and I waited, grinning for the few seconds it took Mom to realize what was happening. Finally, Mom's eyes widened. "Oh, my God. Oh, my God. Barb!"

We laughed and visited for hours. Afterward, Mom said it was the best part of any Michigan trip we'd taken with her these past years.

Day 282: August 20

DREAM:

Down a quiet residential street, I saw a lost, dapple haired dachshund. When I called, he hesitated. To make him less afraid, I lay down on my stomach and called more cheerfully. He rushed to me and let me pick him up.

Looking for a clue to where he belonged, I noticed his dog tag. As I read the name Fritzle on the tag, a car approached and the middle aged driver rushed toward me.

"Fritz!" she shouted through tears. She took the dog and kissed him. "I have three dachshunds I got all at the same time," she told me.

"How old is Fritz?"

"A year."

I couldn't hear her with her face buried in Fritzle's coat. "How old?"

"He's one."

"He's just a baby!" I felt an overwhelming rush of love. "We have two dachshunds, but one of them, Rex, died in May." Overcome by sadness, I couldn't form a fluid sentence. "He got sick so fast . . . we took him to the doctor . . . he had a tumor behind his heart . . . in two days from the time we realized he might be sick, he was gone."

The woman stepped toward the curb and turned her ankle. She paused, then tried to put weight on it.

"Stand still. Give it a moment. You might be fine," I assured her.

While we talked and waited to determine if she was injured, a grocery delivery truck parked beside us.

"I need to get some milk before I take Fritzle home."

The driver opened a sliding door of the truck and began unloading gallon jugs of milk and juice.

Other workers from a nearby grocery store formed a line to pass groceries from the truck to the store. A young man behind me set his feet firmly and twisted left and right to pass the crates. I cautioned him not to lift and twist, but to turn his entire body both ways or he'd strain his back.

Meanwhile the woman's ankle was no better. So I suggested, "Don't purchase a whole gallon. Buy a quart to do just for today. It won't be that heavy to carry and you can get home without putting excess strain on your ankle."

Instead of replying to my recommendation, she said, "Wait here. I want to give you something." Then she hobbled off, I suspected to ask her spouse if she could give me Fritz.

The sidewalks now teemed with people hurrying to work. Overwhelmed with grief for Rex, I sensed the sadness everyone was carrying. So I pictured everyone stacking all the happy events of their lives and all the sad events of their lives beside each other. Though the happy stacks would tower many stories higher, I felt overcome by the fact that sadness weighs so much, and happiness is so light.

As people passed, I grieved for them all. I found a quiet corner against the yellow-brick exterior of a bank, and bawled. When I finally got control of the tears, I checked my eyes in the smoky glass above an ATM.

I turned and, to my surprise, Jerry approached with a fair-skinned red-haired woman who looked vaguely familiar. Both were smiling expectantly.

"Hi," Jerry said. "I came to tell you something."

Because Jerry was dressed in a suit, he must have interrupted his work day to give me this news. My heart sank. Despite their smiles, I worried that Jerry came in person because he had bad news. Perhaps someone in my family died.

Jerry hugged me as the woman pulled out what looked like a National Honor Society graduation cord and draped it around us as she began, "Congratulations, Roger, you have been . . ."

And I awoke.

I felt so eager to discover the good news, I tried to will myself back to sleep to continue the dream. Though I've been able to do it in the past, this time it didn't work.

INTERPRETATION:

This dream reinforces my guiding principle that everything is perspective. Somehow, I made all the wrong emotional choices and blessings still kept coming my way. Joy approached me in the form of a new puppy. Instead of relishing my new discovery, I worried about returning him to his rightful owner. When his owner reclaimed him, I succumbed to the sorrow of missing Rex.

The woman's twisted ankle forced us to stand still, enabling us to see the cooperative effort of many people transporting milk. Instead of marveling at their teamwork, I focused on preventing one young man from suffering future pain.

Jerry's arrival portends wonderful news for me, yet I worry he'll tell me that someone I love has died.

So many blessings keep appearing throughout the dream. The puppy brings joy. His owner, I suspect, is planning to give me the dog. A chain of people work together to get milk to the store. Jerry and a woman arrive beaming and congratulate me for some great honor.

But throughout the dream, my focus is on helping, or fixing, or preventing, or fearing problems. Clearly there is balance in all of us: there is a yin and yang of happiness and grief, support from and help for others, peace of heart (the solitude of the street at the beginning of the dream) and full throttle activity of the mind (the bustle of the same street as hoards of people rush to work). Even though my focus in this dream swam against it, a current of blessings keeps streaming forth. It's so powerful that I tried to will myself back to sleep to receive the last one.

I love the overriding lesson of this dream: Blessings perpetually stream toward us and emanate from us; they are our essence. To be fully alive, we need only focus on the blessings in the present. We deplete our own spiritual power by inventing—and they are our own invention—problems and sorrows by anticipating something to fear or lingering in past grief.

Unexpected events (a twisted ankle) invite new solutions (get only a quart of milk) that return our focus to the present. The solution works as a metaphor to savor life in small increments. All we have is this moment.

Day 290: August 28

My first last year has reminded me not to take time for granted and made me aware that no one is long for this world. Comfortable talking about end-of-life decisions, I fulfilled a special request for my mother this weekend.

On Saturday I took my camera and laptop to my parents' house to photograph and record the history of items that had a meaningful story Mom wanted my siblings and me to know. For example, she bought ceramic bride and groom salt and pepper shakers for the bridal table at my parent's wedding reception. Other meaningful items included a cross that adorned her brother's casket, a cup and saucer from a set of china that belonged to her grandmother, and gifts from my brothers, sister, or me. In part Mom wanted us to know the monetary value of some of the items, but I was more interested in the emotional value they had as part of our family's history.

As I've reached the last quarter of my first last year, I have worked on loving each day I live, rather than counting down days before my year is up. I find it interesting that part of my mind wants to go in that direction—watching, and sometimes fretting and even grieving a little—about the fact that, if this were actually my last year, I'm down to my last three months. As a person who believes in the power of the mind, I have made an effort to avoid creating a self-fulfilling prophecy and inadvertently communicating to the universe that I want this to be the end. If anything, this experiment has deepened my appreciation for life and made me hunger for more.

I began another project to leave a family legacy. Last summer, my Aunt Arlene gave me scrapbooks and antique photos that once belonged to my grandmother's older sister, Angie, because of my interest in our family history. Some of the photos, you may recall, I sent to my Aunt Lenore last Christmas. After Ciocia Honey died, Arlene found her scrapbooks and gave those to me, too.

I bought new photo albums intending only to reorganize the hodgepodge of pictures. Sorting through old photos, I selected the best to create a single scrapbook of my family beginning with my great grandparents' immigration to the United States 100 years ago. When it's completed, I'll produce multiple copies to give relatives.

Working on the book has expanded my perception of being present, a goal of my first last year. While identifying and organizing photos from eras that precede my own lifetime, I am immersed in the present moments of chronicling my family's history. When I think of life only from the physical plane, my heart grows melancholy about the loss of so many who've lived and moved on. From a spiritual perspective, I'm uplifted by new details about my ancestors that extend our relationship. As I work, the past and present merge because both exist within me.

Whenever the past brings something new to my awareness, my perception of eternity expands. Our souls—the energy of who we are—have always existed and been united. In linear time, they have been before, are now, and ever shall be. But in spatial time, there is no mystery to the question of whether we existed before or some piece of us will live on or move to another plane after our physical body dies. As spiritual entities, our souls have no past or future to traverse. Everything is now, and every time is now.

Creativity thrives in spiritual time. I have felt time's malleability when researching my movie reference books. Although many actors I write about have died, their legacy keeps them alive in the public's consciousness. When their work inspires my creativity, our mutual impact on eternity grows. Like Rex and Ciocia Honey in The Rex Meditation, the actors are balls of light individually distinct, yet merged through creative links to those still influenced by their contributions. The fact that I recently discovered and have been inspired by silent film stars Ramón Novarro and Harold Lloyd, for example, pulses new life into their film legacy while expanding mine as a writer.

To thrive, Spirit needs a vehicle. Most obviously, it is life: human, animal, or plant. But the mind is a vehicle: it houses memories that perpetuate life, and it creates new vehicles, such as movies or books, to extend memories over eons. Articulating this concept might seem to negate any need for a first last year. As eternal beings, our physical death is an illusion. But eternity is comprised of infinite individual moments, as distinct as each ball of light in the Allsoul. Awareness of physical death makes living the individual moment imperative.

This exploration of time has brought new insight about the sadness I believed was about missing what is gone and cannot be retrieved. I now think it's more about how often I am asleep to the awareness that my ancestors are always united with me. I recently found a photo of my grandmother that I'd never seen before. In this physical world, my grandmother was plagued by dark moods and troubled thoughts. But after I scanned and enlarged this photo, I saw so much joy and sorrow and hope behind her smile that I loved her more than ever.

 I thought my knowledge of her personal struggles created that effect, but when Jerry saw that photo, tears welled. Jerry never knew my grandmother, who died the year before he and I met. His similar response reinforces my belief in the timeless connection we all have, and the eternity of all souls expressed as love.

22

The Bigger Picture

Day 299: September 6

My movie reference books, including the forthcoming *Countdown to Oscar's Favorite Actors* and *Actors and the Academy Awards*, encapsulate the history of actors' most celebrated work. Like distilling an essence, they highlight their greatest contributions. As I near the final lap of my first last year, I'm imagining what legacy my work will leave. My dream: produce a body of writing that inspires, empowers, and most of all, touches souls.

Is there room for a publishing house in that dream? Because the idea came as a vivid spiritual inspiration, I suspect there is. Rather than dive right in, I will seek guidance through prayer, meditation, and even daily routines.

Living my first last year has helped me value both productivity and calm. So part of me feels enthusiasm about embarking on a new endeavor. But I am equally drawn to the spiritual peace I can sustain when I limit activity, and as Thoreau recommended, "Simplify, simplify, simplify." Both concepts appeal to me, so I have not selected one or the other. Perhaps the choices are not exclusive. If my first last year has confirmed anything, it's that I feel most alive when my spiritual awareness and physical experiences thrive in tandem. Although I don't feel pressured to decide, I believe I've reached a crossroad in my journey that requires prayerfully selecting a path and taking action. How lucky I am to have choices—and they're both inviting!

Milestones encourage us to notice the present moment in larger contexts. Last weekend we celebrated my father-in-law's birthday. He's now only 10 years younger than his mother was when she died. Viewing life on a linear timeline offers a gentle reminder to make each day count. Living this first last year prompted me to identify my values and live them fully, moment-by-moment. I create meaning through loving action, which includes writing. The context of my day is filled with details that, at the end of this journey, whether in two months or decades from now, I can use to trigger memories of the only experiences that mattered—how I loved and what I gave.

We all have interests and passions. Developing them into talents, especially those to which we dedicate our lives, is the loving gift from our soul. What could be better? What else could matter? That energy of love sustains us now and will move us through eternity.

Fulfillment doesn't come by reaching a destination, but appreciating that we're already there. This is heaven. We are not merely in the presence of God, as we always have been; we *are* the substance of God. In the light of that energy, we awaken to one universal truth: all peace, wholeness, and bliss are ours whenever and wherever we are still and know.

23

We are to Live Our Mission

Day 304: September 11

Whenever I resist doing something spiritual, I know an empowering spiritual message awaits me. For no apparent reason, yesterday I dreaded going to church. Uncharacteristically, I even misplaced my keys. As Jerry and I looked for them when we should have been on the road, I knew that I needed to relinquish the search for the keys, plow through the resistance, and go to church.

After the service, a friend of ours who had had cancer presented a workshop about her trip to Brazil to visit John of God for healing. As our friend shared her story, I could feel myself shift to an uplifted energy zone where I can physically sense everything that's going on, but I'm seeing everything in the physical world through thin gauze and hearing everything with a slight echo, as if my soul were hearing it all through an otherworldly veil.

Her presentation ended with a film about John of God, the famous healer in Brazil who has been doing his spiritual work since the 1970s. In interviews John's assistants suggested that we must facilitate our own healing by doing 50% or more of "the work" required to get well, rather than expecting God or an outside force to heal us.

This morning I went for a follow-up appointment with my urologist. In recent years, I have had an elevated PSA and symptoms suggesting possible prostate trouble. At last month's visit with the urologist, he ordered more extensive blood tests, prescribed an anti-inflammatory, and recommended some dietary changes. Today, I told him that the diet shift and medication helped, and I feel fine.

He smiled and said he suspects the new blood work will confirm that I am. But then he added, "If the PSA hasn't gone down, you may have cancer and you'll need to come back for us to determine what to do next."

I had wondered about cancer since my most recent PSA spike, but until this visit no doctor mentioned the word. I wasn't scared. First, my body responded almost instantly to the medication and the diet change, both great signs. Second, I thought about the John of God video and sensed that, no matter what might be going on in my body, I will continue my spiritual work even after this physical journey ends. I didn't feel nonchalant about a possible difficult prognosis. But by looking at the circumstance from the higher spiritual view, I reacted to the doctor's comment as a child of God, not a victim of fear.

I left the doctor's office feeling exuberant. I love life and the adventure I am having throughout this journey. Outside, the weather was cool! Texas had sighed away the sweltering grip of summer. I took my time returning to work to savor the refreshing air. When I arrived on campus, I observed my surroundings, especially the bright sky dappled white and blue. At that moment in that setting I felt my place in the universe. I belonged. I felt happy and alive. How grateful I am for everything. Everything. Everything.

Day 306: September 13

Today I am to email my urologist for results of my blood work. I am not scared, but I am alert. If I've learned anything this past year, now that I am ten months through it, it's that life keeps sending me reminders to live, live, live. Before I began this year's adventure, I would have said that life keeps sending us reminders of its brevity. People and animals I love have died, children have grown and started families of their own. This month Jerry and I have each mentioned past experiences—his heart attack, our tribute party to Ciocia Honey and Ciocia Stas when I dedicated *Drowning in Secret* to them, Rex's passing, funny things Cory and Rebecca said as children—that point to the apparent briskness of life. This time last year, such memories reminded me to appreciate what I have because soon what I now enjoy will pass, too. That vantage point still has merit, but thanks to this first last year, I have a different perspective on the passage of time. Memories do not merely commemorate time lost or spark reminders to live in the present and appreciate every moment I am given. Beyond that divine tap on the shoulder to live each moment in the now is an even bigger reminder to go about the business of doing what I came here to do. However my spiritual quest manifests, I am here to live from my soul and to inspire others to live from theirs.

When life gives us a task, it also provides every resource we need to achieve it. Once we start living our calling, our mind assesses our progress. This year, my brain raised an interesting argument by imagining that some of my family and friends will think ideas I share in this book are proof that I've gone off the deep end. When I started my first last year, one of my first instructions was to be bold. Fear of being ridiculed is a coward's blanket. So I breathed in, reassured the doubting, self-protective part of my brain that this venture is not about gaining worldly approval, but living the promise I made when I came to this life with a spiritual mission, as I believe we all do.

DREAM:

Jerry and I were treading water and wearing foam life preservers in the swimming pool my family had in our backyard when I was a boy. I asked Jerry why the water had remained so clean and clear all these years if no one had been taking care of it. As he ventured a response, I noticed that the tile mosaics all around the pool had crumbled, and individual tiles had fallen away. The perimeter of the pool had shown its wear, but the water remained pure. I then looked at the foam lifejackets we were wearing and realized that we could stop treading water and the preservers would keep us afloat, even in the roughest waves of the largest ocean.

INTERPRETATION:

Worldly mosaics age and disintegrate over time, but the liquid realm of Spirit in which we are always immersed remains clear. The divine support we have even in the physical realm supports us through everything.

I don't know what my PSA results will be. I feel sanguine that the inflammation is not cancer. Whatever the news, I have again been reassured that I'm spiritually supported through anything.

Having my health in question increases my desire to live each moment as vibrantly as I can and to fulfill my spiritual mission. That's our purpose. We reach it by listening to the guidance of Spirit and responding with consistent action. Emptiness and loneliness are signs of our hunger to stay connected to Spirit and live our soul's journey. Achieving supreme fulfillment is as simple and as infinitely, fascinatingly complex as that.

24

My Faith is Tested

Day 307: September 14

For days I've waited for the urologist's email to confirm that my PSA went down and all was well. This morning, his message arrived: *PSA went up; please keep appointment for biopsy.* Below, he pasted my last two test results. Since last month, my PSA rose from 3.2 to 3.5.

On the ride to work I allowed myself to feel whatever came up. I was disappointed, surprised (stunned is too strong a word, though I sometimes felt a little numb), and, to my disappointment, worried. My mind sprang in various directions, even wondering if this test result was the beginning of the end of my life. My soul assured me that the thought was a silly exaggeration of very little information, but that's where my mind went.

It also traced recent health-related experiences. I remembered my resistance before church last Sunday, and how the John of God workshop inspired me. Again my mind wondered if Spirit was preparing me for a cancer diagnosis. When I was re-shelving books in the church library last month, I checked out a CD entitled *Spontaneous Healing*. Recently my car radio and CD player have been volatile, sometimes working, and other times shutting off spontaneously.

Rather than getting the radio fixed, I used it for a spiritual experiment. If the radio or CD worked, Spirit wanted me to get that message. If the radio shut off, I took it as a sign that I didn't need that information or should be focusing on something else. Only a few radio programs really captivated me, and those stayed on until the discussion ended. Yesterday I started the *Spontaneous Healing* CD. The author, Dr. Andrew Weil read from his manuscript for about five minutes, and then the CD popped off. I tried the inspirational radio station I usually listen to, thinking maybe I should be hearing something there instead. It too shut off. So I rode in silence.

On a later ride, I again tried listening to *Spontaneous Healing*. That time, it shut off even sooner. It must not be time to hear this message, I concluded.

During one silent commute, I wondered what message my body is trying to communicate. I believe physical pain or illness mirrors emotional issues I need to resolve. For example, years ago during a period of conflict with a group I trusted, I suffered rotor cuff pain. As a lifelong swimmer, I knew I had not injured my shoulders. At first, I thought the pain reflected the weight of the world I was carrying on my shoulders. That sounded nobler than what I later admitted to myself: I had developed a chip on my shoulder because I thought I'd been mistreated. The pain helped me identify my anger. As soon as I did, the shoulder pain disappeared.

I'm wondering now if prostate trouble is tipping me off to something emotionally unresolved. Because prostate trouble causes bladder irritation, my first guess was that maybe I'm pissed about something and don't even know it. If so, my body might clue me in with a raised PSA. Exploring that possibility so far hasn't brought up anything.

This morning I read an article in a wellness circular that discussed the psychological and spiritual benefits of journaling. I can relate to what the author shared, as right now I'm feeling better just having written about all I've felt since reading the doctor's email.

Another metaphor appeared on the way to work today. Approaching the interstate, I saw a traffic update indicating a major accident and lanes closed along my usual commute. An alternate route via a state highway opened so recently I'd never taken it. As I ascended the ramp to go a different way to school, I wondered if the PSA results are a sign, like the accident sign, that will veer me just slightly from my usual journey through life.

As I glided along empty lanes, my mind wandered through different scenarios. *If I have prostate cancer, I might die. If I don't die, perhaps my sexual function will be compromised.* I took the exit which listed two streets, the latter one nearest my school. It turned out to be the last exit before the highway ends. *Metaphorically, I wondered if this meant that whatever spiritual growth or physical treatment I might take to heal the prostate will go swiftly, and conclude just before I reached the end. (That is, if I do have prostate cancer, it might not kill me).*

As I exited the highway it began to rain, but only a gentle patter on the windshield. *My life's journey includes storms, but this one's light, barely an inconvenience.* When I reached the first street listed at the exit, I couldn't tell which direction to take to get to the street that led to my school. I turned one way, immediately got my bearings and realized I needed to go another way, so a swerved into a gas station parking lot so I could turn around. In the parking lot, I heard thuds and a grating rrrrr under my car. I had hit something. I turned to see that the underside of my car had scraped against three high bumps in the gas station pavement covered by manholes.

As I got out of the car in the drizzling rain, it finally occurred to me how much more upset about the prognosis I was than I first acknowledged. Emotions constricted my throat and my mind grew hazy. Inspecting the underside of my car I saw the plastic guard hanging limply at one end. Given the worried thoughts about compromised sexual function, the phallic metaphor of it struck me as funny, even during this disorienting detour. The humor escalated as I tried to yank the guard free so I could drive the rest of the way to work without it dragging on the pavement. The other side was so secure I couldn't free the guard without damaging the plastic.

So I drove the rest of the way with my flap dragging (ah, the irony!), but was pleased to discover that when I reached 30 miles an hour, the plastic guard must have caught the under draft because the scraping stopped. At work, the auto mechanics teacher removed the guard.

Writing this has lightened my heart. The humor of the metaphor shifted me out of fear, and got my creative mind reeling. (By the way, don't be surprised if this exact series of events doesn't show up in a novel—the phallic metaphor is just too perfect not to use someday.) My mind also has something constructive to focus on now—what spiritual message is my body giving me with these PSA results?

As I have frequently affirmed, I know that I'm a soul, my existence is eternal, and I will continue to pursue my spiritual purpose whenever my work in this life ends. Receiving news that makes imminent death a possibility adds immediacy to my mission. The resounding lesson I keep getting from living my first last year: *determine your spiritual purpose and live it full out now.* Knowing I have a mission that will continue throughout eternity comforts me whenever fear of death looms. I still hold to the hope that my condition is not dire. After all, though my PSA has doubled since last year, it's still within the range some physicians consider normal.

One final erroneous thought bears sharing here. I have often attested to the power of the mind and soul to create our physical reality. Since I began writing this book last November, I have had a fleeting thought: What if I facilitate an early death because I have held in mind these past months that I'm living as if this were my last year? Whenever I have the thought, I backtrack with, "I don't know if my mind and soul have *that much* power."

I know people can will themselves to die, but that's not my mindset. My first last year goals have been to revel in each moment, learn soul-nurturing lessons, and share them with you. That this quest could accelerate premature death seems preposterous. But it's an interesting spiritual question worth digesting. Being bold means exploring any divine messages that could teach me and, in turn, help you.

Day 310: September 17

Jerry's dad is one of the most faith-filled men I've ever known. If I face a challenge and want prayer support, I call him first. This time I didn't need to. On Saturday evening the phone rang. When I answered, he began, "Jerry told us about what's going on with your health and I'd like to pray with you." He said the sweetest prayer. I felt moved and uplifted by the love emanating through the phone. After finishing the prayer, he said, "Thank you for letting me do what God put on my heart to do."

After I hung up, I opened the office door where Jerry was working. "Besides you, your dad is the sweetest man who ever lived." Jerry knew his dad was planning to call, so he understood what I meant. We held each other a moment, then Jerry resumed his work.

Instead of the resistance I felt last week before church, today I couldn't wait to pray about my health with the day's prayer volunteer after the service. I hoped it would be sweet Dixie, but no name was listed in the bulletin. When the platform assistant announced that Dixie would be in the prayer room today, tears welled.

What was happening? I wondered. I hadn't been emotional about the biopsy since Thursday.

After service, I was stopped on the way to the prayer room by a funny woman named Vivien. She had just lost her husband, Ernest to a long battle with cancer.

I hugged her and asked how she was doing. She said that she was great. "I passed," she said proudly. "For years I have been teaching spiritual principles, but they've never been tested as they were by losing Ernest. He died two weeks ago today. I did so much grieving while he was dying that when he finally went, I discovered that I really am living what I've been teaching."

I related to what she said. Since learning about my biopsy, I've wondered how well I will live the principles of faith that I espouse. I hope, whatever physical challenge I face, I grow in health, wisdom, and happiness.

After talking to Vivien, I found Dixie alone in the prayer room. Telling her about my PSA numbers rising and requesting a prayer for my biopsy in two weeks made my eyes fill with tears. I was disappointed in myself for feeling afraid. I wanted my faith to be so strong that I would be unflappable in the face of any challenge. Dixie, of course, was as sweet and supportive as I expected her to be, and I didn't stay frustrated with myself long. However, I did wonder why I felt so sad and scared again.

Even when life challenges me, I want to be so brave I maintain my zest for life. Like Vivien, I hope to pass the tests of faith that I encounter. The tears during my prayer request were tears of fear, not faith. So I left knowing I could think better, feel better (both emotionally and, as was paramount in this lesson's context, physically), and be better.

While listening to Deepak Chopra on the radio Friday, I had planned to find the copy of *Ageless Body, Timeless Mind* I'd cataloged for the church library. After the prayer, I went to the bookshelf but was drawn to another Chopra book, *Creating Health*. I flipped through it and felt a stirring to read it, so I checked it out.

On the ride home, Jerry and I both got a little weepy. I started it by crying when I told Jerry how disappointed I was that asking Dixie to pray with me made my eyes well. My mind was back to worrying about cancer, and even going so far as to be scared of death. Jerry, crying now too, turned to me as he drove and said, "You better not leave me."

"I'm not planning to," I said, and a little of my faith felt restored.

That afternoon I was working on some financial calculations when I heard raindrops tapping on the window as if inviting me to see who was calling. I opened the blinds and watched the rain with the realization that I need to appreciate this in case I don't have many more rainfalls to enjoy. That thought only made the experience sad, reinforcing the idea that something might be wrong with my body and that my life, in this physical form, could soon end.

I recalled my first last year intention to live as though I may never live this date again. From that perspective, my body felt energized, and my spirit nourished. But that was easy because I believed deep down that it was just an exercise to practice living in the present moment. In the back of my mind I suspected I had much more time. As I stared at the limbs of our sycamore tree drooping from the weight of the rain, I realized how I had allowed one suggestion for a medical test to alter my focus, thereby changing how I perceived everything I was living.

I disappointed myself by getting sidetracked from my spiritual focus so easily. Without even a prognosis, I had allowed my thinking to stand at the edge of a quicksand pit of morbid wallowing. What was I doing?

That awareness led me to find a better thought by choosing a better action. Instead of staring at the rain feeling hope drain from me, I spent the evening reading *Creating Health*. Instantly I knew why Spirit led me to that book. When I read about all the factors that contribute to poor health I felt relieved by how life-affirming my mental, spiritual, emotional, and physical habits are. Of all the factors Chopra listed that can cause or exacerbate disease, the only item that applied to me was when he said "Don't limit your diet to the same few foods repeated over and over." For lunch every day over the past ten years, I have almost always eaten an apple, yogurt, and a granola bar. I talked to Jerry about this, and we wondered if even eating the same healthy foods so continually could be harmful.

As I read the scenarios about former patients, I felt even more confident that my mindset and spirituality lend themselves only to vitality. That insight gave me confidence to explore spiritually what next step to take. Do I want the biopsy? At this point, it seems a good idea to confirm what I hope—that I am healthy. Tomorrow I will start my day by meditating about the next best step. I know I will receive the guidance to do what's best for me.

Before we went to bed, I told Jerry, "Whatever happens, it's going to be great."

He looked at me but didn't say anything, as if he worried that I was conveying some fateful message shrouded in a happy spin.

"I believe I'm fine," I confirmed. "I really do. I don't know what will happen, but I believe that I am perfectly fine, and it's going to be great. Period."

In meditation this morning, I sat in silence listening for guidance about what to do next concerning my prostate. My mind wandered occasionally, but I remained calm and patient. While waiting and listening, I noted that I had grown spiritually. In the past when I felt concerned and took something to God in prayer, I remained defiantly grounded in meditation demanding that God give me guidance. I never respond positively to being bullied. What made me think God would? But if I'm asked, or better yet, given the opportunity to feel inspired to do something loving, I do it joyfully.

I didn't come away from the meditation with a clear directive from God, but I decided that was good. Not getting an answer required me to remain open to guidance. All day, every thought and sign that caught my attention suggested that my body has nothing wrong with it or has every resource in its power to heal. Whether that required intervention from a conventional doctor, I didn't yet know. But I did determine to honor my body's natural instinct to live, and live vibrantly.

I agreed with Chopra's mind/body suggestion that healthy bodies do health-enhancing activities. So after I ate a good breakfast, I worked out. As I lifted weights, I affirmed my strong, healthy muscles and organs and internal systems by thinking, *I am able to do this because my body is healthy. And by doing this, I'm helping it perform even better. My thoughts and my actions are support systems that keep my body thriving.*

After feeding our dachshund Joey, I took him into the den and stroked his back, rubbed behind his ears, and kissed him repeatedly on the forehead. So much love passes between us every day. I wanted to relish this moment by being fully present. I contrasted this soul-nourishing interaction with the disheartening few seconds I had standing at the window watching it rain yesterday. The only difference between the two incidents concerned my perception. What I believed going into each experience, and what I thought during each encounter, determined whether it depleted or vitalized me.

Until I looked at the rain yesterday, I didn't know I was holding onto negative, fearful thoughts about life. But because I was paying attention to my thoughts, I was able to think something better and do something different. I could have remained at the window with the new perception and started feeling energized by the beautiful, refreshing downpour. But I didn't feel that power within me at the moment. So I did something just as effective: I chose another action and picked up the Deepak Chopra book. Instantly my mind started ricocheting hopeful thoughts not about my body's ability to heal itself, which it has in the past, but even better, about my body's current wellness.

On the way to work I tried again to listen to *Spontaneous Healing*. My antenna (or whatever the flashing "Aux Input Device" light refers to every time the CD or radio goes off) had not been repaired, but I started the CD. Only a few lines into the audiobook, the CD turned off. This time, instead of taking it as a sign from God that I wasn't meant to hear this yet, I decided to try again. I punched the CD button and the CD played a few more seconds. Then it popped off. I pressed the CD button again. It played a while longer, then popped off. I turned off the radio in hopes of resetting whatever was malfunctioning, and pressed CD again. It stayed on the entire commute to work.

As I listened, I knew why hearing this *after* reading Chopra's *Creating Health* made the CD useful. Chopra's book provided a foundation of ideas that made Dr. Weil's arguments palatable to me. Without Chopra, I might have dismissed Weil's arguments about homeopathy. After learning from both doctors, I concluded that my body is giving me a gift of awareness through the elevated PSA. I had committed to be bold this year, so I will have the biopsy.

Beyond testing my own courage, what spiritual benefit will come from this health challenge? I believe that everything that happens—with our bodies, in our personal and global interactions, on our Earth—is rooting for us at top decibel to wake up and know that what we've always sought is right here, right now. Throughout this first last year, I've felt that spiritual promise come more alive. But the thought of facing death tells me to embrace the philosophy even more boldly than I had before. Live now. Love this moment now. Be joyful now. But don't do it because I fear losing now. Do it because I love now so much I am willing to give it my full attention and embrace.

25

The Courage to Love

Day 313: September 20

It's time to stop absorbing new information and use what I've learned since receiving the email from my urologist. Here's the analogy that reinforced that decision: Prior to a ten-day journey, I wouldn't eat thirty meals so I don't have to stop for breakfast, lunch, or dinner any day. I need the meals as I travel. So it is with spiritual food and inspirations.

So for the past few days I have not sought out new ideas to explore, but instead have continued to seek guidance from God and from my body during meditation and throughout the day. I have also continued listening to Andrew Weil's *Spontaneous Healing*, agreeing with and taking to heart some of his suggestions, questioning others, and saving others for future exploration.

Focusing on the future is a healthy mindset I'm glad to be maintaining.

This week I've been revising *Teach Me SUCCESS*. It's a slow, methodical process of transferring data, reformatting various sections of text, and proofreading to ensure consistency of data presentation. Yesterday, about my eighth day into the task, I sensed my body growing anxious about the impending deadline. The fact that the word deadline begins with "dead" feels burdensome to my soul. Feeling it looming makes me anxious to complete the task rather than excited about the work.

I related this idea to the fear I have felt about potentially being ill, and saw another sign from God that I am fine. I keep getting new inspirations about Paradise Publishing that tell me I have something to do, and more to look forward to. That spiritual assurance reinforces positive expectations for a prognosis of good health. I think my soul is trying to show my mind how to hold onto faith.

If you write, you know the experience of sitting down to compose something and coming up with text that surprises even you. It's your conscious mind that's surprised because the most enlightened writing comes from deeper within—the soul has the knowledge that the conscious mind is surprised to recognize as coming from you. Soul, mind, and body are all connected. The soul is the permanent core of everything you "know" from experience and from your connection to the collective consciousness that is the Allsoul. The mind and body have both permanent and temporary aspects. A body naturally knows how to be healthy. If we act in unhealthy ways long enough, we may interrupt that perfect physical balance and create illness. Or illness may emerge without our ever doing anything self-destructive. But the body and the mind must both be reminded occasionally about what each innately knows—that infinite mass of knowledge stored in the soul.

I committed to start today feeling healthier and more hopeful than I have since I read the urologist's email. The truth of my healthiness will not come from a lab readout after my biopsy. It comes from my soul. I am healthy and whole in body as well as spirit and mind. Evidence of this belief comes as ideas about all I have yet to do to fulfill my purpose in this life. More writing and Paradise Publishing are waiting to be expressed through me. The work is mine to do. I promised God when I first started receiving the inspirations that I am up to the task and am honored to have it entrusted to me.

How wonderful life is! How lucky I am not just to be a part of it, but to be *aware* that I am part of it. Awareness distinguishes living from merely existing, and I'm grateful to be alive.

Day 317: September 24

Friday was the first anniversary of Ciocia Honey's birthday since she died. My family, Jerry and I honored her with a dinner at the only Polish restaurant in town.

I brought a 5 x 7 photo of her and Ciocia Stas to display on the table throughout dinner. I gave a tribute, my mom recited prayers said at Catholic funerals, and we toasted Ciocia Honey just as she would have enjoyed.

I held the 5 x 7 photo in front of Jerry and me as my brother Ray took our picture, and the resulting image staggered my soul. A ball of light like the one I pictured as her in my mediation shone over Ciocia Honey's body, but still revealed her face. The aftereffect of that image has stayed with me, affirming that spiritual moment when the vision came to me in meditation.

Today Jerry had a church board meeting after the service, so I stayed home and cleaned. While working I played an old CD of the *Yentl* soundtrack. I was wiping the mirror when the lyrics, "Tell me where, where is it written what it is I'm meant to be?" made tears stream. The journey that the soundtrack depicts of a young woman who must break out of the restrictions of her culture to fulfill her destiny has always inspired me. Hearing it now, near the end of my first last year with an uncertain prognosis looming, I now felt more grateful for what I have had. The last time I visited my paternal grandmother when she was dying of cancer, she declared, "I love life." I always have, too. But seeing the journey from what could be the end deepens that love. Writing this book has also kept me mindful of how precious is the gift of life.

Earlier this week, I received new lab results from the urinalysis. Everything said "Clear" or "Negative," reviving hope that I'm fine. I don't know if the urinalysis actually meant that. Maybe these tests actually ruled out some less dire prognoses that could come from rising PSA numbers. But I took it as a sign of hope.

I think about my body and keep affirming how lucky and healthy I am. I am more than just active—I'm energetic, even exuberant, and go non-stop from 4:30 AM when I wake up until 9:00 PM when I go bed. I work out nearly every day, have the stamina and motivation to keep altering my workouts, and my body can do everything I challenge it to do. I know that I am blessed, and I feel grateful.

But something more was happening in response to the *Yentl* music. As I knelt scrubbing the floor with tears streaming, I thought of other works that have inspired me to think of my life metaphorically. My lifelong fascination with the movie *The Poseidon Adventure* began when I was 11, about the time I started realizing I was gay. Only later did I see its obvious parallel to my life: my secure and joyful childhood was suddenly turned upside down by a secret realization that left me feeling trapped and needing to wend my way through uncharted emotional territory in a disorienting world inverted from the norm. Those psychosexual reasons for loving the film were reinforced when I began attending *The Poseidon Adventure* benefits in California and discovered how many fans who shared my youthful fascination with the movie at its release were boys between the ages of 10 and 14 who ended up being gay.

An aspect of the film that filled me with hope was seeing how a disparate group of people could work together for a common goal. Over the years, I recognized that I loved other movies and books, including *Murder on the Orient Express,* for the same reason: withdrawing from others to hide who I really was left me lonely, but seeing strangers working together helped me feel less alone.

That loneliness really resonated when I read *The Great Gatsby*, especially the scene where Nick promises Gatsby's corpse that he will find people to come to his funeral. While the overriding plot concerned Gatsby's ill-fated love for Daisy, what struck me was Nick's eternal love for Gatsby and his ideals. Acknowledging both the magic and the destruction of Gatsby's vision, Nick headed back to the Midwest believing only Gatsby rose above his unadulterated scorn for everything that transpired that summer. When I first read the novel at 17, Gatsby represented the power of a dream that could have lived if he entrusted his heart to Nick, not Daisy.

Throughout my teens, the relationships I did not develop with other people I established with God. It was then that I began journaling. In my written dialogues with God I began seeing my physical life as part of a longer spiritual journey. During that time, I also got the inspiration to become a writer when it became clear that hiding a spiritual journey was like Gatsby's reaching for the stars alone. To live my dream, I had to develop the insight to know who I was and the courage to share that with others.

So many years later, my first last year experience has made that lesson even clearer. Part of embracing life fully is being entirely accepting of myself and what I love, and being open about it and letting others respond as they may.

That idea was reinforced this weekend in two related examples. On Saturday, I watched Irwin Allen's *The Sea around Us*, a 1952 documentary based on the book of the same name by marine biologist and conservationist Rachel Carson. Even though I wasn't sure how much I personally would enjoy a science-based film made 60 years ago, I had high expectations because it had won the Oscar for Best Documentary Feature. I found the movie interesting throughout, and I marveled at how technologically advanced some sequences seemed for its day, especially when showing microscopic organisms or sea creatures that the narrator said most people, including many scientists, had never seen before. The end of the film described melting polar ice caps and warned of potential consequences that seemed far ahead of their time, as the message is now being echoed in reports on global warming.

After the movie, as I often do when I watch a film or am doing research about one, I read about the work online and in movie reference books. Even though the film was impressively lauded in its day, I was surprised to discover that Allen's adaptation so disappointed Rachel Carson that she thereafter refused to let any of her books be adapted to film. Because I appreciated Allen's ability to keep me interested in the topic, I held to its Academy Award-quality filmmaking rather than find fault with it because he apparently disappointed the person whose concepts he had filmed.

Reading about Carson's displeasure with Allen reminded me that Isaac Bashevis Singer, who wrote the short story "Yentl the Yeshiva Boy," the original source material for the movie *Yentl*, reviled Streisand's adaptation. Understanding and even appreciating Singer's points of contention did not diminish the impact the movie's soundtrack has had on me. Like my decision about *The Sea around Us*, I decided to continue revering *Yentl*'s songs for the gift of inspiration they give my soul.

The example helps me appreciate the value of differing opinions about a work, and challenges me to have the courage to accept that *My First Last Year* may (I hope, for this is my dream) touch many souls and catapult readers further along their journey toward greater awareness of their enlightenment. On the other hand, some may perceive the anecdotal account of my year as valuable only to me. I'm aware that the insights I share in this book are not research based, are not scientific, and do not fall within the realm of traditional religious scholarship. I wonder how it will resonate with readers, but I was told to be bold, and sharing my personal story is an exercise in courage.

Thinking of *The Poseidon Adventure* brings me hope. I have studied movies since I was 14, so I know that the general consensus about the film is that it's a fun pop culture phenomenon, but nowhere near a great classic movie. I know that and I don't care. I love it just as much regardless of what scholars think because of the emotional connection I made to it as a boy.

Since writing *Film Stars and Their Awards*, I have been known as a movie expert. During book tour interviews, people asked me my favorite movie. The look of consternation I got for being a movie expert who would pick *The Poseidon Adventure* as his favorite led me to apologetically explain my boyhood response to the film before giving the title. I know the difference between what scholars might consider an excellent movie versus one they would not. I like many of both.

For the longest time I discounted the lesser works and shied away from admitting that I liked them. But I accept now that there is just as much value in a unique spiritual or emotional response to a product of someone's creativity as there is in something that is universally lauded as a classic. Because I'm writing *My First Last Year* from my spiritual core, I believe that it will resonate with many people even if religious or scientific scholars find no grounds for anything I've shared. I understand their perspective, just as I appreciate Rachel Carson's frustration with Irwin Allen's documentary of *The Sea around Us* and Isaac Bashevis Singer's arguments against turning "Yentl the Yeshiva Boy" into a musical. I agree with and value their arguments, just as I can appreciate the view of scholars who may take issue with the lack of scientific support for my ideas in *My First Last Year*. But I also believe that spirituality and science will ultimately bear out some of the ideas I've shared about life, death, and spiritual energy that I've shared for others to read and, I hope, recognize their own enlightenment.

A lesson I hope you learn from my insights is to love unabashedly whomever and whatever you love. Some people won't get it, but they don't need to get. If you know who you are and love as you want to love, then all criticism is inconsequential. To live fully, as I've striven to do this year, requires being *wholly* you (the spiritual pun is not coincidental) whether or not anyone else approves of what you think or feel or believe.

Even as some may judge or discount you when seeing you fully expressing yourself with joyous abandon, others whose hearts want the same for themselves will be inspired to tap into their own best self and start living it because you had the courage to model it for them. To me, that's what being fully alive requires. Now more than ever, I am grateful to be alive.

Is *The Poseidon Adventure* a four-star quality film classic? No. Did Irwin Allen express Rachel Carson's conservationist philosophies to her satisfaction? No. Was Barbra Streisand's musical adaptation true to Isaac Bashevis Singer's characterization of his central character? No. Do all have valid points worth considering in creating works of artistic merit? Absolutely. But the value we extract from a work is entirely individual. If we have the courage, we can love something or even someone for reasons that only matter to us.

Consider some people that others choose as spouses. Is there anyone who seems an ideal mate for everyone? No. Even dream archetypes of cultures change as society evolves. Intellectually some people may have no idea why other people choose to love whom they love. What does anyone else's opinion matter? If you regularly explore your own thoughts and feelings to dig deeply enough to know your soul, you come to realize that it would still be nice to get general approval from others, as we are all part of each other in the Allsoul. But if meeting with disapproval is holding you back, you're not giving yourself the opportunity to align with people who appreciate you exactly as you are. The only way to open that invitation is to be you with full reverence for yourself, your ideas, and your passions. Honoring your journey invites you to honor others' unique paths as well.

Love what you love unashamedly. Love whom you love unabashedly. Some people may question and, from their perspective, may have valid arguments for why they don't appreciate your choices. But they are not living your life, you are. If you hesitate for fear of being ridiculed, you'll never take the opportunity to relish life as fully as your heart desires.

People's opinions of you say nothing about you, and everything about them. That awareness may not eliminate the sting of rejection or criticism, but it may hold your focus on what feeds your dream rather than what dampens it.

As soon as you take that leap of faith to embrace fully whatever and whomever you love, people who had the courage to do the same before you will come forward and become part of your life immediately. In time, others who find their resolve thanks to your example will align with you, too. In that process, you will get validation reminding you that integrity and happiness are natural consequences of being true to yourself. Love in all its forms requires risk and courage. You have it, we all do, but you cannot reap its rewards until you step out in faith—in yourself and in whatever you perceive to be the source of all Spirit—and find your own unique way of expressing that love for who and what fills your soul.

26

SUCCESS

Day 323: September 30

It's two days before my biopsy and I am excited about moving forward with my life. Already I have learned many valuable lessons from the magic of living since the urologist recommended the procedure. That first week, I processed many feelings and thoughts. Most empowering, I acknowledged the fear that arose when I asked Dixie to pray with me after church and when I was in my office working alone all day and called Jerry to share with him my sadness. Since then, I have moved forward on my spiritual journey and am watching my life unfold. In the process my spirit is emerging brighter than I ever recognized it doing before.

In the past when I have had to face changes in my life, I remember wanting to get through the crisis or challenge so I can return to being the happy person I was before. I was at a lecture once when the speaker shared about being awake and not taking things for granted. Although it seemed to contradict the point the lecturer was making, I thought, *but that's my goal. I want to get back to being in a place where I can take things for granted because that means I'm back in balance.* There is a difference between taking life for granted (which I agree is really not an enlightened goal) and being so grounded in the spiritual awareness that whatever happens, I know I'm fine.

For the past few days I've determined that I do not want to get through this health challenge in order to return to how happy I was. I want to come out the other side even more enlightened, spiritually powerful, and faith-filled.

Many spiritual teachers talk about the limitations of our mind and the mindtalk that can keep us distracted from our true spiritual nature. I have had experiences where my mind initially takes me into fear or temporarily appears to derail progress along my spiritual journey. Ultimately, however, my thoughts have always supported the idea of returning to the innate spiritual knowing that there is something more to me and to this life than my physical senses experience.

Over the past three weeks I have tilled ideas and feelings as a result of my urologist's email that could amount to nothing. Because my mind went places that brought up many feelings, including fear and anxiety and dread, I have already reached a higher spiritual plane. I am not the person I was before I read the message right before I raced out the door to work that drizzly morning.

The pinnacle observation I have made is that the goal is *not* to get out of a challenge or crisis so we can return to life as it had been before. It is to get through it and discover ourselves as someone spiritually brighter than we previously realized we were. Maybe we make that breakthrough even if we die.

When I receive the excellent health results that I'm anticipating after my procedure Monday, I have no desire to sigh back into complacency. I want the joy of this experience to be more powerful than that. For most of my adult life, I couldn't imagine being happier than I am—but I can envision it now. This experience has already peeled back the gauze I have kept as an unnecessary protector of my soul. Whatever news I receive, I commit now to using it to nurture my soul and find new ways to recognize my power as a dazzling, vibrant piece of the Allsoul.

Day 325: October 2

I re-watched the movie *Harper*, which features Shelley Winters at her boisterous best as a washed-up former starlet now bingeing on the excesses of food, alcohol, and delusion. In one scene she lies passed out on her sofa, draped like a stuffed down comforter, while above her fireplace in the same shot is a portrait of her in her glamorous youth.

Seeing that image reminded me of what Deepak Chopra said about how all the cells of our body are replaced every 11 months so that we are literally not the same person we were a year ago. That lesson flashed from the television in one still shot from *Harper*. In the years that separated the person Winters was in the portrait to the character who lay sleeping, she had transformed into someone else.

The image brought to mind a lecture by Isabel Allende, discussing her transformation after her daughter's death, which she wrote about in the memoir, *Paula*. She described the person she had been while enjoying her early success as a writer, floating egotistically among people impressed by her brilliance, to the more grounded and world-weary person she became since Paula's death. In stories such as Allende's, I latched onto what people lose as they become someone new.

I had a great aunt named Esther who, when asked how she was doing, would bypass details and merely shrug, "The old gray mare ain't what she used to be." Many times when I watch awards shows a presenter will enter the stage with scenes from a lifetime career punctuating the passage of time. Not long ago, Dick Van Dyke came out to such a montage and began his speech with, "Hi, I'm what's left of Dick Van Dyke."

Again, my mind picked up on the undercurrent of what one loses. Turning the prism toward the facet of Spirit, I think now not what I've lost over time, but what I've gained. Recently I've been doing interval training in the pool, timing my laps for the first time since I competed in swimming as a teenager. My 50 freestyle and breaststroke are both at least 10 seconds slower than they were when I was 17. At first, my mind observed the difference and I felt unmovingly reconciled to the fact that I am over 50 now. I believe wholeheartedly that if I felt inspired to train hard enough, I could return to, or at least come close to, the same time I reached in high school. But I have no desire to do that because, although my body physically is not doing what it did back then, I'm not missing having that skill. That's what the 17-year-old Roger could do. That same teenager was the one who sat home on weekends not knowing how to reach out to others, did not know I could embrace my right to love and be loved by the person I'm attracted to, and had so vague an awareness of my soul that I did not know how to nurture or expand it.

Turning 50 was the greatest experience of my life because I am so much more at home as a soul than I was before. That perspective came as a conscious decision. I wanted turning 50 to be a great experience, not the beginning of the decline into aging infirmity. As a soul I decided that my 50s would be about reaching greater heights of being joyful, appreciative, vibrant, and spiritually attuned. My heart danced from this opportunity, and my mind reeled with ways to create evidence of my decision.

Thanks to Shelley Winters, my Aunt Esther, Isabel Allende, Deepak Chopra, and Dick Van Dyke, I have a new appreciation for being someone new. I am not who I was cutting through the water between lane ropes during a high school swim competition. I'm not even the guy whose picture still appears on the home page of my author website. I see now that every day my body is replenishing itself. Now that I'm aware of that fact, I don't want to focus on what my body could do before that it doesn't do as much, as fast, or as well now. If I wanted my life to be about the physical, I could concentrate all my energy toward that and come pretty close to having much of the physical conditioning I did at any peak period of my life.

But I have chosen what I believe to be a more expansive focus—on my soul. Who I am spiritually does not age, but grows in wisdom. To me, that's the fountain of youth that so many throughout the ages have misinterpreted as a way to keep physically alive. When we're awake to Spirit, we are alive, no matter what our body may do. Physically this life crescendos like the effortless rise and fall of the chest during a single breath. In the eternal scheme of our existence, this life is about that long. But it is a breath in the life of our soul, and so it matters, we matter, and people and animals and objects, all vibrant with their own life story, matter. Death is not an end but a reimagining of the cells that came together as a physical creation of a spiritual idea. When the spiritual idea evolves, as it always will because it is life, the mind, heart, and body evolve naturally to manifest the new creative idea spoken into being by the soul. Who I am today is a mirror of my soul right now. Thank God the image evolves.

Day 328: October 5

Life continues to take interesting turns. On Saturday night, I had a dream consistent with my recurring dreams: *I was lost. This time I was trying to get to the doctor's office where I needed to go for my biopsy, but I couldn't find the way. Every familiar direction I headed turned into unrecognizable territory.*

Here's the sweetest part of the dream:

As I left work to meet Jerry and head to the doctor, two librarian colleagues from my district arrived to lend support by going also. I was touched.

On my trek to find the doctor, I was on my own for a good while. En route, I saw from a distance two more fellow librarians heading toward my doctor. Their enthusiastic wave left me awash with a feeling of being loved. It then occurred to me that all the librarians were going to be there for me. Seeing in which direction they sprinted showed me how to get to my doctor's office.

Later in the dream I ran into one librarian who asked me what was most helpful for getting this procedure done? Choked up, I told her,

"Having the support of all of you showing up to be with me, and the prayers that people have been saying for me."

I woke in the middle of the night with an excruciating headache. I hadn't had a headache in months. When Jerry awoke and asked me what I thought caused it, I admitted, "I think I'm scared again." Because the procedure requires refraining from taking ibuprofen for 7-10 days, I nursed the headache with a heated eucalyptus pad, which helped a little.

Before 8:00 a.m., the receptionist called from the urologist's office to postpone my procedure until the following Monday. The instant she told me, I knew the most important reason for the postponement: I had another spiritual lesson to learn first. That lesson came yesterday.

Since learning I need a biopsy, I have prayed alone, have been prayed with, and have been prayed for. I asked Dixie at church to pray with me. Out of his own sweet spirit, Jerry's dad prayed for me over the phone. I haven't told many people about the procedure, but I've asked a few people to pray for me. The other day, Ms. Bhetti, a community advocate for our school district, stopped by the library to say hello. We had had so many enriching spiritual discussions in the past, I told her about the biopsy and asked for her prayers. Without hesitating, she pointed upwards and said, "He's taking care of everything. You know that."

I agreed. I was aware that I knew it intellectually, but emotionally I still feared.

This past weekend a minister friend stayed with us. As she was leaving, Jerry reminded her of the procedure and asked for her prayers. Her sweet, smoky eyes locked onto mine and she smiled. "You already know what the results are going to be. It's done." The words reached my ears with smooth assurance. I trusted what she said, but a nagging "What if . . ." shook my faith.

Yesterday I told an administrator that I'd be out next Monday. I shared about my PSA because he was trying to figure out how best to monitor his own health situation. His office door was open, as was the door to the adjoining assistant principal's office. When I left the first AP's office, I went in to visit the other. She's a sweetheart of a woman whom I've known for decades. Although we rarely talk directly about spirituality, we talk about food with a reverence that always assured me she was definitely a spirit-centered woman.

"I guess you overheard what I just shared," I began, "if you would, keep me in your prayers Monday."

Before I even finished my request, she replied, "It's done." Like Ms. Bhetti, she pointed upward. "He's taken care of it. You spoke it and He took care of it. It's done," she repeated with such conviction that something shifted in me. For the first time, the doubt was gone.

It took me until that moment to learn a lesson of faith that I really never got before. I could feel fully trusting of faith in either my heart or my head, but rarely did that conviction fill me so thoroughly that I knew the truth of my faith both intellectually and emotionally at the same time. In the past, I might believe something in thought, but still feel fear. Or, I have believed something in my heart so fully that all fear vanished, but my mind still recognized the window of possibility that new information could change how I felt.

This time, I got it. The spiritual message permeated my soul, heart, mind, and body. I "knew" the truth spiritually, I felt light of heart, clear of mind, and strong in body. For the first time I tore through the veneer of concern to realize that it doesn't matter what the biopsy shows. I know as a soul connected to the Allsoul that I am fine and will always be fine, and no diagnosis can alter that. If a test result indicates more is required to take care of my body, I will soulfully explore options and do what I need to bless my body back to the conditions of health I have inherited as a child of God. Meantime, I have the work I have been called to do, and I am doing it. A test result will not keep me from my spiritual mission in life, which I am in part fulfilling this very second by writing to you.

Day 330: October 7

It's the weekend before my biopsy and, only one week later, I feel completely transformed from the person I was last week going into the same procedure. As a result, I appreciate even more the value of trusting God's timing of everything, and accepting that, when things don't happen exactly when I thought they would or should, higher wisdom is available for me to absorb.

I am going into this procedure more faith-filled than I could have last week. Another simple metaphor has added a new perspective to the results of my PSA tests. These past two weeks I have felt and looked how I wanted when I started eating healthier after my summer vacations and since my new interval training workouts. I stepped on the scale this morning and weighed 156, three pounds higher than my ideal. That number did not match how I felt and looked.

My mind drew the parallel to my PSA numbers not revealing my true health and vitality. Even with my PSA rising, I feel as energetic, strong, and healthy as ever. Ready for the procedure, I go in with mind and heart open, convinced my body will reflect the spiritual truth of my being. No matter what the results, I know the news will be good, because it will lead me to a clearer understanding of who I am as a soul, and how to fulfill the mission I came to this life to complete.

Life is an exciting adventure, always! What a blessing to know that fact intellectually, feel it emotionally, and sense it spiritually. In combination, those three aspects of the trinity within help me realize my full vitality. I am not just connected to my creator, I am also contributing to what my creator is—the Allsoul that feeds us spiritually, and that we, in turn, feed to illuminate ourselves and others. How exciting to see life from that vantage point. To me, it's the ideal position of spiritual empowerment and altruism. I am being filled spiritually while simultaneously feeding other's souls the very concepts for which they've been hungering.

Writing this book is one link that connects the transmitting of spiritual gifts. I am certain it's happening in myriad other ways as well. To be aware of this process and to observe my part in it brings an ecstasy of gratitude. Feeling more alive than ever required exploring the possibility of death on a level I'd never gone before, and which I wouldn't have been prompted to venture into intellectually, emotionally, or spiritually without a looming biopsy.

Occasionally my mind raced to the most fatal conclusion with too little justifiable evidence. So be it. Because the gift has still been received, none of this self-examination has been histrionics. Instead, it encouraged me to advance along my spiritual path and find footprints of similar travelers that I wouldn't have seen if my mind hadn't raced to extremes.

Rather than regret the worry, I now thank God that my mind doubted until it compelled me to discover the truth. The breakthrough led to peace.

Day 336: October 13

During the ultrasound on Monday I felt hope when learning that, on initial screening, my prostate looks healthy, but was warned that it's twice the size it should be. Instead of worrying, I redoubled my commitment to faith in God and in my body to support what is most rejuvenating for a long life. The doctor told me he would call with results of my biopsy in 3-5 days. Day four has just begun and I've received no word yet.

Meantime, I did learn some encouraging news about my family history. At dinner with my father Wednesday, he remembered something that he hadn't thought to tell me previously: his father suffered prostate problems and had his removed in the 1950s. I asked if my grandfather had cancer, and Dad assured me he didn't. Whatever the trouble, his symptoms were best treated at the time by removing it. I then asked my dad when his prostate troubles began, and, like mine, his started in his early 40s. He has contended with prostate issues for over 40 years, and has never developed cancer.

I've noticed how naturally my life has shifted this week to other future-oriented goals. For the past month I was immersed in praying and gathering information about health, focusing primarily on natural healing and wellness. Without my consciously noticing, my energies have shifted to developing ideas for my new publishing house.

This week I've investigated starting the new business with many people, including a friend in independent publishing, my brother who recently started a new business with his wife, my father who has been a business start-up advisor through the SCORE organization for years, and my accountant. Most of this journey has been thrilling, and occasionally surprising. I didn't expect it to be so challenging to secure a name for the business, but now that I've come up with Paradise Publishing, I feel better.

Yesterday an email from my accountant initially left me overwhelmed by how much there is to learn just about applying for and then filing taxes for a business. Instead of entertaining concerns about not knowing enough yet to start a business successfully, I knew to give myself time to process that instant spike in anxiety.

In recent weeks, Jerry has shaped his church messages around Wayne Dyer's *Excuses Begone!* Within minutes of leaving the computer with the prayer, "God, if this is too much and it's not the right path for me to take, please let me know," I recognized two familiar excuses from Dyer's book: *I don't know how*, and *This sounds financially overwhelming*. Without my effort the fearful energy of those excuses dissipated. I concluded, *If I don't know how, then I'll learn*. Feeling overwhelmed about money made my spirit exhale in exasperation with a "Really? That? Again?" I knew I had to move forward.

To do so I only needed to remind myself of the seven SUCCESS traits I researched in my dissertation and wrote about in *Teach Me SUCCESS*. Starting this business requires that I am:

Self-motivated: I received the inspiration and have been taking steady action for over a year.

Undeterred: Dyer's book reminded me to excel rather than make excuses.

Creative: If what I've done in the past won't work in this new context, then I will have to find another way to pursue my goal.

Courageous: The email left me overwhelmed, my most familiar signal that it's time to step through my fears to achieve what I dreamed was possible.

Egalitarian: My primary inspiration for starting the publishing house is to get more books to readers with timeliness and abundance. Following the standard publisher route has not accomplished that goal to the satisfaction of my dream.

Sanguine: To make this effort work, I need to stay optimistic and enthusiastic. A positive attitude will help me learn new information and overcome old financial fears.

Self-Aware: In this process, I have been invited to look at myself to determine what in me might be holding me back. Acknowledging what I don't know is the first step to learning it; admitting what scares me creates new hope for empowerment.

These seven traits help us achieve what we want. On a grander scale, they also empower us to live more fully because they require being spiritually awake to inspiration, mentally and physically engaged in responding to it, and metacognitively attuned to who we have been, who we are now, and who we are becoming. It is a process that gives us the vision to plant seeds for our future, the patience to let

Spirit germinate it, and the excitement of seeing what emerges. The process brings our ideas, and us, to new life. Being spiritually awake to this process allows us to not only live our life, but also to thrill at its adventure. It sounds demanding, but it's actually natural. Delete the unproductive or destructive distractions, and the awareness appears with vibrant, elated energy.

Though positive, feeling lucky to be alive is a passive observation. Being grateful for the awareness that we are alive requires awakening to Spirit, but it, too is passive, and therefore will not spark true fulfillment. But experiencing gratitude for knowing that we actively participate in the creation of our life and the unveiling of our Spirit takes us toward the heights of enlightened self-actualization.

I am certain that I will gain even more understanding of life and Spirit than these three stages of gratitude, for I believe that the soul's journey is endless and there is no one spiritual completeness to ultimately achieve. Every time we express our fullest concept of godliness to date, new potential opens to expand the universal energy we call God.

Believing there is no end to the journey reinforces the idea that death provides an imaginary threshold to greater expression of our true essence, Spirit. When that awareness alone is strong enough to impel us to those heights of enlightened self-actualization, death is a portal, not an end.

Meantime, at least through the experience of living this life as my first last year, as if time is linear and life is temporal, I have tapped into my own fear of death. That experience, even before I receive my biopsy results, has accelerated my exploration of what life and God really are and have led me to where I am now.

I see that the goal of living fully that prompted this book is based on the false perceptions that time is limited and that what I am experiencing now as a physical being encapsulates my life. An ideal of humankind has always been to discover the secret to immortality, a quest often prompted or intensified by fear of dying. This year I have lived from both the excitement of being present with each moment as if I will never experience it again, and from the anxiety that I will lose what I love in this life. Both perspectives are facets of the same prism, and both are useful.

However, fear is only useful for helping us tap into the courage we've always had, but have not yet used to the extent necessary to reach the next level of evolution. We may start any stage confused and concerned, but we will develop the power to master that stage just as we have every other. Once we have, our soul fills us with the desire to expand further. The new inspiration will initially excite us, but then require us to utilize all seven SUCCESS traits, starting with self-motivation and culminating with self-awareness.

So here I am, one month to the day until my first last year experiment ends. I choose now to see that fear of death can spark my love for life only as a shocking splash to the face; it cannot serve my spirit if I lose myself in its tide.

Always, my Spirit walks several strides ahead of my experience to clear the path toward eternal growth. By looking at the bigger picture, I see that long ago Spirit provided the catalyst that would now redirect my thinking away from death and toward my commitment to contribute something permanent to others. Many months before I read the email that sparked an exploration of my fear of death, I had an inspiration to write this book. Because I acted on that inspiration, it became my next spiritual task to complete. In the process, it diverted my focus from me and redirected toward my desire to contribute to the Allsoul.

I look forward to good news from the urologist, but I am not dwelling on the call. I am excited to write to you now and to find a way to publish this work, perhaps through my own publishing house. My reaction to the accountant's email has given me new obstacles to conquer, which will require tapping into energy sources I haven't before.

I used to think life was an endless adventure that I joined for my brief span on this earth. Now I believe my life is the endless adventure to which I have finally woken. The vastness of it lies before me. And to know it never ends . . . Wow, gratitude never felt so enriching.

27

The Entire Picture

Day 346: October 23

Last Saturday I finally received an email from the urologist. It said simply, "Good news, Roger. No cancer." Like a deflating balloon, my anxiety whooshed out of my body in a palpable sigh.

I emailed him back and asked what I was to do next. He suggested only that I get my PSA checked again in three months. I didn't know what to make of that reply. Until then, I had believed that together the doctor and I were partnered in determining what was wrong and working to remedy the problem. But instead of reacting to what I initially interpreted as the doctor's indifference, I decided to explore with God in meditation what to do next to facilitate my healing. In prayer, I suspected that the urologist would merely prescribe a pill, which would provide no solution from the perspective I shared earlier: I believe physical imbalances are my body's signals to grow spiritually. So instead of focusing on getting the PSA numbers down, I'm going to explore what this health episode is teaching me as a soul.

Since the "no cancer" news, I have felt surges of joy. I'm grateful that the doctor's email eclipsed having to weigh drastic measures, such as chemotherapy or radiation, and instead allows me to concentrate on my spiritual calling to write and share my message.

To that end, I have accelerated my efforts to start Paradise Publishing. Concurrently processing my health concern and acquiring spiritual guidance and practical advice about the publishing house have taught me that Godtime has no urgent deadlines. When I'm attuned to the spiritual guidance propelling me to fulfill my dreams, everything occurs in a genuine flow. It never demands swimming upstream, but requires finding balance at the crest of the current we're riding so that we move naturally, can breathe easily, and feel no inordinate strain to stay afloat.

The most important lesson from this past month: really living and remaining present impacts more than the individual moments of life; it requires us to see how every stage teaches us to live as a soul. Recently I saw a girl about 8 years old with a touch of makeup coloring her face and highlights in her long auburn hair. It reminded me of the advice that Grandma gave me as a boy, and which my father reiterated at different stages of my adolescence: don't rush to grow up because you'll miss some of the wonder of childhood that you can never recapture. I have appreciated those wise words through many stages of human life; I see now they also apply to our eternal spiritual journey.

During a meditation this week I heard my loving grandmother's voice echo advice I offer you now: don't rush to self-actualization or push toward enlightenment. It's coming as inevitably as childhood becomes adulthood. Follow the innate rhythms of your own path and develop however is natural for you. In the process savor each stage of this life, be spiritually awake every step of the journey, and let yourself be exactly who you are at each interval of your mental, emotional, and spiritual development. Race past any stage of your journey and you risk missing gifts that can enrich every stage beyond it.

Fully embody each stage. Love yourself without judgment as you work through the emotional limitations of fear and the mental constraints of confusion and doubt. The fastest way to grow: re-interpret the qualities you've judged about yourself and see them as tools for spiritual development. As you may recall, I felt disappointed in myself for the tears that welled when I asked Dixie to pray with me about the biopsy. I judged the tears as weakness, but I had mislabeled them. They were my body's physical affirmation of how much I love life. My judgment emerged from my own spiritual immaturity. I didn't know in that moment what the tears really meant. Less than a month later, I understand better now, and I appreciate why I had to sit with the fear instead of rushing to get over it. In that space of fear, my spiritual understanding grew.

Human strife is fertile ground where spiritual seeds flourish. I believe this philosophy applies as much globally as it does personally. Last night Jerry and I watched *Ethel*, a documentary by Rory Kennedy about her mother, and in many ways, about her father, Bobby, who was assassinated just months before Rory was born. During the civil rights episodes especially, I thought about how societal conflicts have always surfaced in human coexistence. The intensity of such strife may shift or abate, and the victims of such hatred change, but the struggles will always be there for people who strive for spiritual enlightenment, the springboard for universal human respect and equality. But enlightenment, at any level of our development, occurs through natural processes for all life. In that process, darkness plays an integral, meaningful role.

The friction of strife, the struggle with sadness or fear, the vagueness and worry of inexplicable discontent carry the resources we need to be transformed. Like soil for a seed, our social problems and internal struggles are not just the setting from which we must emerge. They are the sustenance and the suppliers of every nourishment we need to become more fully who we came to this life to be.

Before embarking on this leg of your spiritual journey we call life, you, as a soul, in full accord with the Allsoul of which we are all a vibrant and necessary part, determined your mission in this life and structured your spiritual DNA. Picture your DNA as a ladder that takes you to the heights of eternity. As you develop you will break through old beliefs and misinterpretations of life just as a seed transforms into a stem that stretches through the soil and reaches upward until it breaks free to feel the radiance of the sun.

A seed cannot rest atop the ground to fulfill its destiny. It needs to burrow into the darkness and temporarily immerse itself in it. Through the innate struggle, which is actually a gift of the darkness, the seed discovers that survival requires action. The source of that action comes from within, and ultimately, the seed will look there and become aware of its DNA. Only then does it remember the spiritual plan it co-created. In that discovery, the seed knows instinctively to reach upward. In that reach, it is transformed.

Blooming, however you interpret that for yourself, requires multiple stages that we each must go through. As I experience the final month of my first last year, I am not seeking to feel enlightened or to be self-actualized. Instead my goal is to relish my newfound appreciation for even those moments when I am uninspired, shine less than brilliantly, and get a glimpse of how much farther I have to travel along my spiritual journey. To appreciate that awareness and to savor life, even in moments devoured by darkness, requires knowing that I am Spirit, that my soul contains in it the DNA that I am here to climb, and that everything that surrounds me is providing the nourishment I need right here, right now to fulfill my destiny. Ironically, that appreciation is the embodiment of self-actualized enlightenment.

I see now that enlightenment is not a holy grail for which we must search, but a realization of what we've always had. Spiritual journeys take us to many new, exciting places, but ultimately lead back to ourselves.

Day 353: October 30

When I called my sister-in-law to tell her I was cancer-free, our conversation evolved to details about the last stages of life, and death. She told me that her once tall and powerful uncle died this weekend. Her dad was grieving the loss of his beloved younger brother, and feeling guilty for having outlived him. The euphoric flight of my good news had been grounded by the sadness I felt from her story.

In meditation after the call, I realized how all year I hoped to create endless bliss. But living as if each day could be my last showed me a bigger picture. Being fully alive requires savoring present joys AND facing the sad, potentially frightening prospect of physical death. It may be comfortable and manageable to observe and even comprehend a small portion of the overall picture that colors the canvas of our lives. But taking it all in, even the dark shades and obscured shadows, demands a higher level of appreciation. When we view that portrait through wisdom, we see the value of it all and can accept that every shade and shadow is beautiful, even as it illuminates fear and sorrow.

The challenge of this past month has given me a gift—new insight about the darker side of mortality. In every leg of our journey through life we choose a focus, as I did when embarking on my first last year. With concentration the view expands, like pulling back from a pinpoint focus on an object in a painting, to see how surrounding details color our perception of it. With experience, we adjust and appreciate how both the object and its adjoining details create multiple effects of perception.

The true power of joy comes from seeing more of the entire canvas and realizing that what we see is only part of the entire picture because we too are in the picture. Through human eyes we cannot see what is behind us or, more intriguingly, within us and thus projecting from us so that we know that a picture even exists to comprehend. The process of that gradual understanding is the divine journey we are all on, and it includes awareness of loss and of death. The process of letting go of what we used to think we needed flings aside the curtain to unveil the picture that we spend this life watching, marveling at, and, as we grow in spirit, appreciating. Ultimately, as our spiritual eyes open, we discover that we are not looking at the painting, and are not even in the painting. We are the painting.

Mine is not a new story, just one version of the story we all live, learn from, and can tell about our universal journey. With my first last year, I expressed from my Spirit the desire to press forward, and not wait until life forced me to move. Along the way I encountered uncharted territory. Sometimes moving forward required tapping into wells of strength I didn't know I had. Other times, it revealed to me fears that I judged as weakness. I see now that fear reverberates only as proof of how much I love life and want it to continue. I have not overcome my fears, but I have developed a new appreciation for them.

When we are bold, however boldness looks to us, we step into the center of our spiritual path. There we bask in the life-sustaining warmth of the light showing us our way. As we step forward, we kick up the debris of everything we have avoided, or ignored, or did not even know was underfoot. Just like the sun, the debris is also there to serve our highest good, to help us find sure footing as we reach higher ground.

In the broader, more nuanced view of eternal life, there can be no first last year because time is not linear. But for the purpose of my experiment, perceiving it as such invited me to reawaken every day and to feel the perpetual pulsating energy of life that transcends time. In my human-ness, I didn't always achieve it. But throughout the year I recognized and accepted the invitation more readily.

I contrast where I am now on my spiritual journey to where I was a year ago. I am not the same man, but I am the same soul. That's the point! Human expression is ultimately one of those aspects of "self" that we shed because it's unnecessary. But while we have it, it is serving us every day to explore, to connect with others, and to ultimately see the oneness of all, and the completeness of being an individual expression of the Allsoul.

There is nothing we must do or have, only the exciting discovery of what we've always been. As humans, we express ourselves individually until we learn to express "Ourself" collectively. For this reason I believe we have always had locked in our hearts the innate desire for peace, cooperation, and belonging. Separation, discord, and individualism are illusions. Allness and harmony are spiritual reality. Some still living the human existence already understand that truth and are expressing more fully as Spirit than others. But we are all evolving, unfolding, emerging. The idea of who we are and what life is remains obvious but abstract, close but elusive, constant but evolving. That abstractness feeds the hope that we are forever on the precipice of our grand epiphany.

Last night I had a new variation on my recurring dream. I was in a school, but this time I was not lost and anxiously wandering halls that transformed into something unfamiliar each time I turned a corner. To my relief, I was already in my first period class, a student, not the teacher. I was far enough into the semester to know my class schedule and to realize that I didn't need all the books I was carrying from class to class. In possession of a locker pass from my teacher, I reorganized my books, putting those I needed for upcoming classes in one bag, and placing into another those I could set aside for good. I woke from the dream before I finished reorganizing the books, so I never made it to the locker. In the classroom, I couldn't know if the school halls would transform and confuse me again, and I had not yet opened the locker and unburdened myself of the excess books. But in the dream I knew what I did and didn't need for the next semester. The next leg of my journey would be lighter.

What I know is not all that makes life worth living. What I don't yet know remains just as valuable. The halls may shift again. I may not be able to unlock the locker and keep my books organized and my schedule as efficient as I anticipate. But with the wisdom I've acquired so far, I have faith to head into the mystery of what lies ahead.

———•◆•———

EPILOGUE

Up Next

When I started my first last year, I committed to set priorities, do only what really matters, and let the rest go. During my twelve-month experiment, I only succeeded intermittently. I did set priorities, but too many. I continue to pare down my commitments and focus on what I value most, one activity at a time.

When the year was up, I committed to writing fewer books at once and setting fewer goals. Both changes stilled the mind torrents that overwhelm the first half of this book and have improved the quality of my day-to-day life. The book I will continue after this one is *Actors and the Academy Awards.* That keeps alive my original goal to ask Gene Hackman to write the Foreword. Because Hackman is in his 80s, Spirit prompts me to resume the work soon.

I never heard from the excised administrator I emailed. Like all loving intents, I trust that my communications were well-received and that they blessed him as intended.

At some point while reading this book, you probably turned to the title page to see if I started Paradise Publishing. I am proud that I did. I broke through waves of feeling overwhelmed before settling into learning publishing a little at a time. Early demands of the business helped redouble my commitment to keep my writing my first priority. Paradise Publishing exists to facilitate, not usurp, my writing career.

My public profile has exploded since Jerry's coworkers told me they didn't know I was already a speaker. I've traveled the globe in person and online sharing my research on the SUCCESS traits. Highlights of my adventures include sharing my SUCCESS research with renowned scholars from universities around the world at the international Association of Moral Education conference in Montreal, Canada and igniting a passion for success with a TED Talk that introduced "7 Skills for Success" (www.RogerLeslie.com).

In fulfillment of Spirit's instructions, I am offering in-person workshops (MyFirstLastYear.com) where I guide others through their own First Last Year so they too can not merely live, but FLY. Not surprisingly, sharing the journey is enriching me as much as the spiritual travelers who've joined me so far. Recent dreams suggest that I expand my mission to teach others to FLY through online webinars and a series of FLY books comprised of essays and personal stories from workshop participants. In my first FLY group are several aspiring writers who have yet to be published. Through me, Paradise Publishing, and *My First Last Year*, Spirit is about to make their dreams come true. I couldn't be happier.

APPENDICES

Index of People Connected to Roger Leslie

—A—

Alfonso (Mexican restaurant waiter) 39-40
Anna (Roger and Jerry's niece) 47
Angie (Roger's great-aunt) 192
Arlene (Roger's cousin) 2, 159, 160, 192
Assistant principals 1 (Roger's assistant principals) 224-225
Assistant principals 2 (Jerry's assistant principals) 36, 49, 242

—B—

Baka (Roger's maternal grandmother) 27, 35, 112, 132, 167-168, 169, 174-175, 183, 194
Baka and her sisters (Roger's grandmother and his great-aunts) 20, 35, 103, 131, 132, 139, 159, 167
Barbara (Roger's mother's friend) 2-3, 187-188
Bhetti, Ms. (community advocate at Roger's school) 224, 225
Bonita (Roger and Jerry's friend; Manuel's wife) 62, 172
Bonnie (Roger's childhood dog) 167-168, 174-175, 183

—C—

Cancer surviving friend 197
Caroline (Roger and Jerry's niece) 47
Charlee (Roger and Jerry's niece) 100, 123
Constance (Roger and Jerry's friend) 102
Coogan, Dr. (Rex and Joey's vet) 8-9, 19, 163, 170
Cory (Roger and Jerry's son) xii, 19, 30, 33-34, 70, 199

—D—

Dad (Roger's father) 13-15, 19, 40, 97-98, 100, 102, 126, 184, 227, 234
Debbie (Roger's cousin) 2, 4
Dennis and Ann Marie (Roger and Jerry's friends) 39-40, 59-60
Dixie (church prayer team member) 138-139, 205-206, 219, 224, 234
Donna (Jerry's paternal aunt) 76
Doris (Roger's publicist) 35-36

—E—

Ernest (Vivien's husband) 205
Esther (Roger's great-aunt) 221, 222

—G—

Gloria (Roger's former student) 5
Grandfather (Roger's paternal grandfather) 227
Grandma (Roger's paternal grandmother) 27, 167-168, 169, 183, 184, 213, 234

—H—

Hannah (veterinarian's daughter) 19
Honey (Roger's great-aunt) 2, 159-161, 167-168, 169-171, 173, 174-175, 183, 192, 193, 199, 213

—J—

Jacob (Roger's teaching colleague) 13-14
Jake (Jerry's uncle) 76
Jeanette (Roger's lifelong friend) 27
Jeff (Jerry's youngest brother) 70
Jerry (Roger's husband) viii, 1-13, 17, 19-20, 25, 26, 29-34, 36-41, 43, 45, 47, 48-49, 50, 53-54, 59, 60-62, 64, 66-67, 68, 69-70, 75, 78, 83, 84-85, 91, 94, 98, 100-101, 102-103, 107, 115-116, 123, 125, 126-129, 132-133, 134-136, 137-138, 139, 140, 145-146, 154, 155, 159, 160, 161-168, 171-172, 181, 182, 183-188, 190-191, 194, 197, 199-200, 205, 206, 213, 219, 223, 224, 228, 235
Joey (Roger and Jerry's black dachshund) 8-10, 11, 19, 20, 21, 31-32, 67-74, 78, 162-166, 170, 173-174, 189, 208
John (Dennis and Ann Marie's son) 39-40, 100-101
Judy (Roger's sister) 3, 40, 100, 192

—K—

Karen (Roger's sister-in-law) 100
Kate and Darryl (Renaissance bride and groom) 1-2, 6-7
Kelly (Constance's sister) 102

—L—

Larry (Barbara's husband) 187-188
Lenore (Roger's aunt) 4, 43, 192
Lindsey (Roger and Jerry's daughter-in-law) 60, 69-70
Lorette (Jerry's aunt) 30
Lori (Roger's secretary) 55, 171

—M—

Manuel (Roger and Jerry's friend; Bonita's husband) 62, 72-73, 172
Marita (Mexican restaurant waitress) 39-40
MawMaw (Jerry's mother) 2, 25-26, 31-32, 71, 98, 127, 132, 184-185
Max (Roger and Jerry's first black dachshund) 27, 163, 167-168, 170, 174-175, 183
Maycee (Roger and Jerry's niece) 3, 100, 123
Miami-based travelers in Rome 186-187
Minister (smoky-eyed friend) 224
Mom (Roger's mother) 2-3, 4, 11, 40, 97-98, 100, 102, 126, 159-160, 187-188, 213
Mocha traveler (mudslide drinker) 186, 192

—N—

Nancy (Roger's cousin) 2

—P—

Patrick (Jerry's previous relationship) ix-xiii
Patty (Jerry's cousin) 76
PawPaw (Jerry's father) 2, 25-26, 31-32, 71, 76, 98, 127, 132, 184-185, 196, 205, 224
Phil (Roger's brother-in-law) 40, 100
Pricilla from Manila (cruise bartender) 186
Principal (Roger's excised administrator) 22-24, 52-53, 241

—R—

Randy (Roger's older brother) 41, 71, 192
Ray (Roger's younger brother) 41, 100, 123, 192, 213
Rebecca (Roger and Jerry's daughter) xii, 19, 30, 33-34, 60, 69-70, 162, 199
Rex (Roger and Jerry's red dachshund) 9-10, 11, 20, 31-32, 67, 100-101, 161-168, 169-171, 172, 173-175, 183, 189-190, 193
Rita (Roger and Jerry's travel agent) 3
Roberts extended family (Jerry's paternal relatives) 25, 29-30, 67, 76
Roberts immediate family (Jerry's parents and siblings) 29
Romie and Ted (Roger and Jerry's friends) 62
Russian traveler 185

—S—

Stas (Roger's great-aunt) 2, 161, 199, 213
Students 1 (Roger's library assistants) 66
Student 2 (Roger's mentally handicapped student) 88-89
Student 3 (Roger's student relishing the rain) 109-110
Sue (Roger's sister-in-law) 71, 236
Superintendent (Roger's school district superintendent) 68

—T—

Tom (Roger's uncle) 159

—U—

Urologist 198, 201, 211-212, 220, 227, 233

—V—

Vestal family (Jerry's maternal relatives) 25, 29-30
Vivien (church member) 205-206

General Index

—A—

Actors and the Academy Awards 4, 74, 195, 241
Ageless Body, Timeless Mind 206
AIDS ix-xii, 47
Allen, Irwin 215-217
Allende, Isabel 221, 222
Allsoul 32, 140, 175, 212, 218, 220, 226, 238
Arkansas Razorbacks 32-33
Association of Moral Education 242
"Auld Lang Syne" 102-103

—B—

Bacon, Reverend Ed 48
Bayou Publishing 115
Beatty, Warren 180-181
Bennett, Tony 138
Brickman, Jim 39, 59
Brontës, the (authors) 171
Byrne, Rhonda 145

—C—

Carson, Rachel 215-217
Charlie Brown Christmas, A 21
Chödrön, Pema 141, 143
Chopra, Deepak 206-209, 221, 222
Christmas Tidings 47-48

Countdown to Oscar's Favorite Actors 195
Creating Health 206, 207, 209

—D—

Day, Doris 84
"Dead, The" 53
Drowning in Secret 60, 199
Dyer, Wayne 141, 146, 228

—E—

Eat, Pray, Love 41
Emerald Lake Lodge 3
Emerson, Ralph Waldo 171
Energy of Money, The 142
Ethel 235
Excuses Begone! 228

—F—

Film Stars and Their Awards 102, 180-182, 216
Fitzgerald, F. Scott 140
Fondas, the (actors) 180
"From Inspiration to Publication" 65

—G—

Gilbert, Elizabeth 41
God xi, xiii, xiv 3, 40, 42, 48-49, 51-52, 53, 60, 61, 87, 103, 115, 118, 122, 132, 134, 135-136, 138, 139-140, 146, 150-152, 159, 166, 168, 171, 179, 196, 197-198, 208, 209, 211, 212, 215, 223, 225, 226, 227, 228, 230, 233, 234
Goethe, Johann Wolfgang von 117-118, 124, 128
Great Gatsby, The 87, 88, 140, 214-215
Guess Who's Coming to Dinner 112

—H—

Hackman, Gene 4, 241
"Happy Birthday" 160
Harper 221
Hawaii Five-0 184
Henry VIII 8
Hepburn, Katharine 112
Hill, Napoleon 26, 131, 139, 142
Houston Livestock Show and Rodeo 123-124
Hustons, the (actors) 180

—J—

Jameses, the (authors, philosophers) 171
Jesus 17, 24
John of God 197-198, 201
Joyce, James 53

—K—

Keurig coffeemaker 71-74
Kennedy, Bobby 235
Kennedy Center Honors 101, 104

Kennedy, Ethel 235
Kennedy, Rory 235

—L—

Lapine, James 85
Last Lecture, The ix
Late Night with David Letterman 181
Lee, Harper 75, 140, 151
Letterman, David 181
"Live Like You Were Dying" 14
Living the Wisdom of the Tao 146
Lloyd, Harold 193

—M—

Ma, Yo-Yo 104
MacLaine, Shirley 180-182
Magic, The 145-146
Maria Full of Grace 92
McGovern, Maureen 69, 138
McGraw, Tim 14
Moses 58-59
"Moonlight Serenade" 138
Murder on the Orient Express 214

—N—

Novarro, Ramón 193
Nemeth, Dr. Maria 142
Nepo, Mark 50
Notes from the Universe 141

—O—

"O, Come, All Ye Faithful" 19
Oates, Joyce Carol 75
"O, Holy Night" 17, 103
One Sister Left series 75, 101, 131
One Sister Left the Gun 20, 25, 46, 63, 68, 74-75, 86-87, 101-102, 103, 107-108, 113, 131-132, 138, 141-142, 151, 159-161

Oprah's Soul Series Sunday 41
Oprah Winfrey Show, The 41

—P—

Paradise Publishing 61, 135-136, 212, 228, 234, 241-242
Paula 221
Pausch, Randy ix-x
Peters, Bernadette 85-86
Philadelphia Philharmonic Orchestra 19
Plato 174
Police officer (highway patrolman) 121-122
Poseidon Adventure, The 214, 216-217
Providence 117

—R—

Redgraves, the (actors) 180
Rollins, Sonny 101-102, 104
Rubens, Peter Paul 87
Rules of Money, The 146

—S—

Samson and Delilah 87
SCORE 228
Sea around Us, The 215-217
Seurat, Georges 85
"7 Skills for Success" 242
Shakespeare, William 2
Shirley Valentine 183
"Silent Night" 30
Simon, Carly 138
Singer, Isaac Bashevis 216-217
Socrates 114
Sondheim, Stephen 85
Spirit 1-2, 17, 30, 31, 61, 70, 75, 83, 87, 103-104, 107, 109, 118, 124, 128, 136, 138, 140, 150-152, 172, 175, 182, 186, 193, 200, 201, 207, 218, 221, 222, 230, 236, 238, 241, 242
Spontaneous Healing 201-202, 209, 211
Starbucks 43
"Sto Lat" 160
Streisand, Barbraa 216-217
"Sunday" 85-88
Sunday Afternoon on the Island of Grande Jatte, A 85
Sunday in the Park with George 85
Super Bowl 118-119
Super Soul Sunday 48, 50, 141
Success Express for Teens 26, 115, 187
Superman 177, 179

—T—

Taylor, Jill Bolte 126, 132
Teach Me SUCCESS 12, 18, 21, 45-46, 63, 74, 81, 115, 211, 228
TED Talk 242
Teresa, Mother 137
Texas Library Association 147
Theory of Forms 174
Think and Grow Rich 26, 131, 139, 142
Thoreau, Henry David 195
To Kill a Mockingbird 75, 140, 150-151
Tracy, Spencer 112

—U—

Unity Circle of Light 1, 127-128, 134, 137, 138
University of Houston x
University of Houston—Clear Lake 86

—V—

Van Dyke, Dick 221, 222
Von Oech, Roger 155

— W —

Weil, Dr. Andrew 202, 209, 211
Whack on the Side of the Head, A 155
White, Barry 40
Winfrey, Oprah 15, 24, 48, 121-122
Winters, Shelley 116, 221, 222

— Y —

Yentl 213-214, 216-217
"Yentl the Yeshiva Boy" 216-217
Yuletiders, The 17-18, 30

— Z —

Zukov, Gary 113, 121-122

Dream Chronicle

My First Last Year	vii-viii, xii, 1
"What is the core of the universe?"	17
Peanuts lunchbox	21-22
Restaurant gift cards	79
Terrorist on plane	92-94
Going through customs with young cousins	93-94
"Open House" at my childhood home	98-99
Ill at school	113
Lost at school, then floating over the Michigan coast	153-158
Flying, healing the doctor, thinking I'm invisible	176-180
Shirley MacLaine promotes Film Stars and Their Awards	181-182
Lost dachshund, injured lady, milk pass-along	188-191
Jerry and I treading water in crumbling pool	199-200
Lost on the way to the doctor's office for my biopsy	223-224
Not lost in school, but already in class sorting my books	239

Roger Leslie's Workshops

Time to FLY® — Join the growing legion of spiritual adventurers by embarking on your own First Last Year journey. You will live more fully as a soul through these exhilarating workshops that deepen your spiritual appreciation and strengthen your connection with others.

I became one of Dr. Leslie's FLYers at age 83, and my life was transformed.
—Barbara Nelson

Live the Life You Dream — Achieve any goal or lifelong dream with "The Goal Guy," Dr. Roger Leslie, whose original, research-grounded techniques enable you to use both sides of the brain to discover your passion and fulfill your destiny. Believing it's never too early or late to set new goals, Leslie teaches these workshops to all age groups.

The best speaker on goal setting is Dr. Roger Leslie. He taught me goal setting in high school and I use those strategies 20 years later. — Dr. Stephanie Hatten

SUCCESS in Education — Let character education and children's literature scholar Dr. Roger Leslie empower your school with innovative approaches to build a foundation of success for all educators and students.

Dr. Roger Leslie gave a fantastic presentation on inspiring and giving hope to children through character education. I was WOWED! —Mari M. Serrano

Fun in Cinematic Proportions — Get entertained and awed by the massive body of film knowledge Leslie unveils through joyous keynote speeches and movie night celebrations for any organization, business, or special interest group.

Dr. Leslie gave an amazing presentation. I could have listened to him for hours! It's remarkable the data he has in his head. I loved all the stories, as did the entire audience. He was definitely a HIT!!! —Susan Shelander

To book Roger Leslie for speaking engagements,
you can contact him via his website,
www.RogerLeslie.com

Dr. Leslie also customizes workshops and speeches on most any topic.

www.RogerLeslie.com

www.MyFirstLastYear.com